D1759722

303902091

Explorations in Philosophy

Essays by J.N. Mohanty

Professor J. N. Mohanty

EXPLORATIONS IN PHILOSOPHY

Essays by J.N. Mohanty

Volume II

Western Philosophy

edited by Bina Gupta

OXFORD
UNIVERSITY PRESS

OXFORD
UNIVERSITY PRESS

YMCA Library Building, Jai Singh Road, New Delhi 110001

Oxford University Press is a department of the University of Oxford. It furthers the
University's objective of excellence in research, scholarship, and education
by publishing worldwide in

Oxford   New York
Auckland   Bangkok   Buenos Aires   Cape Town
Chennai   Dar es Salaam   Delhi   Hong Kong   Istanbul
Karachi   Kolkata   Kuala Lumpur   Madrid   Melbourne   Mexico City   Mumbai
Nairobi   Sao Paulo   Shanghai   Singapore   Taipei   Tokyo   Toronto

and associated companies in Berlin Ibadan

Oxford is a registered trade mark of Oxford University Press
in the UK and in certain other countries

Published in India
By Oxford University Press, New Delhi

ISBN 019 565 0867

Typeset in Giovanni Book
By Eleven Arts, Keshav Puram, Delhi 110035
Printed at Roopak Printers, Delhi 110032
and published by Manzar Khan, Oxford University Press
YMCA Library Building, Jai Singh Road, New Delhi 110001

Contents

PART II

Preface

Of the twenty-two essays collected in this volume, ten are directly concerned with Edmund Husserl's phenomenological philosophy, while the remainder are concerned with systematic philosophical questions. With the exception of the essay entitled 'Phenomenology and Psychology', all the essays collected in this volume were initially delivered as lectures and subsequently published between 1970–97. Some of these essays on Husserl have been read and cited by scholars all over the world.

One hardly needs to explain Mohanty's status as one of the leading writers in this field. Collecting all these essays in one volume will be welcomed by contemporary scholars in the area of phenomenology, and may be perceived as a fitting recognition of his life-long work, the planned final achievement of which will be a two-volume book on Husserl—as Mohanty himself puts it, a *Gesamtdarstellung* and *Kritik*—which will serve as the culmination of his years of textual, archival, and interpretive research.

Bina Gupta

Editor's Introduction

I t is not an exaggeration to say that J.N. Mohanty is the leading and the most influential expositor of Husserlian phenomenology of our times. I know of no one who has done more than Mohanty to make Husserl accessible to the philosophical and the intellectual world. Some of his important works on the subject are: *Edmund Husserl's Theory of Meaning* (1966), *Phenomenology and Ontology* (1970), *The Concept of Intentionality* (1972), *Frege and Husserl* (1985), *The Possibility of Transcendental Philosophy* (1985), *Transcendental Phenomenology* (1989), *and Phenomenology between Essentialism and Transcendentalism* (1997).

Mohanty has devoted his entire life to understanding and interpreting Husserl. He himself concedes that he is 'Husserlian of a sort' and acknowledges the impact of Husserl on his way of thinking:

. . . It is often surprising for me how in these more than three decades of concern with various powerful philosophical schools, Husserl fares so well. If one test of a great philosopher is that he lets us be free to pursue our own interests, Husserl certainly satisfies this test. He taught us how to think with a sensitivity to phenomena and with a self-critical attitude.[1]

This, however, is not to suggest that the goal of Mohanty's writing is simply to give an exegetical commentary on Husserl's writings or dogmatically defend Husserl against his critics. Mohanty is not afraid to take Husserl to task, if the situation so warrants. For example,

Mohanty repeatedly criticizes Husserl for holding the view that Indian thinking was practically oriented, (How to get rid of suffering, and to attain *mokṣa* or *nirvāna*?), whereas western thought, beginning with the Greeks, developed a purely theoretical thinking, i.e. a purely interest-free contemplation of the nature of things.[2] Mohanty is a philosopher in his own right and provides his readers with a version of transcendental philosophy that is sensitive to both relativism and historicism, an account that cuts across both East and West.

The collection of essays in this volume provides an insight into Mohanty's vision of phenomenology in general and Husserl's ideas in particular. The essays cover a span of over 25 years; the earliest was published in 1970 and the latest in 1997. The essays are divided in two sections: the first section contains essays that are directly concerned with Husserl's phenomenological philosophy, while the essays in the second section focus on some philosophical themes, generally from the perspective of phenomenology. To be specific, in these essays Mohanty applies the phenomenological method to certain general philosophical problems and concepts such as 'time and history', 'religion', and 'psychology'.

I

Readers of this volume who are not familiar with the philosophical ideas of Edmund Husserl may find it useful to have a general account of Husserl's philosophy, which I hope would serve as a frame of reference for my comments on the essays included in this volume. We know that Husserl is one of the most influential philosophers of the twentieth century. Among those who were either his students or were seriously influenced by him are Sartre, Heidegger, Levinas, Gadamer, Ricoeur, and Derrida, to name only a few.

Husserl was born in 1859, in Prossnitz, a village in present Czechoslovakian Moravia, then a part of Austria. After completing his schooling, Husserl studied mathematics, physics, and astronomy at the Universities of Leipzig and Berlin under Kronecker, Kummer, and Weierstrass. In 1881, he transferred to the University of Vienna and received his doctorate from there in mathematics in 1883. Though Husserl pursued his formal education in mathematics, he became interested in philosophy very early in his life. His interest in philosophy was kept alive by the lectures he attended by Wilhelm Wundt at the University of Leipzig and Friedrich Paulsen at the University of Berlin. Eventually, he decided to complete his education in philosophy and from 1884 to 1886 attended Brentano's lectures in philosophy, which were also attended by Sigmund Freud. On the advice of Brentano, in 1886, Husserl accepted a position at the University of Halle as the assistant of Stumpf, which provided him with a thorough grounding in psychology. A year later, he was offered a teaching position in philosophy at Halle. The same year, he published his first major work entitled *Philosophie der Arithmetik*. He published *Logical Investigations* in 1900, which earned him a great deal of reputation and he was invited to be a Professor at the University of Göttingen in 1901, where he stayed until 1916. From 1916 to 1928, he taught at the University of Freiburg. After his retirement in 1928, he remained at Freiburg, during which time he published some of his major works. He died in 1938.

While it is not easy to summarize Husserl's philosophy in a couple of pages, I will nevertheless make an attempt here. I myself find Husserl fascinating partly because of the many parallels that I find between his philosophy and Indian philosophy. One central concern in both Indian philosophy and for Husserl is the nature of consciousness; later in this section, after providing a general account of Husserl's philosophy, I will briefly review some of the parallels.

For this exposition of Husserl's philosophy, I will begin by following the brilliant and almost incomparable 'Preface' that Merleau-Ponty wrote for his *Phenomenology of Perception*.[3] In the 'Preface', he discusses four different themes that are central to phenomenology.

First, phenomenology is intended to be a descriptive philosophy and so rejects all attempts to reduce, deny, or theoretically explain the data of experience. This programme not only rejects scientific reductionism, but also idealistic reduction, that is to say, the reduction of the world to consciousness, for phenomenology has to be descriptive, not speculative.

Second, one must not lose sight of the fact that describing experience and what it delivers is not as easy as it might seem to be. What stands in the way is both our built-in and acquired preconceptions and prejudices. Phenomenological description therefore requires that we be able to put under brackets all our preconceptions and then to return to the experience of the world with a new innocence. This is the famous phenomenological reduction or *epoché*. In Merleau-Ponty's language, the phenomenologist refuses the natural complicity with the world. He tries to put it 'out of play', he does not withdraw from the world but 'slackens the intentional threads' which attach to the world and thereby brings them to our notice.[4]

Third, phenomenology is supposed to be concerned with essences and not with particular facts. To detach the essences from the particular facts, Husserl also proposes a methodological reduction, sometimes called eidetic reduction. Following the programme, the phenomenologist asks such questions as: What is the essence of consciousness? What is the essence of a work of art? What is the essence of moral experience? To follow Merleau-Ponty's interpretation of this move, this recourse to essences does not mean that philosophy is not concerned with the world in which we live, but on the contrary the essences are the means of 'becoming acquainted with and to prevail over its facticity'.[5]

Lastly, perhaps the most important and the central theme of phenomenology is the concept of intentionality. Brentano had held that all mental phenomena are distinguished by the fact that they alone are directed towards an object. Husserl further developed this idea through various phases. First of all, he points out that what is essential to consciousness is what Husserl calls correlation between *noesis* and *noema*. By this he meant that to every intentional act there is a correlative meaning which is the way its object is presented or intended through that act. Later on, Husserl extended the concept to horizon intentionalities. An object is presented always within a horizon, such that the presented object refers to the other possible experiences that are indicated by the presentation. The utmost limit of these horizons is the world which may be described as the horizon of all horizons, the ultimate background within which things stand out as objects.

This leads me to the fifth theme, not mentioned in Merleau-Ponty's account of phenomenology: the idea of the life-world, of which Husserl gave a classic account in his book *Die Krisis der europaischen Wissenschaften und die transzendentale Phänomenologie*. In this work, Husserl shows how modern science arises out of the life-world and through a process of idealization and mathematization constructs the scientific world. The life-world nevertheless continues to remain the foundation, even if forgotten, of all scientific construction.

These four (a philosophy of essences, a descriptive method, a theory of intentionality, and a conception of life-world) perhaps sum up the major thematic concerns of Husserl's philosophy. To these, I would like to add one more fundamental concept of Husserl's phenomenology, if not of all phenomenology. Husserl called his phenomenology 'transcendental phenomenology'. His use of the word 'transcendental' clearly has Kantian overtones. What he meant was that everything in the world, and the world itself, derives its meaning from consciousness and its intentionality. The purpose of this programme is to demonstrate that all things are constituted in consciousness and in this sense consciousness is said to be transcendental. But consciousness is not only intentional but also temporal so that the process of constitution is a temporal process giving rise to the historicity of the transcendental consciousness and the world which it constitutes. We are also confronted with the question of how I as a transcendental ego come to share a common world with other co-constituting transcendental egos.

These last questions have led to many severe criticisms of Husserl's thinking by his closest followers, most notably by Martin Heidegger and Emmanuel Levinas. It is not possible to recall these criticisms in this introduction. Suffice it to say that some of these criticisms, if not all, were too hasty and do not stand careful examination. For the present, I will next recall some of the points on which the Indian philosophical tradition overlaps with the transcendental phenomenology of Husserl. They concern the nature of consciousness, the distinction between the empirical and the transcendental, the idea of the world being constituted in consciousness, and the problem of inter-subjectivity. Here I can only provide brief outlines of Indian thinking on these issues.

In general, the Nyāya-Vaiśeṣika system of Indian philosophy took consciousness to be intrinsically intentional; Yogācāra Buddhism, denied the external object, and insisted upon a distinction of subject and object within consciousness, which looks like the *noesis-noema* structure; the Advaita Vedānta denied intentionality and took consciousness to be definable as self-shining or self-manifesting and explained its objective directedness to be the result of ignorance *(avidyā)*. The one philosopher who sought to combine both the self-shining nature of consciousness and its object directedness was Rāmānuja, who took these two features to be mutually dependent. Consciousness, he held, reveals itself to its locus (owner or ego) only when manifesting its object.[6]

Another important question that must be considered in this context has to do with how the distinction between the empirical and the transcendental consciousness is explained in both these traditions. Whereas in the Husserlian tradition, consciousness is transcendental in the sense that it constitutes the world, it may be said following the great contemporary Indian philosopher K.C. Bhattacharyya that in the Indian tradition, especially in Advaita Vedānta, consciousness is transcendental in as much as it detaches itself or dissociates itself from the world and enjoys its freedom within itself. It is only in Sāṃkhya where the empirical world is taken to be a product of *prakṛti* and *puruṣa* that the philosophical problem that if each puruṣa has its world, how could there be one common world was confronted and sought to be solved. Finally, I would only point out that it does seem as if only in one system of philosophy, that is the Kāshmir Śaivism of Abhinavagupta, which is a form of Advaita Vedānta, that the pure consciousness itself was construed as being temporal, or better still, as time itself. Some of these parallels need to be developed in detail; that task, however, is beyond the scope of this introductory essay. However, before concluding this section, I will develop one of these themes a little further in the context of the overall framework of Husserl and Advaita Vedānta. To be specific, I am going to consider the following question: Is Husserl's transcendental 'I' something like the Advaita Vedānta's *sākṣin* or witness consciousness?

Etymologically the term *'sākṣin'* means that which directly or immediately perceives, the agent of such perception. Accordingly, the term *'sākṣin'* also stands for a witness. In the context of epistemology, it refers to a witness in the sense of the phenomenologically pure observer; the observer who observes without the mediation of any process. It signifies the self, which though not itself involved in the cognitive process, functions as a disinterested, uninvolved onlooker. A phenomenological exploration leads to the recovery of this principle as a necessary ingredient in any epistemological process. In simple terms it represents an attempt to understand experience and its implications. The object as such is not the focus of attention. Rather, the focus of attention, *vis-à-vis* the object, is consciousness which functions as the medium for the manifestation of the object. Sākṣin, in other words, is a form of apprehension, direct, non-relational, non-propositional, and non-evaluative in both cognitive and practical affairs. In the absence of this notion, no knowledge at all would be possible.

In order to understand the parallels between sākṣin and Husserl's transcendental 'I', one must keep two important concepts of Husserl's phenomenology in mind: the transcendental ego or the transcendental 'I' and intentionality of consciousness.

The transcendental ego, argues Husserl, is 'purified consciousness' or 'transcendental consciousness'. It is reached by a conscious reflective methodological move called *epoché*. Husserl describes *epoché* as follows:

By phenomenological *epoché* I reduce my natural human ego and my psychic life . . . to my transcendental-phenomenological Ego, the realm of *transcendental-phenomenological self-experience*. The Objective world, the world that exists for me, that always has and always will exist for me—this world with all its objects, I said, derives its whole sense and its existential status, which it has for me, from me myself, *from me as the transcendental Ego*, the Ego who comes to the fore only with transcendental-phenomenological epoché.[7]

It involves complete suspension of all presuppositions, a 'bracketing', i.e. a setting aside of all beliefs about the world by the knowing mind. Such an attitude, argues Husserl, establishes phenomenological truths about consciousness.

Consciousness, maintains Husserl, is intentional; it is always of an object. In fact, Husserl even goes a step further and asserts that a certain type of intentional act corresponds to each type of object. J.N. Mohanty explains this aspect of Husserl's position in the following words:

On the one hand, there is, for Husserl, a correlation between types of objects and types of intentional reference in the sense that to each type of object there corresponds a certain mode of givenness. In fact the mode of givenness characteristic of a certain type of object may be used to bring out the phenomenological distinctiveness of that type. In the second place, to each particular object there corresponds a whole series of actual and possible intentional acts which have precisely that object as their intentional object. Two typically Husserlian notions arise out of this latter situation: the notion of noesis-noema correlation and that of the constitution of objects in the acts.[8]

The point that is being made is as follows: if we succeed in setting aside all presuppositions of our conception of the world as well as of consciousness as a part of the world, then there would result an experience of one's own consciousness which does not belong to this body, or person, and the consciousness so experienced, as the 'transcendental I', which sounds very much like the witness-consciousness of the Advaita Vedānta.

Let me elaborate on this further using what Eugen Fink, Husserl's close co-worker and assistant during the last years of his life calls 'the ego-splitting' or 'the paradox of the three egos'. Fink describes the transcendental reduction or *epoché* thus. It

. . . is not a 'direct' refraining from belief paralleling the believing life of the thematic experience of the world which directly enacts its beliefs, but—and this can not be overemphasized—is a structural moment of transcendental reflection. The *epoché* is a reflexive *epoché*, it is a refraining from belief on the part of the reflective observer, who looks on the belief in the world in the actuality of its live performance *without taking part in it*.[9]

Fink's point is as follows: in the natural reflective attitude a human ego reflects upon herself within the confines of the natural attitude. Bracketing the world establishes a reflective ego which is outside human apperception:

This ego knowingly directs itself toward the universal world apperception as its theme. The disconnection of the world, however, not only makes possible the formation of a nonworldly reflecting-self, but . . . also makes possible the discovery of the true subject of the belief in the world: the transcendental subjectivity which accepts the world.[10]

So, he argues that there are three egos in Husserl's thinking:

1. the ego which is preoccupied with the world (I, the human being as a unity of acceptance, together with my intramundane life of experience); 2. the transcendental ego for whom the world is pregiven in the flow of the universal apperception and who accepts it; 3. the 'onlooker' who performs the epoché.[11]

Thus, there are three egos: the empirical ego which is engaged in the world, the transcendental ego, which is involved in the constitution of the world and so is not in the world, and the transcendental ego as the 'on-looker' for whom this distinction between the first two egos holds good. In other words, it is possible for me, a reflecting philosopher, to distinguish within me two I's, the empirical I and the transcendental I. The former belongs to the natural order, the latter, however, is the same I but purified of all natural presuppositions. The observer who apprehends this distinction must be a pure disinterested spectator, an 'on-looker'. Such a concept of phenomenological 'on-looker' who does not participate in the world belief perhaps comes closest to the Advaitic notion of sākṣin or the witness consciousness, the disinterested witness. Finally, it is worth noting that in the Preface to the article in which Fink introduces the notion of disinterested spectator, Husserl himself acknowledges that he agrees with Fink's interpretation of his philosophy. Husserl writes: 'I am happy to be able to state that it contains no sentence which I could not completely accept [as] my own or openly acknowledge as my own conviction'.[12]

The above analysis, however, should not be taken to imply that there is a complete agreement between Husserl's disinterested 'on-looker' and the Advaita notion of disinterested witness.[13] In the Advaita account, in every cognition, of whatever sort and of whatever object, besides the cognitive process appropriate to that kind of cognition and to that object, there must necessarily be an accompanying witness-consciousness. The witness-consciousness, for the Advaitins, is the presupposition of all knowing; it illuminates all that is known as well as the process of knowing, thereby making knowledge possible. Husserl's transcendental I, unlike the Advaitin disinterested witness, is not merely a spectator; it is also a constitutive ego. This on-looker, argues Husserl, is revealed in reflection. The existence of this on-looker, however, is not, for Husserl, a necessary condition for the occurrence of any cognition. Nonetheless, the fact still remains that what Husserl calls the 'disinterested on-looker' very closely captures the concept of the witness-consciousness.

Although this volume of essays concerns western philosophy, Volume I being devoted to Indian philosophy, it is only natural, almost unavoidable that the essays concerned with Husserl's transcendental phenomenology should be understood by many readers against the background of Indian philosophy. This explains why I have decided to mention some of these parallels, and discuss in some detail a specific parallel, i.e. between the Advaita notion of witness-consciousness and Husserl's transcendental 'I'. Notwithstanding the fact that a comparison of the western thinkers with the Advaitins is not intrinsically necessary to expound western phenomenology, I believe that such a comparison will help Indian philosophers gain an access to this central concept around which Husserl's phenomenology revolves and make this collection of essays accessible to Indian philosophers. I hope the above remarks will also help the readers to appreciate the contribution of Mohanty's essays not only to the understanding and interpretation of Husserlian phenomenology, but also in the long run to appreciate their relevance for understanding Indian thought though the latter is not the explicit goal of these essays.

II

The essays in the first part are directly concerned with Husserl, especially with his concept of intentionality, theory of meaning, and phenomenology of time. The first six essays deal with intentionality. The first four essay go back to the 1970s: (1) 'Husserl's Concept of Intentionality' (1970); (2) 'Can Intentionality be Explained Away?'

(1972); (3) 'On Husserl's Theory of Meaning' (1974); and (4) 'Husserl and Frege: A New Look' (1975). I will begin with these four essays first because they are clearly separated from the remaining two essays on intentionality both by virtue of the time period in which they appeared and also in their concerns.

These essays provide an interpretation of Husserl's phenomenology in the context of his theory of meaning thereby making possible a conversion from the natural to the phenomenological attitude. Such an interpretation distinguishes Husserl's theory of meaning from the naturalistic accounts of meaning as components of mental states on the one hand, and the formalistic account of meaning according to which the meaning of a word is determined by the rules of its usage, on the other. Mohanty's analysis underscores not only Husserl's conception of meanings as ideal entities (that is to say, entities which are not, unlike real entities, spatio-temporally individuated), their differences from mental states, and the relation that exists between meaning and experience, but also affirms Husserl's anti-psychologistic position and his thesis of the intentionality of consciousness.

For Husserl, consciousness is characteristically intentional, i.e. directed towards that which may or may not exist. Mohanty's essay 'Husserl's Concept of Intentionality', written in the late 1960s in Calcutta, analyses this important Husserlian concept. This essay might have been an early account of what later became *The Concept of Intentionality* (1972). It undertakes to do several things: it first explores the relationship of Husserl's concept of intentionality with that of Brentanos, then traces the development of that concept in Husserl's writings, finally, it looks at Husserl's thoughts in the light of its criticisms by Heidegger, Sartre, and Merleau-Ponty. It is well known that Brentano changed his views in later years partly in order to respond to criticisms of his early formulations of intentionality. Husserl believed that Brentano's locution of mental 'inexistence' was misleading. One of the goals of Husserl's philosophy was to free it from the naturalistic presuppositions of Brentano's psychology. Tracing the development of Husserl's own ideas on intentionality, Mohanty first distinguishes between a static analysis of the second *Logical Investigation* and a dynamic analysis of the sixth *Logical Investigation*. Whereas for the former, an intentional act has its own correlate which he terms its 'intentional object' (later to be called the *noema*), in the sixth *Logical Investigation*, the act develops from an original empty intention towards gradual fulfillment in intuitive experience. The development takes place in time and the question of time naturally came to occupy a central position in Husserl's thinking. The next stage of the development is the famous doctrine of the correlation between *noesis* and *noema*, the Kantian-like thesis that intentional acts confer meanings on the sensory data *(hyle)*, and finally, in the introduction of the idea of constitution, Mohanty distinguishes between two senses of constitution in these writings: constitution₁ in which to constitute means to confer meaning *(Sinngebung)* and constitution₂ meaning bringing the object constituted into evidence. The second notion, constitution₂, was possible only after Husserl rejected his own notion of *hyle* as phenomenologically unwarranted. In light of this, Mohanty examines the criticisms of Husserl by Heidegger, Sartre, and Merleau-Ponty and argues that while some of these criticisms highlight obscurities in his thoughts of different phases, further development of his thoughts renders many of these criticisms pointless. As a result of examining these criticisms, Mohanty develops his own thesis which may be regarded as his own contribution to this theme, namely that there are degrees of intentionality, just as there are degrees of reflexivity or transparency of consciousness. One could say that such intentionalities as those of bodily movements, the intentionality of emotional and affective life, are less transparent than the intentionality of knowledge. Mohanty argues that the degree of intentionality in his scheme varies with the degree of transparency of consciousness and both depend upon the presence or absence of the *hyletic* component in the intentional experience. In other words: '. . . to the extent to which a state is intentional, i.e. to the extent to which it excludes opacity and approximates towards the completely empty consciousness, a consciousness that is in itself nothing, that is fully exhausted in its intentional function, is also the most intentional.'[14] This scheme helps Mohanty to find a place for the Freudian theory of the unconscious within Husserl's phenomenology, following certain suggestions of Paul Ricoeur. In Mohanty's words:

This principle helps us to grade the intentional states in a certain scale at the one end of which are the so-called unconscious states, followed by the purely bodily intentionality, the horizon or preconscious intentionalities, conscious intentionalities with their various gradations leading up, at the other end, to *knowledge*, the most free from any content, the most transparent of all intentionalities at the same time.[15]

Mohanty returns to this idea of the 'degrees of intentionality' and the 'degrees of reflexivity' in the 1990s in the essay 'Phenomenology and Psychology', I will return to this essay later.

xx • EDITOR'S INTRODUCTION

Whereas 'Husserl's Concept of Intentionality' traces the development of the concept of intentionality from Brentano through Husserl's mature period, in contrast, the essay 'Can Intentionality be Explained Away?' considers some prevalent strategies for getting rid of the notion of intentionality, advanced by behaviourists and extensional logicians in the 1960s, and demonstrates why these attempts were unsuccessful. To be specific, it examines the attempts of contemporary philosophers, such as Carnap and Quine, to eliminate intentionality either by replacing it by appropriate stimulus and response or by giving linguistic translations of psychological sentences which dispense with the need to posit an intentional relation. Mohanty argues that these reductions cannot be carried through, and moreover, are not necessary. They cannot be carried through because what acts as a stimulus on the subject is not a physical object as such but that object as interpreted or taken by the subject to be such and such. Chisholm's tiger-response example illustrates this point. Tiger-response may be brought about by an actual tiger or by something that is believed to be a tiger. This latter belief reintroduces intentionality which shows that the translation into the language of stimulus and response does not work all the times. This reduction, Mohanty believes, is also not necessary unless one is concerned with preserving a prior physicalistic ontology. It seems to me that Mohanty's own position on this issue would be to maintain that ontology should come after phenomenology and not prior to it. A philosopher must find a place for both causality and intentionality in her scheme and not deny one and absolutize the other.

Husserl's theory of intentionality has important ramifications for his theory of meaning, which the essay 'On Husserl's Theory of Meaning' demonstrates. It would have been more appropriate to call this essay 'Husserl's Theory of Meaning Revisited', given that it first appeared nearly ten years after Mohanty's own (now classic) work, *Edmund Husserl's Theory of Meaning*. This essay was occasioned by two discussions which were going on in the early 1970s. One of them was the relationship between Husserl and Frege (to be discussed next), the other was the appearance of the English translation of Jaccque Derrida's French book under the title *Speech and Phenomenon* (1972). As regards the former, Mohanty shows that the Husserlian meanings should not be construed as essences, and that the difference between noema and essence is fundamental to understanding Husserl. At the same time, it is misleading to suppose, as Hubert Dryfuss did, that Husserl's notion of perceptual meaning as developed by Gurwitsch makes direct seeing impossible and would involve an infinite regress. Even if perception is an immediate and direct encounter with its object, there is nevertheless a distinction between perceptual adumbrations and a total presentation of the object. The latter becomes a goal that is never reached so that there is always a distinction between the meaning-intention and its fulfillment. Mohanty's response to Derrida's criticisms of Husserl's theory of meaning may indeed be one of the first to be offered. Derrida argues that Husserl's turning away from communicative speech to monologue, in the first *Logical Investigation*, already contains a reduction of all factuality and worldly existence. According to Derrida, Husserl not only abstracts all relations of meaning to empirical existence but also reduces the complete speech act to the inner voice. As we know now, this criticism lays the foundation for Derrida's later attempt to deconstruct Husserlian phenomenology. Mohanty shows that Derrida's reading of Husserl is mistaken—what is bracketed is what Husserl calls the function of indicating to the hearer the speaker's mental life, but the function of referring to a worldly entity is not meant to be excluded from the monological speech. In other words, even the monological speech remains a real concrete event and not a transcendental non-empirical act. As a result, the novelty of Husserl's thesis that there is a correlation between real temporal intentional acts and ideal meanings is missed by Derrida's interpretation of Husserl's move from communication to monologue.

Mohanty has returned several times to this theme of Husserl's theory of meaning. I would refer to two other occasions: one of them is his introduction to the third edition of his book *Edmund Husserl's Theory of Meaning*, in which he takes up the various lines of criticism of Husserl's theory, especially those offered by both Derrida and Habermas. The other is a reformulation of the theory published in Elliston and McCormick (eds). *Husserl: Exposition and Appraisal*.[16]

The essay 'Husserl and Frege: A New Look' (1975), seeks to determine what bearing, if any, Frege' conception of meaning, psychologism, epistemology, logic, etc. have on Husserl. This essay is part of Mohanty's larger project to revise accepted views regarding the relation between these two thinkers. This essay is the first published version of his thesis that the account of the relation between Husserl and Frege, which was widely prevalent at the time, was mistaken. It must have been in the early 1970s that Mohanty discovered that already in his 1891 writings, Husserl had arrived at many of those views which were generally ascribed to the influence of Frege; that they really ante-date Frege's 1892 paper on sense and reference. As

Mohanty recalls in a conversation, it was while reading the then-unpublished correspondence between Husserl and Frege (which Mohanty later translated into English and published), that he came across evidence against the traditional view. He showed it to Aaron Gurwitsch at the New School for Social Research; Gurwitsch's enthusiasm and excitement led him to further explore the matter. We now know that the theme of this essay was later expanded into the book *Husserl and Frege* (1982), which gained wide recognition upon its publication. Its thesis still remains unchallenged.

Regarding the relation between Husserl and Frege, it had been taken for granted by scholars that Husserl in his first book on philosophy of arithmetic had defended a theory of psychological origin of arithmetic. It is well known that this book was reviewed by Frege. In this review Frege had subjected Husserl's thesis to a devastating criticism and had shown the absurdity of a theory of psychological origin of mathematics. It was then taken for granted that it was Frege's devastating review which led Husserl to retract his position and in the *Prolegomena to Pure Logic* to have a systematic critique and rejection of psychologistic theories of logic. I think Mohanty was the first one to have pointed out on the basis of a close and critical study of all documents, including the correspondence between Husserl and Frege, that the above account was mistaken. Not only is it inaccurate to say that Husserl's theory of number in philosophy of arithmetic was psychologistic, it also seems to be the case that Frege did not quite understand Husserl's project. Their correspondence shows that the two of them independently of each other had arrived at the distinction between meaning, reference, and presentation. Once this distinction was made, overcoming of psychologism followed as a corollary.

In an important paper, Dagfinn Føllesdal held that the Husserlian *noema* is the result of extending the Fregean concept of *Sinn* to all intentional acts. If Mohanty's argument is correct then Føllesdal's reading is misleading. Mohanty proposes that instead of understanding the Husserlian *noema* as an extension of Frege's *Sinn*, it is preferable to understand Frege's *Sinn* as a special case of Husserlian *noema*. As would be known to all Husserl scholars today, it is common to distinguish between Føllesdal's Fregean reading of Husserl and Gurwitsch's understanding of meaning as perceptual meaning. Mohanty argues for a distinction between perceptual meaning and conceptual meaning in his book *Husserl and Frege*. It seems that both Gurwitsch and Føllesdal recognized only one kind of meaning to the exclusion of the other. Husserl's own questioning was about how conceptual meaning arises out of perceptual meaning.

Mohanty returns to this important concept of intentionality in two others pieces included in this collection, namely 'Levels of Understanding Intentionality' and 'Intentions of Intentionality: 20 Theses'. The former appeared in Monist in 1986, almost ten years later than the first group; and the latter was presented as the basis of a lecture given at Bryn Mawr College in 1996. These two essays provide a systematic and independent exposition of Mohanty's own position on the concept of intentionality.

In the first essay, Mohanty distinguishes between four levels of understanding intentionality: (1) the way it is understood in cognitive science (note that by this time a lot of philosophical concerns had moved from behaviourism to cognitive science, especially in the works of Fodor, Dretske and Sellars); (2) the understanding of intentionality in a phenomenologically descriptive psychology, for which Mohanty focuses on John Searle's work on intentionality; (3) an existentialist phenomenological account of intentionality in terms of the place of intentionality in the life-world; and (4) a transcendental constitutive account of intentionality. All these involve a discussion of the relation between intentionality and causality, and between *de re and de dicto* intentionality. There is an overall path that Mohanty traces from a naturalistic-causal to an information-theoretical to an existentialist and from the last to a transcendental interpretation of intentionality. He emphasizes that the lesson we learn from this path is that there is no route from object to sense. We have to move unavoidably from sense to object. This blocks all naturalistic interpretations of intentionality.

The 20 Theses give a schematic representation of the implications and significance of the idea of intentionality and in so doing Mohanty takes into account various critical discussions that have been going on for nearly half a century. For example, in thesis number 6, he recognizes that intentionality should not be taken to be merely cognitive; there are also practical and affective intentionalities. By this he seeks to bring together Husserl, who emphasizes the cognitive, Ricoeur, who emphasizes volitional, and Heidegger, who emphasizes the affective intentionalities called by him *Befindlichkeit* or moods. The theses 7 through 10 reconcile two different points of view which are taken to be antagonistic: that meanings originate from an ego and that meanings always belong to a culture. Likewise number 12 accepts two kinds of intentionalities: I-intentionality and we-intentionality. I think the most novel thesis that Mohanty proposes

xxiv • EDITOR'S INTRODUCTION

is expressed in 14 through 16; 15 *seems to* reverse 14, primarily because the sense of 'constitution' has been reversed so that even for transcendental phenomenology it makes sense to say that the world and consciousness are inseparable. I will only draw attention to the last thesis, number 20, in which he asserts that the empirical is the transcendental, which only *seems* to be a surprising twist to the meaning of transcendental phenomenology. For more on this, I would refer the reader to Professor Mohanty's book entitled *The Possibility of Transcendental Philosophy*. I wonder if in the formulation 'the empirical is the transcendental', Mohanty was not influenced by Nāgārjuna's thesis that *saṃsāra* and *nirvāṇa* are identical.

Mohanty's account of the 20 Theses included herein is meant to capture Mohanty's own position, carefully considered through other Husserlian pieces, for example 'The Problem of Relativism in Husserl's Late Manuscript' (read at Göttingen, Tübingen, and Konstanz in a German version) and 'The Relevance of Husserl Today' (first presented as a lecture in St. Edmund Hall, Oxford, England). These essays are concerned with showing that contemporary relativism and historicism do not present any serious challenge to transcendental phenomenology.

Regarding historicism and relativism, Husserl's thesis that the world, both the perceived world as well as the world of science, is constituted in transcendental subjectivity was severely criticized by Heidegger. Heidegger argued that the source of all constitution is *Dasein*, regarded as a mode of being in the world and as historical. From this it followed that the *Dasein* could not be a presupposition-less and ahistorical thinker, thereby making all knowledge including science and philosophy to be grounded in the historical perspective of *Dasein*. Such a conception results in relativism and historicism, implying that all truths are relative to the perspective of the age and so to the historical condition under which one thinks. There is no purely objective, disinterested, ahistorical truth. The proponents of the Heideggerian perspective used this criticism to undermine the entire Husserlian project of transcendental phenomenology which was taken to provide the foundation for scientific knowledge. For those who are familiar with Mohanty's writings know how much of Mohanty's work, including some of the essays in this collection, is intended to meet the Heideggerian objections.

The essay 'Husserl on Relativism in the Late Manuscripts' takes into account Husserl's late manuscripts, especially from the late 1920s and early 1930s, and brings to light many different ways in which the old philosopher, during the last decade of his life, under persecution by the Nazis, reflected on the question of relativism which he had once, in his youth, claimed rather hastily, to have finally resolved. The essay shows that although he had abandoned the early programme of simply refuting relativism, he did not reject the idea of absolute and objective truth. It appears as though in his old age, Husserl was oscillating between the ideal of the absolute objective truth and the relative truths which we actually attain, and tried to show that we cannot give up either of the two. The actual truths that we reach in every day lives are what he calls 'situational truths', but these situational truths tend to be 'idealized' such that they tend to suggest truths that are not bound to situations. Absolute truths are the ideals towards which all truth-seeking is oriented.

'The Relevance of Husserl Today' was a lecture Professor Mohanty delivered at Oxford on the occasion of the 50th year of the death of Husserl. The article focuses on the then-prevalent philosophical climate at Oxford on the one hand, and across the channel on the other. In Oxford, he draws attention to the growing interest in the idea of the content, and surveys this concern in Michael Dummett, Garrett Evans, John McDowell, and Christopher Peacock and evaluates this theory of content in light of the Frege–Husserl theory of *Sinn* and *noema*. The study of consciousness along with its content which at that time occupied many Oxford philosophers is shown to be closer to Husserl's philosophy. However, on the European continent, the story was quite different. There Husserl is perceived as a foundationalist and the new forms of historicism are used to challenge this foundationalism. This point of view is particularly represented in the US by Richard Rorty and on the European continent by Foucault. The common idea is that there is no grand history but only historical epochs which are divided by radical discontinuities. Mohanty offers criticisms of this point of view and argues that this or rather any relativistic philosophy of history presupposes an absolutist point of view from which the various discontinuities can be described. He also advances the argument that since there are only histories and not one History and since histories are constructed by the historian's interest, project, and methodologies, no historicism can claim ontological primacy and so cannot be a challenge to transcendental phenomenology. Mohanty further develops these ideas in some of his later writings especially in 'Phenomenology and History' and 'Some Thoughts on Time, History, and Flux', two essays included in this collection.

In the essays concerning time and history, Mohanty demonstrates the limits of a historicist reading of experience, argues that temporality includes duration and permanence as its dimensions, establishes that the thesis 'everything is in flux' is a metaphysical thesis, and proposes that history implies an ideal meaning which delimits the field of historical research.

In an earlier paper on history written in the late 1960s included in the Bilimoria volume, he had argued that philosophy of history required an intentional concept of consciousness. But that paper did not go beyond this simple claim. Now in the 1990s he goes back to the question: what is the place of history in a transcendental phenomenology? It is well known that Husserl's early thinking was essentialistic and ahistorical. It is only gradually that he began to think about history. On this path, his lectures on internal time consciousness provide the connecting link between early essentialism and the later concern with history. Mohanty first tries to ascertain the nature of Husserl's concern with history. Husserl was concerned not with actual history of the historians but with historicity. This distinction was taken over and developed by Heidegger when he claimed that human existence is characterized by historicity. In the second place, Husserl was concerned with what may be called *intentional history*. Starting with an already accomplished interpretation of the world as is to be found, for example, in modern physics, Husserl asks what kind of thinking process must have led up to it. In the third place, as Derrida has brought out, in Husserl's view history is always history *of* an ideal meaning or essence. For example, it is history of 'music' or of 'art' and 'music' and 'art' are ideal essences. Of bare particulars, there is no history, there is only arising and perishing. After having shown this, Mohanty compares Husserl's understanding of history with Heidegger's and I think what he tries to show is that Heidegger's understanding of history is heavily influenced by the western, especially Christian experience of history. Accordingly, Mohanty concludes that if we take an ontological point of view and ask whether history is a phenomenon, even after we bracket all ontic knowledge of history that we have, then all that we can find are either temporality or historicity. We cannot use any specific historical cognition to understand the nature of transcendental subjectivity or, in Heidegger's case, *Dasein*.

Given that consciousness is not only intentional, but is also temporal, the problem of time is more fundamental to phenomenology than that of history. In the essay on time entitled 'Some Thoughts on Time, History, and Flux', Mohanty provides a series of reflections on the thought of Joseph Margolis who holds that everything is in flux. Mohanty therefore distinguishes between the claim that everything is in a flux and that everything is temporal. To be enduring or permanent is also a mode of being in time. It would therefore be a mistake to hold that whatever is in time is involved in a ceaseless flux. Next, he takes up the conception of time and points out that there is no one, unique conception of time and goes on to distinguish between cosmological time to which all natural processes belong, the physical time, i.e. the time of physics, the historical time, and the time of internal stream of consciousness. Each one of these may be understood again in different ways. Given the multivalence of the idea of time, the philosophical thesis that all things are in time cannot be satisfactorily formulated, for one would still like to know 'in which time'. The same, he argues, is also true of history. There are, as the post-modernists have been insisting, histories rather than one grand History. This again makes the thesis that everything is historical ambiguous and even difficult to formulate. One may even want to argue that any history must be 'history of—' and the concept which would fill in this blank must be an ideal meaning and in that sense invariant. Mohanty's point is that these considerations set a limit to Margolis' thesis of universal flux and historicism.

Mohanty is critical of Husserl's presupposition of linear time. He voices these criticisms in 'Time: Linear or Cyclic, and Husserl's Phenomenology of Inner Time Consciousness' which is one of the few essays Mohanty has published on Husserl's lectures on the inner time-consciousness. The one included in this volume was written on the occasion of the 60th birthday of Elisabeth Ströker, a leading Husserl scholar in Germany. Mohanty in this essay argues that however penetrating Husserl's description of inner temporality may be, his account still suffers from a deep unthematized prejudice in favour of the predominantly western conception of time as linear progression. Given a different conception of time, for example as cyclic, the experience of time, as has been described by phenomenologists of religion such as Eliade, would possibly result in a different account of time-consciousness. Mohanty questions whether or not Husserl's famed 'phenomenology of internal time consciousness' can account for the experience of the cyclic character of 'sacred time' (à la Eliade).

Mohanty takes up the concept of the sacred again in the three essays on religion included in this volume. He questions whether there is a distinctive, irreducible mode of intentionality to be called religious intentionality and argues for the objectivity of the concept of the 'sacred'. The three essays on phenomenology of religion in this collection constitute perhaps everything that Mohanty has written on that topic. His interest in phenomenology of religion, however, goes back to the 1960s, to Temple University, where he held several seminars on this subject. These essays give an idea of the direction in which he might develop this topic.

'Phenomenology of Religion and Human Purpose' is the earliest of the three, written in the 1970s but published in 1986. The essay is rather a general review of what could be the subject matter of the phenomenology of religion. He takes it to be concerned with religious acts and religious intentionality. In order to understand what the religious acts are, he first discusses the views of Max Scheler, According to Scheler, religious acts are very different from intellectual acts in that their intention is more global. They also intend to transcend the world. Furthermore, the religious acts demand a reply, for example a response from the God to whom you pray. However, he finds Scheler's account of phenomenology of religion insufficient owing to his commitment at that time to Catholicism. More promising is Rudolph's Otto's emphasis on the idea of the holy rather than on the idea of God. Others like Van der Leew emphasize the centrality of the concept of power for religious consciousness while Mircea Eliade emphasizes the concept of the sacred. Using these concepts and relating them to the concept of intentionality, Mohanty argues that the religious phenomena exhibit a form of intentionality which is *sui generis*.

In the second essay 'What is Special about the Phenomenology of Religion?', written about twenty years later, Mohanty calls into question the last-mentioned thesis and raises the following questions: Is there any specific form of religious intentionality? One speaks of love, faith, prayer as religious acts. But they are not presumably specifically religious acts because they may take objects which are not religious. If there are no specifically religious acts, then there are two alternatives to choose from. One may deny that religious experience is a kind of intentionality (this is the route Levinas takes); or, one may hold that religious experience rather be construed as distinctive interpretation of the totality of one's intentional experiences. It would seem that Mohanty's sympathy lies with the second alternative.

The third essay 'Religion and the Sacred' locates the notion of the sacred in the very heart of the religious experience. Using Brentano's distinction between modifying and determining predicates, Mohanty regards 'is sacred' to be like 'is beautiful' and argues for the objectivity of those predicates which are grounded in an original experience of sacredness or the experience of beauty as the case may be. The experience of the sacred, he claims, is the experience of a power, not of a thing; a power acts upon you as sacred. This brief essay perhaps contains the rudiments of an entire phenomenology of religion which it may be hoped Professor Mohanty will develop sometime.

The essay 'Phenomenology and Psychology' argues that contemporary psychology, especially psychoanalysis and cognitive psychology, can profit from a strictly Husserlian phenomenology. The essay in fact formed the content of a lecture given at the annual meeting of the American Psychological Association in 1996 and is being published for the first time in this volume. While phenomenological psychology has grown into a wide-ranging discipline, Mohanty begins by pointing out that most of those who work in this area get their methodological ideas from Heidegger rather than from Husserl. Mohanty focuses on Husserl in order to demonstrate in what ways Husserl's ideas can be significant for psychology. One should not be deterred from this project by Husserl's well-known critique of psychologism, for that critique should not be construed as a critique of psychology but rather of a philosophical position known as psychologism. What Mohanty does first is to show that what phenomenology can contribute to psychology, to begin with, is to provide an initial determination of the field of psychology. We need this determination in order to be able to test the claims of various philosophical theses as to their adequacy. The field of psychology is regarded by Mohanty as the domain of subjectivity (to be distinguished from consciousness) and subjectivity cuts across the Cartesian distinction between mind and body. The subjective, for phenomenology, consists of pre-intentional *hyletic* experiences and also the intentionalities which confer meaning upon the *hyle*. These meanings have to be considered initially from the perspective of their producer, that is to say, their subject. In order to make it possible for these meanings to enter into a psychological theory we need to reject the naive assumption that the mental is private. On the contrary, although the acts are private, their meanings are public and can be expressed in language. After defending these claims, Mohanty proceeds to show to what extent today Husserl's phenomenology can be of use to understand and interpret both cognitive psychology and psychoanalysis. It has been noted by such philosophers as Hubert Dreyfus and Jerry Fodor that there is a close affinity between what cognitive psychology calls a representational theory of mind and Husserlian understanding of intentionality in terms of noemata. The cognitive psychology wants to retain both physicalism and what Fodor calls methodological psychologism, whereas phenomenology is not anxious to preserve physicalism, and therein lies the difference between the two theories. The main focus of phenomenology is to be faithful to experiencing in all its dimensions. Similar remarks may be made in relating phenomenology to psycho-analysis. The phenomenologists would not posit the unconscious as a theoretical entity whose use is simply explanatory. When Husserl in his late life begins to talk about the unconscious, he was interested in finding out an experiential access to the unconscious. Following the work of Aaron Mischara, this access to the unconscious was to be found in the way retentions gradually became modified and receded into the darkness of the unconscious. Mohanty also looks into the structure of the *hyletic* data and shows how there is always an element within the *hyle* pointing to the unconscious. The relation between Husserl's idea of *hyle* and Freud's unconscious had already been noticed by Paul Ricoeur and stressed by Mohanty in his early book on the concept of intentionality. However, in this essay he suggests a more concrete path from the *hyle* to the unconscious.

It is well known even to a beginner in phenomenology that phenomenological philosophy claims to be descriptive in its method and therefore is opposed to the construction of systems. Three essays in this collection, 'The System and the Phenomena: The Kant Interpretations of Nicolai Hartmann and P.F. Strawson', 'Thoughts on the Concept of World', and 'On Philosophical Description' take up the issue of description as a philosophical method. In the first of these three essays, Mohanty takes up the case of Kant and considers to what extent within Kant's philosophy one could separate descriptive from speculative components. In the second essay on philosophical description, he goes on to distinguish between various kinds of descriptions that philosophers may or actually have undertaken. In the third, dealing with the concept of the world, Mohanty shows how this highly metaphysical concept, namely of the world as a whole, which Kant regarded as giving rise to antinomies, may be salvaged on a descriptive basis.

Let me elaborate on Mohanty's central theses in these essays. In the essay on Kant (which was his contribution to the *Festschrift* for Hermann Wein), Mohanty considers two attempts to separate the descriptive core in Kant's thinking from speculative and system-building motives. These are the attempts by Nicolai Hartmann and Peter F. Strawson. Hartmann distinguishes between what he called historical elements in Kant's thinking which are determined by the metaphysical standpoint of transcendental idealism and the elements which are grounded in genuine philosophical problems and some of which are descriptions of undeniable phenomena. Likewise, Strawson aims at disentangling 'the two faces of Kant': Kant as a transcendental idealist and Kant as a descriptive metaphysician. Mohanty separates these elements in both Hartmann and Strawson, puts them side by side, compares their descriptive soundness as well as their metaphysical validity, all of which lead him to raise certain fundamental questions about philosophy as a truly descriptive enterprise.

The questions that he raises are as follows: If idealism is a metaphysical theory, then its opposite, namely realism, may also be taken to be a metaphysical theory. Why is it then that both Hartmann and Strawson regard Kant's transcendental idealism alone to be a departure from descriptive philosophy? Is it possible that a truly descriptive philosophy has to reject both idealism and realism and look for a common neutral core which both must accept? Is it possible that even Kantian idealism along with its concept of transcendental unity of apperception has its basis in a descriptive account of our experience? Some of these questions lead us to his essay on philosophical description.

The questions raised in that essay are as follows: how is a philosophical description different from non-philosophical description? How is a truly philosophical description different from a philosophical statement which only purports to be descriptive, but is not really so? How are the descriptive and the speculative components of a system related to each other? The last question clearly refers back to Kant.

If the sentence 'I have a toothache' describes my present experience, it is surely not a philosophical description. But the statement 'all conscious states are *of* something' would seem to be descriptive as well as philosophically interesting. It would seem then that a philosophically interesting description would not merely describe a particular bit of experience but must be able to describe the *essential* structure of some experience or the other. Additionally, he points out that a genuine philosophical description requires that we look at the experience we have to describe independently of any prior scientific or other theoretical prejudice. A philosopher must develop the skill of looking at his or her experience without being prejudiced by any of her theoretical beliefs.

With regard to the third question, namely the relation between the descriptive and the speculative components of a system, Mohanty sorts out various ways in which a genuinely descriptive finding may be used for speculative purposes. For example, a philosopher may generalize his descriptive finding beyond the region where he first ascertains it and extend it over other regions. Good examples of this kind of philosophizing are to be found in philosophers like Whitehead and Charles Hartshorne, both of whom generalize the Brentano thesis about intentionality for all things in nature, a thesis which results in a kind of panpsychism. Finally, one of the most useful contributions of this essay is to distinguish between various kinds of descriptions undertaken by philosophers. Some descriptions are pure, i.e. direct, others are descriptions by negation (one may describe an X by saying what X is not), still others may be descriptions by a series of approximations (which point towards X as its limit) or there may be classificatory descriptions, or what he calls, following Heidegger, 'hermeneutic descriptions', to name a few.

The essay on the concept of the 'world', which was originally given in Santiniketan in 1978, tries to rehabilitate the concept of the 'world' as against the Kantian critique. Mohanty in this essay argues for two theses. If we understand by world 'scientific nature', then, as against Kant, he argues that it is not constructed out of sensations but rather out of prescientific life-worlds. However far back from scientific nature we may go, we would always find a world and these prescientific worlds are not eliminated by the scientific but coexist with it such that we actually exist in many different worlds. His second thesis is that the one world which we sometimes refer to is really the concept of the ultimate horizon within which both science and common sense have their moving space. This horizon is always there in the background but can never be thematized. Kant showed that the idea of the world as a completed totality generated antinomies. Mohanty argues, following certain suggestions of Heidegger, that the totalization of the world takes place not in cognitive thinking but in non-cognitive, rather affective experiences. These are the experiences in which nothing makes sense or perhaps in experience of great art such as epic poetry in which a tradition comes first to be constituted.

The essay on Wilfred Sellar, originally a commentary on Sellar's paper on consciousness presented at a meeting of the APA, is intended to demonstrate that physicalism does not pose a serious challenge to phenomenology. Mohanty critically examines Sellar's failed attempt to keep physicalism and phenomenology together. In order to reach the pure element of sensation involved in perceptual experiences, Sellar does employ a kind of Husserlian reduction but

EDITOR'S INTRODUCTION • xxxiii

when he reaches a given sensation as such, he proceeds to identify that sensation with an element in the brain of the perceiver. Mohanty challenges this position. According to Mohanty, Sellar preserves his physicalism because he does not appreciate the role of Husserlian *noema* in a perceptual situation.

'A Case for Idealism' was presented in the All Souls College, Oxford. This occasion had a particular significance as Professor Mohanty recalls. Matilal had arranged this meeting to celebrate the birth centenary of S. Radhakrishnan, a former fellow of All Souls College. Among the speakers were Mohanty, Davidson, and Strawson. It was also the last occasion for Mohanty to be in the company of Matilal at All Souls College. In this essay, Mohanty presents a case for idealism. He begins by distinguishing two versions of idealism, one of which follows Hegel's *Phenomenology of Mind*. In this version, every form of consciousness—perceptual, scientific, or religious—has a realism built into it, for example perception always regards its object to be out there independently of the perceiver, the scientist in his naivete is a realist with regard to his discoveries, but so also is the religious believer. But critical reflection would abolish this realism in each case and would show that a domain of objects necessarily refers back to a form of consciousness. The second version makes use of the phenomenological thesis that an object is constituted by intentional experiences of a certain kind in which that object is presented. Consciousness and the world are correlates in so far as consciousness both belongs to the world and presents the world. In the first respect, it is mundane, in the second respect, it is transcendental. After making this distinction between two forms of idealism, Mohanty proceeds to develop an argument for idealism. The argument is primarily based upon the defense of idealism in the Indian tradition. It makes use of two premises: one of which is the principle of transparence *(svaprakāśavāda)*, the principle that every consciousness is *eo ipso* conscious of itself. The other is what he calls the principle of content *(jñānsākāravāda)*, namely that every state of consciousness has an intentional content internal to it. Add to these two, a third premise, namely the principle of intrinsic truth *(svataḥprāmāṇyavāda)*. Mohanty argues that these three premises yield a strong idealism. In substance, the argument reformulates and strengthens (by adding the third premise) the Yogācāra Buddhist defense of idealism as against the Nyāya positions. These three premises are further developed by Mohanty in the light of modern phenomenology. Thus, the first premise is reformulated as the principle of phenomenological accessibility which says that consciousness *can* be made transparent by reflection, while the second principle is reformulated by distinguishing between surface and deep contents of consciousness. In this way, the argument for idealism is strengthened. However, Mohanty ends by insisting, along with Hegel, that although idealism in principle may be a sound theory, we still do not know how it can be true *in detail*. As Hegel puts it 'idealism only gives the assurance about its truth, but does not comprehend this fact', that is, whereas in general an idealist can say that the spirit alone is real, it is difficult to assess with certainty what is entailed in such a claim when applied to particular instances. It would appear nevertheless that Mohanty has a strong leaning towards a kind of idealistic philosophy while he restrains his realistic intuitions by bringing them under the scope an overarching idealism.

This brings me to the essay that compares Kant and Husserl, which was presented at the International Kant Congress in 1995. It shows that if Husserl had aimed at writing a critique of reason and Kant had thought of writing a phenomenology of consciousness and if they had carried out these two programmes where they would have met and with what differences. Mohanty shows that Husserl's Transcendental Aesthetic would have contained, besides the theory of perception as with Kant, also the beginnings of mathematics of continuity and its limits. Similarly, Transcendental Analytic for Husserl would have dealt with logic and mathematics—in the long run, with what he calls formal ontology. Kant had, as is well known, a different understanding of both the Aesthetic and the Analytic. Mohanty traces this difference to Husserl's different understanding of formal logic as well as of pure mathematics, which he shared with contemporary workers in those fields. Kant's understanding of logic remained Aristotelian and of mathematics Euclidean.

III

These essays should not only be of immense help to scholars in phenomenology, but also make evident Mohanty's complex philosophical agenda. They not only provide a preliminary orientation to Husserlian phenomenology but also insights into hermeneutics, post-structuralism, and deconstuctionism in the context of the philosophical views of Heidegger, Sartre, Merleau-Ponty and Ricouer. In *Phenomenology: East and West*, a collection of essays published in his honour, the editors begin their introduction in the following words:

To know the work of Jitendra Nath Mohanty even slightly is to commence to appreciate it immensely. Lucidity and sagacity have been its armor; originality and ingenuity have been its strength . . . It has fulfilled the most welcomed promise of striking the chords of both imagination and reason by exposing Husserlian phenomenology to the concerns of both the so-called 'analytical' and 'continental' traditions and by exposing the philosophical tradition of Indian thought to the intricacies of Husserl.[17]

I concur with the above assessment. The clarity, lucidity, and comprehensiveness of his thought is phenomenal. Irrespective of whether the language is German or Sanskrit or English, this clarity comes through.

A little later, the editors further note that 'Mohanty's career in phenomenology can be characterized by three phases, each concentrating on different themes, but the later two epitomizing a more incisive and deeper discussion of the issues raised in the first.'[18] I must say that in reviewing Mohanty's writings carefully, I do not see any marked split of the sort that the editors attribute to him. It seems to me that there are some central concerns that appear again and again. His writings exhibit various attempts to understand the motives and central issues—*noema*, intentionality, descriptive philosophy, essence and meaning—which form the foundation of Husserlian transcendental phenomenology in order to put them in proper perspective. Mohanty's writings demonstrate a deep thinking, a constant revision and expansion of his views.

Mohanty is one of the most prolific philosophers of our times. He has spent virtually all of his philosophical life engaging in conversations with philosophers of different beliefs and persuasions. The diversity of the topics on which he has written attests to the multidimensional character and the fecundity of his work. He qualifies for the highest marks, irrespective of whether one is judging him by the insightfulness of his work, the depth of his work or the breadth of his work. I hope that these essays facilitate the sort of 'comparative philosophy' which Mohanty himself has pursued so vigorously, and provide the impetus, for further research into directions which his work brings—and continues to assist in bringing—to full brilliance.

Before closing, I would like to bring to the attention of my readers an issue which requires some attention. Much has been made of the impact of Husserl's thinking on Mohanty's interpretation and understanding of Indian philosophy. He himself concedes that he is 'Husserlian of a sort' and accordingly follows this approach in his interpretation of Indian philosophy. It remains to be assessed how his training in Indian logic and Vedānta impacted his choosing to work on Husserl and phenomenology, rather than, say, on Descartes. In other words, did his study of Vedānta in any way predispose him towards Husserl, as well as influence his understanding of Husserl? A review of the biographical details of his life reveals that Mohanty was trying to come to grips with issues such as the intentionality of consciousness, reflexivity of consciousness, and the locus of consciousness in the context of Advaita Vedānta, long before he ever picked up a copy of Husserl's *Ideas* at the home of his teacher, Rash Vihari Das. One would like to believe that his study of Śaṃkara's *Brahmsūtrabhāṣya* played a decisive role in his study and interpretation Husserlian phenomenology.

Since beginning to work on this introduction, I have tried to press this point several times with Mohanty; however, no answer was forthcoming for some time. But, to my pleasant surprise, at the American Philosophical Association Pacific Division meetings in Berkeley, California, 2 April 1999, after Mohanty finished his lecture on 'The Other Husserl', a member of the audience asked Mohanty about the possible influence of Indian philosophy on his reading of Husserl. He again avoided a direct thematic answer to the question and simply supplied a few biographical facts. Subsequent conversation with him seemed to bring out something like the following account. His choosing to read Husserl was not inspired by any of the concerns in Indian thought of which he was aware. But it is also true that once he got hold of some components of Husserl's thought, the latter continued to suggest inner affinities with Indian philosophy. We know that in the early fifties, Mohanty had already written his first essay on phenomenology and Indian philosophy—a theme to which he has returned time and again. More specifically, Husserl's concern with consciousness, his distinction between transcendental and empirical consciousness, and the thesis that all objects owe their constitution to consciousness, could not have endured without awakening the interests of the one who was already steeped in Vedāntic learning. A young European scholar is very likely to find these aspects of Husserl's phenomenology highly problematic, but not so the Indian philosopher. However, the Indian Vedānta scholar may have to avoid taking an opposite step, i.e. to completely 'Indianize' the key Husserlian notions. I think Mohanty consciously tried to avoid doing so. But, it is nevertheless quite possible that Vedānta of some variety or other has continued to shape his sensitivity for phenomenology. When one, especially Mohanty, talks about this subtle influence, he is afraid lest he may turn it into an explicit comparison and also be tempted to reconstruct a story which would replace the subtle and slow fusion of interests.

Mohanty of today, as I see him, is neither a Naiyāyika, nor a Vedāntin, nor a Husserlian, but rather a 'Mohantyian' in whom one finds a fine assimilation of all three.

NOTES

1. Frank M. Kirkland and D.P. Chattopadhyaya (eds), *Phenomenology: East and West* (Dodrecht: Kluwer Academic Publishers, 1993), p. 292.

2. J.N. Mohanty, *Self and Its Other* (New Delhi: Oxford University Press, 2000).

3. M. Merleau-Ponty, *Phenomenology of Perception*, (tr.) Colin Smith (London: Routledge & Kegan Paul, 1962).

4. Ibid., p. xiii.

5. Ibid., p. xv.

6. See Bina Gupta, 'Phenomenological Analysis in Husserl and Rāmānuja: A Comparative Study', *International Studies in Philosophy* (Binghamton: State University of New York, 1983).

7. Edmund Husserl, *Cartesian Meditations*, translated by Dorions Cairns (The Hague: Martinus Nihjoff, 1973), p. 26.

8. J.N. Mohanty, *The Concept of Intentionality* (St. Louis, Mo: Warren H. Green, 1972), p. 56.

9. Eugen Fink, 'Husserl's Philosophy and Contemporary Criticism', in *The Phenomenology of Husserl*, ed. R.O. Elveton (Chicago: Quadrangle Press, 1970), p. 115.

10. Ibid.

11. Ibid., pp. 115–16.

12. 'Preface', to Fink's 'Husserl's Philosophy and Contemporary Criticism', p. 74.

13. For further details, see Bina Gupta, *The Disinterested Witness: A Fragment of Advaita Vedānta Phenomenology* (Evanston, Illinois: Northwestern University Press, 1998). Also see, J.N. Mohanty, *The Concept of Intentionality*.

14. Mohanty, *The Concept of Intentionality*, p. 171.

15. Ibid.

16. Elliston amd McCormick (eds), *Husserl: Exposition and Appraisal* (Nortre Dame: University of Nortre Dame Press, 1977).

17. Kirkland and Chattopadhyaya, *Phenomenology: East and West*. p. xi.

18. Ibid.

Author's Prologue

E ach of these essays has its own biographical contextual origin. In any case, these origins—as the author gets older—tend to recede into the increasingly forgotten past while some broad outlines contine to permit 'Vergegenwärtigung'. By putting these essays together, both the editor, Professor Bina Gupta, and the publisher, Oxford University Press, have made it possible for me, and my readers, to hold fast to some segments of my creative life and prevent them from receding into the darkness of anonymity. But, however much the author's personal life may have been responsible for the composition of each of these pieces, it still remains and deserves to remain on an outer horizon. To the inner horizon belong how the community of thinkers and their thoughts determined their origin and formation. The editor, Bina Gupta, a friend and colleague and increasingly a participant in my life of mind, has been able to preserve some of these stories and illuminate the origins of some of the essays that go into these volumes. For this I am thankful to her.

J.N. Mohanty
April, 1999

part

one

part

one

chapter

one

Husserl's Concept of Intentionality*

I t may not be an overstatement to say that the development of Husserl's thought can be adequately grasped if only we followed the development of his concept of intentionality. The same could also be said of the development of phenomenology after Husserl. There are no doubt some excellent studies on Husserl's concept of intentionality,[1] but what is still lacking is a comprehensive account which would take into account the total *Husserliana* which are only now coming to be made available to scholars. Furthermore, we also do not have a study which undertakes to assess Husserl's concept of intentionality from the point of view of the criticisms and challenges emerging out of the writings of the post-Husserlian phenomenologists. This essay will make an attempt to fulfil these two needs but only within the brief compass permissible here. There will be first an attempt to explore the philosophical relationship of Husserl's concept of intentionality to Brentano's. An exposition will next be given of Husserl's concept through the various phases of its development. This will be followed by a reference to the criticisms and challenges made by the later phenomenologists like Sartre and Merleau-Ponty, and the concluding part of the essay will seek to evaluate the points made by the critics and in that

*Tymieniecka (ed.), *Analecta Husserliana*, Vol. I, 100–132. All Rights Reserved Copyright © 1970 by D. Reidel Publishing Company, Dordrecht-Holland

connection take a fresh look at Husserl's thought against the new perspective gained thereby.

I

While making out his case for regarding intentionality as a distinguishing feature of what he calls 'mental phenomena', Brentano makes use of such locutions as 'intentional inexistence of the object', 'relatedness to a content', 'direction towards an object' and 'immanent objectivity'. However, he is also aware that these expressions are not free from equivocations. The scholastic notion of 'inexistence' dominates his way of speaking about intentionality, and he even speaks of a mental state as 'containing' something as its object, or of the psychic 'Einwohnung'. For a proper understanding of Brentano and also for a correct appreciation of Husserl's relationship to the Brentano thesis it is necessary to be clear about Brentano's uses of 'object' and 'content' and to ask: (a) did Brentano, like Twardowski and Meinong, distinguish between object and content, and also (b) did he regard intentionality as a relation? With regard to (a), it would seem that Brentano did at first draw some kind of distinction between the mere object ('Gegenstand schlechtweg') and the intentional or immanent object, in which case the latter (e.g. this-tree-as-an-object-of-my-present-perception) will seem to be the content having a sort of mental or quasi-mental existence.[2] However, we learn from Kraus as also from Brentano's later writings, especially from his letters, that his view on this matter underwent a radical change. In his letter to Marty, dated 1905, he not only rejects this view but strangely enough contends that he never held it. The immanent object is now said to be the same as the thing itself. When, for example, I think about a horse the object of my thought is the horse itself, not a contemplated horse. Brentano however continues to call this thing, the horse in our example, an 'immanent' object, and to hold the view that such a thing need not exist. The latter view is explained by the fact that he uses 'thing' or 'real' in a specific sense according to which a thing or a real need not exist or need not be actual (wirkliches). The word 'immanent' does not any longer mean 'mental' or 'quasi-mental', and is in fact a redundant qualification of 'object'; and being an object 'is merely the linguistic correlate of the person experiencing having it as object'.[3] We need not recapitulate here Brentano's interesting attempts—anticipating Russell's theory of incomplete symbols—to get rid of the curious Zwischenentitäten by distinguishing between 'autosemantic' and 'synsemantic' expressions; but one has to recognize that although he continues to use misleading language he does come to reject the so-called contents, and that the more successfully he does so, the more he approximates towards an adequate formulation of the concept of intentionality.

As regards (b), again, Brentano no doubt *speaks* of intentional relatedness. But here also he shows keen awareness of the difficulties likely to arise out of treating intentionality as a relation. Brentano tells us that whereas for a genuine relation to hold good between two terms both these terms should exist, this is not the case with mental directedness.[4] In other words, my thought may very well intentionally refer to something nonexistent (e.g. a golden mountain). Brentano therefore suggests that what we may have here is not something *relatives* but *relativliches*.[5]

It would seem then that in Brentano's view all mental phenomena but no non-mental phenomena are characterized by a peculiar, not further analysable, directedness towards an object, a directedness which is not mediated by a mental content as distinguished from the object intended, and which seems to be a relation but is not really one. In view of this, we may now turn to Husserl's criticisms of Brentano.

We may for the present leave out of consideration Husserl's comments in the *Logische Untersuchungen*[6] on the inadequacies and equivocations of Brentano's terminology. The really pertinent challenge to the Brentano thesis, however, concerns its validity as a thesis about the alleged criterion of the 'mental'. Husserl asks,[7] is everything mental intentional? Or, even, are all *Erlebnisse* intentional? Are not sensations—which undoubtedly enter into intentional acts as their components—themselves non-intentional? Further, are there not objectless feeling, e.g. anxieties? Now it would seem that although in the *Logische Untersuchungen* Husserl did hold that not all that is mental is intentional, only the so-called acts being so, he gave up this reservation in the later writings. As he extended the sphere of intentionality beyond the narrow region of what he called acts, as he undertook to lay bare the intentional structure even of the sensible data in the lectures on time-consciousness, he surely came nearer to accepting the Brentano thesis that everything mental is intentional. But at the same time he seems to have moved away from the other half of the Brentano thesis and, as we shall see later on, come to hold that body, and not merely the mind, is characterized by intentionality.

Thus, even with Husserl, as with Merleau-Ponty, that aspect of the Brentano thesis in which it offers a criterion of the mental comes to be abandoned in the long run.

The rest of Husserl's comments are consequences (i) of his total rejection of the naturalistic-causal framework for a philosophy of mind, and (ii) of the fundamental methodological notion of phenomenological reduction. Brentano was operating within the framework of a naturalistic psychology which accords a pre-eminent place to the causal mode of explanation. For Husserl, the concept of intentionality demands a complete abandonment of the causal attitude in connection with whatever is intentional.[8] This change also makes way for the idea of intentional implication and intentional unity amongst mental states and later on for the very important phenomenological notion of motivation which both takes care of and goes beyond the old empiricist notion of association. Conscious states imply each other, lead to one another, are synthesized with each other, and thus constitute a unity—both at the formal level of time-consciousness and at the contentual level—not by mechanical association, nor by logical entailment but by motivating, anticipating and fulfilling each other. To *understand* a conscious state in this sense would require following up all its intentional implications, unravelling its motivations, etc. But it is the reduction which for the first time enables us to appreciate the full significance of the notion of intentionality.[9] Brentano was of course aware that the object intended may or may not exist, and he also saw that the intended reference *qua* reference is not affected by the existence or non-existence of the object of reference. But this indifference cannot be fully appreciated so long as we do not give effect to the reduction by bracketing all positing of transcendent things, and do not view the object *qua* object, i.e. as it is being intended. In other words, it is the reduction which first makes possible the key phenomenological concept of *noema*, a concept which cuts across ontological regions of individual facts and essences, the existent and the non-existent, simply because it itself is not an ontological but a genuinely phenomenological concept.[10]

Gurwitsch has shown the affinity between the method of reduction and the concept of *noema* with the gestaltist's rejection of the constancy hypothesis and the consequent notion of *theme*.[11] While thus Husserl's thesis receives confirmation from the side of the psychologist, a no less interesting confirmation announces itself from the side of the linguistically-oriented philosopher. It has lately been emphasized that intentional discourse—as contrasted with the non-intentional discourse—is characterized either by (i) existence independence (in the case of simple, declarative sentences with a substantival expression functioning as the object of the verb), or by (ii) truth-value indifference (in the case of non-compound sentences containing a propositional clause), or by (iii) referential opacity (in the case of cognitive verbs like 'know', 'see', 'perceive', etc.) or, finally, by (iv) a certain peculiar pattern of implication obtaining amongst the quantified forms of sentences with intentional prefixes.[12] Now it would seem clear that at least the first three criteria are closely connected with the phenomenological distinctions between the intended object and the object *qua* intended, and between the real and the intended objects. What an intentional act does entail—not logically, to be sure—is an intended object but not a real object *qua* real. It may even be that the reality of the intended object is precisely the object of belief, etc., but even in such cases one has to distinguish between its reality as such and its reality as intended, i.e. as believed, imagined, thought of, etc. The concept of intentionality implies neither realism nor idealism regarded as ontological theses: it is this ontological neutrality whose linguistic correlate is brought out in the first two criteria, namely in the alleged facts of existence independence and truth value indifference.

However, while thus Husserl did in many ways go beyond Brentano and refined and improved upon his concept, many of the criticisms made by phenomenologists against Brentano are far from being fair. It has, for example, been contended[13] that Brentano knows only of intentional relation between two entities, and—as a corollary of this—that Brentano's concept of intentionality is based on an assumption of epistemological realism. Now it is surely true that Brentano was a realist but it has also to be admitted that in the formation of his concept of intentionality, especially in its more mature form, he did not let this belief influence him. He does say, for example, that the existence of the object is not necessarily entailed by the fact that it is the object of a certain mental directedness. He did realize the difficulties that arise in case one understands intentionality as a relation. Phenomenologists would do well to take Brentano's later theories and self-criticisms more seriously.

Again, Herbert Spiegelberg in his admirable study of 1936 recognizes that Brentano had abandoned the use of 'mental inexistence', but notes that he had also dropped the adjective 'intentional' and retained only 'psychic relatedness to the object'. It does not however seem correct to say, as Spiegelberg does, that Brentano almost gives up the use of 'intentional' 'um nur die mental Immanenz der psychischen Phänomene noch stärker hervortretenzulassen'.[14] Brentano in fact did most explicitly reject the conception of 'mental inexistence', and if he also ceased to make use of 'intentional' it must be due to the apprehension that this word was—or had been through his own writings—associated with the idea of mental inexistence. It may also be that when Brentano did speak of 'mental inexistence' he did not mean a sort of literal 'being contained in'.

Just as we are after the integral Husserl, so it is only fair that we should look out for the integral Brentano: in both cases the complete philosophical works of the two authors are just being made available, making possible a reassessment of our usual understanding of the two philosophers.

It has already been emphasized that intentionality cannot any longer be regarded as a distinguishing mark of the mental. For though all that is mental may well be intentional, yet not all that is non-mental is non-intentional. Just as the thesis of intentionality is neutral as against realism and idealism—in fact leads beyond both—so also it is neutral as against body–mind dualism and behaviourism. What it surely is incompatible with is a mechanistic interpretation of human behaviour, but not all forms of behaviourism. A philosophy of mind which reduces mental states to bodily behaviour but at the same time replaces an intentionalistic framework for study of behaviour for the Watsonian naturalistic framework is indeed compatible with the intentionality thesis. This point is worth bearing in mind, for it is, or at least used to be, rather rashly supposed that the phenomenologist's interest lay in consciousness and not in bodily behaviour. That this is not so hardly needs to be said today, and this is not true even of Husserl as we shall see in this study. The phenomenologist need not even totally reject the S-R formula, just as Husserl did not totally reject Hume's laws of association. Just as Husserl showed that the concept of association needs to be taken up into the phenomenological concepts of motivation and intentional implication, so we may show that the very concept of stimulus is a covertly intentional concept. Thus suppose there is a mental verb m with an intentional object o, and suppose its behaviouristic translation into the language of response is $r(o)$. Let us grant also that the translation is adequate, in other words that the mental word m is dispensable. But $r(o)$ is no less intentional. The truth of the statement 'S makes the response r

(o)' logically entails neither the existence nor the non-existence of o. The response r is directed towards o, and the sense of this directedness is closer to the mental directedness, and is radically different from the relation of 'being caused by'. To bring in the concept of 'being stimulated by' is of no help, for a stimulus *qua* stimulus is not a cause. Being a stimulus of a response reposes basically upon intentionality.[15]

II

Husserl's concept of intentionality may be said to have developed in several stages though a strict line of demarcation is indeed difficult to draw amongst these. We shall here divide our exposition of Husserl's concept under three heads: the concept of intentionality in the *Logische Unter suchungen*, in the *Ideas* I, and in the works after the *Ideas* I.

A. THE CONCEPT OF INTENTIONALITY IN THE *LOGISCHE UNTERSUCHUNGEN*

In the *Logische Untersuchungen*, II.1., we find what has been called by Diemer[16] a static analysis of intentionality, whereas in the next part of the second volume of the same book we are given what may be called a dynamic analysis. This distinction is useful no doubt, but we have to remember that the two do not exclude but rather supplement each other.

The static analysis lays bare the structure of what is called an intentional act whereby the word 'act' has to be taken not in its ordinary usage as meaning an activity or a process, but simply as standing for all intentional mental states. Intentionality is not a kind of activity, but the ordinary concept of action is itself an intentional concept. The distinction that dominates the static analysis and is carried over into the *Ideas* I, but first explicitly abandoned in the lectures on inner time consciousness is that between the *'reell'* component (Husserl does not say 'real' as he is afraid the latter word may suggest the notion of thing-like entities) and the intentional correlate of an intentional experience. By the former he understands all those *Erlebnisse* which themselves are parts of the act under consideration taken as a totality, as an object like any other, but not particularly regarded as an intentional experience. However, the other, i.e. the intentional correlate, concerns an intentional experience *qua* intentional. But under the intentional correlate, again, Husserl proceeds to distinguish between the intentional object, the intentional matter and the intentional essence of an act. The two judgements '2 + 2 = 4' and 'New Delhi is the capital of India' are said to have the same act-quality in so far as both are judgements, but they differ in their intentional matter. The judgement 'There are living beings on Mars' and the question 'Are there living beings on Mars?' differ in their qualities but are said to agree in their intentional matter. Any two acts having the same quality and the same matter may be treated as being identical even if they, regarded as real events in the mental lives of two different persons, may be numerically different. While the quality of an act indicates the peculiar way of its being concerned with the intentional object (its 'Weise der gegenständichen Beziehung'), the matter determines its objective direction (its 'bestimmte Richtung auf ein Gegenständiches'). Thus, though the two concepts 'equiangular triangle' and 'equilateral triangle' have the same quality and refer to the same object, yet, since they are not identical representations, we must suppose that the intentional matter in the two cases is different. The intentional essence of an act is next defined as the unity of its quality and matter: this gives us a concept of identity to be applied to the domain of acts for the purpose of phenomenological description.

The sixth Investigation introduces a new concept, namely that of the epistemic essence (erkenntnismäßiges Wesen) of an act, but this applies only to those acts which are here called 'objectifying acts', which are in fact the theoretical and cognitive acts as distinguished from the affective and the volitional ones. We need not consider here Husserl's theory that only the objectifying acts (which are either nominal or propositional, and in either case either positing or non-positing) are the primary bearers of meaning.[17] For the present, we may mention that while all acts are intentional and possess intentional essence, only objectifying acts possess an epistemic essence. If we remember that the objectifying acts are the cognitive ones, then the above contention that they possess an epistemic essence would appear to be trivial. However, Husserl's thesis here is important: he is by implication saying something more than this apparently trivial thing. He holds that every objectifying act necessarily has an intuitive basis. The nature and the role of this intuitive basis surely differs in the case of the different kinds of objectifying acts. It may, when the act is symbolic, serve as a mere sign of the intentional matter; in the case of knowledge in the strict sense it may serve to fulfil the meaning intention. While the intentional essence of an act was defined as the unity of the act-quality and act-matter, the epistemic essence is now defined as the unity of quality, matter and the intuitive content. Just as the concept of intentional essence provides us with a concept of identity of acts in general, so the concept of epistemic essence enables us to speak of *the same* knowledge, howsoever this knowledge may otherwise differ.

This static analysis of intentional act is supplemented by a dynamic analysis in the sixth Investigation. This new point of view brings to the forefront *the dialectics of intention and fulfilment*. This dialectics shows that the intentional act involves an aiming at, a project, an active thrust demanding actualization, fulfilment or satisfaction.[18] In it we begin to gain two fresh insights, both definite advances: for one thing, the minimum sense, or rather the central core of temporality involved in intentionality, in fact the essential relationship between the two concepts, begins to reveal itself before our eyes; for another, the early phenomenological notion of absolute givenness, of total intuitive grasp, makes room for the ever receding goal of absolute fulfilment or complete coincidence of the originally empty intention with intuitive fulfilment. Indeed, though the spectre of a total coincidence persists in the *Logische Untersuchungen* where 'knowledge' is still defined in terms of it, yet Husserl soon abandons it as a description of what is ever happening when we are said to know, but continues to retain it as an ideal towards which our intentional life asymptotically aims. We learn both that the *presence* has to be measured by the sense; i.e. the intention it fulfils, and also that the sense, the intention, has to be appraised by evidence, every claim to be measured by 'seeing'.[19] What is of still greater contemporary relevance is that Husserl goes beyond the positivistic restriction of all evidence to the sensuous, and leaves room open for different kinds of fulfilment and for different strata of verification.

B. THE CONCEPT OF INTENTIONALITY IN THE *IDEAS I*

The structure of the intentional act as revealed by the static analysis is basically retained in the *Ideas* I. The *reelle* components of the act are now grouped under two heads: the *hyle* and the *noesis*. As contrasted with them, the intentional correlate is now called the *noema*. Just as with the concept of the *noema* we get into the real heart of the concept of intentionality, so with the concept of the *hyle* we face one of the chief bugbears of the later-day phenomenologists. Many have found in the latter a trace of uncritical sensualistic empiricism, others have found in it a survival of the Aristotelian–Kantian hylo-morphic scheme. Whatever may be the value and the historical affiliation of this concept of *hyle*, the fact remains that it is there and also that Husserl himself came to suspect it later on, and it is doubtful if he was ever able to do away with it entirely.

While the *noema* as the sense (as distinguished from the intentional object which is the reference: Husserl uses 'meaning' for both) is both subjective and objective, *'ein Zwitter subjektiver Immanenz und transzendenter Objektivität'*[20], the *noesis* is both psychological (being a real component of an act) and transcendental (being meaning-conferring) at the same time. Their correlation constitutes the wonder of wonders, one of Husserl's most significant discoveries. But even this correlation (succinctly summed up in Husserl's sentence: 'No noetic phase without a noematic phase that belongs specifically to it')[21] has various aspects which may be distinguished as follows:

(a) Each act has its own intended object;
(b) Each act has its own *noema*;
(c) Different acts may have the same *noema*;
(d) Different *noemata* may refer to the same object;
(e) Each act-phase has its noematic-phase.

In any case, at the noematic level there is achieved a unification which raises the *noema* above the temporality and particularity of the noetic acts, but which also brings to light the fact that the noetic act is not the merely psychological, temporal event that it at first appears to be but is also psychological–transcendental in one.

While the *irreal noema* stands over against a multiplicity of real acts, a multiplicity of *noemata* refers, through passive synthesis of identification, to an identical object, real or ideal. Thus the *irreal noema* mediates between the real intentional act and the real (or ideal) intended object. In relation to the acts the *noema* is an identity, in relation to the noematic multiplicity the intentional object is an identity. To put it in the language of the later phenomenology of constitution, the constitution of the intended object by its correlative noetic acts is mediated by the constitution of the *noema*.

It would be an error to suppose, as Gurwitsch does, that the noetic-noematic correlation constitutes the central core of Husserl's notion of intentionality.[22] The relation of *noesis* to *noema* is not the same as the relation of consciousness to its object.[23] The reference of consciousness to its object is *made possible* through (a) the correlation and (b) the noematic 'nucleus' by virtue of which the *noema* also refers to the object, and (c) the consequent noematic intentionality. It should also be borne in mind that the correlation characterizes only the act-intentionalities, and cannot be meaningfully extended to intentionalities other than acts. Thus, for an adequate understanding of Husserl's concept of intentionality we need to go beyond the correlation thesis.

C. THE CONCEPT OF INTENTIONALITY IN THE WORKS PUBLISHED AFTER THE *IDEAS I*

There is no doubt that the two primitive notions of the *Ideas* I, the noetic act and the *hyle*, lose their privileged status in the lectures on inner time consciousness: they also are now shown to have been constituted in the inner time consciousness. The act-matter scheme, the hylo-morphic framework dating back to the *Logische Untersuchungen* now collapses. Acts and data are also immanent objects, they are possible objects of inner reflection. They are temporal unities. As such they both are to be analysed into primal impressions *(Urimpressionen)*, the *nows* with their retentional and protentional horizon. Husserl, in these lectures, seems to be oscillating between a real and an intentional analysis. When, for example, he decomposes a total act into partial acts or act-phases—the tendency is there in the *Ideas I* also—the analysis seems more *reell* than intentional; when the total act-intention is decomposed into partial intentions which remain anonymous behind it, the analysis is intentional. The former decomposition may be misleading in so far as an act may be regarded as having no temporal stretch at all, it may be concentrated in one moment. The second decomposition would still hold good of it: the partial intentions would not break up this momentary character of the total intention. The partial intentions are not phases of the act, but its media, conditions of its possibility. As the act is to be traced back into partial intentions that are not acts, so the supposed datum, the unmeaning stuff, the sensory manifold—as a temporally enduring object—is resolved into momentary phases each with its retentional–protentional horizon. However it should be borne in mind that when the *datum* is said to have an intentional structure, that is so in a sense radically different from that in which acts are intentional. Its intentionality is simply its temporality, it is not intentional in the sense of being *of* anything.[24]

It has been pointed out[25] that this formal analysis fails to account for the material, i.e. the contentual aspect of the hyletic datum. It would then seem that even if we discard an absolute dualism between form and matter, we cannot do away, at any given stage, with a dualism relative to that stage. The phenomenologist has to retain this relative dualism without succumbing to an easy sensualistic empiricism with regard to the *hyle*, and without identifying all intentions with acts. This indeed is a problem for both Husserl and the later-day phenomenologists.

Intentionality as Constitution

We are thus led from the conception of intentionality as a self-transcending reference to the conception of it as noetic-noematic correlation, and then from the latter to the concept of it as constitution. The last conception, anticipated in the *Ideas I* and also in the lectures on time consciousness, receives much extension in the later works. In fact we may distinguish between two senses of 'constitution': constitution as *Sinngebung* and constitution as transcendental production. Let us call these 'constitution$_1$' and 'constitution$_2$'. The former is a consequence of the doctrine of correlation, it presupposes the hylomorphic scheme, and it applies only to act-intentionalities and so is valid only within a limited perspective.[26] Fink holds constitution$_1$ to be indeterminate *(unbestimmt)*, neither fully receptive nor fully creative, and constitution$_2$ to be productive and creative. However, while it is true that Husserl came both to suspect and give up his earlier hylo-morphic scheme, we should also remember that he never overcame his deep distrust of the notion of *creativity* of consciousness.[27] One cannot but agree with Berger that the notions of 'production' and 'activity' are mundane conceptions and do not apply as such to the transcendentally reduced consciousness. One has also to remember Ricoeur's insightful remark:

What interests Husserl in consciousness is not its genius, its power to invent in every sense of the term, but the stable, unified significations into which it moves and becomes established . . . Phenomenology is a philosophy of 'sense' more than a philosophy of freedom.[28]

We shall point out, in a later context, the rather strange fact that with the development of the doctrine of constitution Husserl also came to abandon the idea of total bodily givenness of objects and that of complete transparence of consciousness to itself: this also corroborates our thesis that even constitution$_2$ does not amount to creation or production.

But the transition to constitution$_2$ is made possible through several lines of thought: first, the discovery of the intentional structure of the hyletic stratum; then, the exhibition of the constitution of the acts; the resulting abandonment of the hylo-morphic scheme; the eventual coming into prominence of the intentionalities other than acts, and emergence of a host of new concepts like those of 'genetic constitution', 'passive synthesis', 'pre-predicative intentionalities', 'horizon intentionalities', 'unconscious intentionalities', 'anonymous intentionality' and 'operative intentionality'. These concepts not only lead to the concept of constitution$_2$ but also make possible the very different philosophies of the later-day phenomenologists like Merleau-Ponty. They deserve therefore our careful attention.

The idea of 'passive' synthesis is already to be met within the *Ideas I*, but in the form of that *(passive)* synthesis of identification by which various *noemata* coalesce so as to make reference to one identical object possible. The *Ideas* I also contains the idea of horizon as what is in an improper sense given with all things *(uneigentliche Mitgegebenheit)* but with more or less indeterminateness to be determined in accordance with a pre-given style *(Bestimmbarkeit eines fest vorgeschriebenen Stils);*[29] also the idea of the three-fold temporal horizon of every experience,[30] worked out in greater detail in the lectures on time consciousness. We also meet there with the distinction between theoretical (doxic) and not-theoretical acts,[31] the former being held to be the basis of the latter; but this distinction is not quite the same as that between act-intentionalities and intentionalities other than acts. The primacy of the theoretical acts persists in the *Ideas* I.[32]

The *Ideas* II proceeds to found theoretical acts on *'vorgebende'* intentionalities which are not themselves theoretical.[33] But the specific sense of an operative intentionality is still lacking.

The overall importance of 'passive synthesis' comes to light only later on, first in the lectures of 1918–26,[34] then in the *Formale und Transzendentale Logik* and in the *Cartesian Meditations*. The *Cartesian Meditations* distinguish between active production of abstract entities like collections, numbers or inference-structures and passive constitution of pre-given things like the physical objects which confront us in life as ready-made.[35] A reconstruction of the sense of their reality, of their pre-givenness, of their ready-made character would reveal their constitution: in this constitution, association no doubt plays a major role but so does anticipation as well. In fact, whatever else Husserl may be doing in his analysis of the passive constitution of pre-given things, his ground had been covered partly by Kant's notion of the transcendental synthesis of imagination and partly by the more modern notion of logical construction The *Phänomenologische Psychologie* regards the passive synthesis as belonging to experience itself and as forming '*die Unterlage für das Ins-Spiel-setzen der Aktivitäten des beziehenden, logisch verallgemeinernde Allgemeinbegriffe und-sätze konstituierenden Tuns*'.[36]

'Passive synthesis' is also called in the *Cartesian Meditations* 'passive genesis'. The typically new element in the notion of genetic constitution is the element of historical achievement. Thus in the *Formale und Transzendentale Logik*, referring to judgments and their constitution, Husserl writes:

Es ist eben die Wesenseigenheit solcher Produkte, dass sie Sinne sind, die als Sinnesimplikat ihrer Genesis eine Art Historizität in sich tragen . . . dass man also jedes Sinngebilde nach seiner ihm *wesensmäßigen Sinnesgeschichte* befragen kann.[37]

To uncover the genetic constitution is to lay bare these sedimentations of meaning, 'to reactivate the original encounter'.[38] The idea of hidden achievements which have to be uncovered by phenomenological reflection is not far away.

The idea of genetic constitution applies to the pre-given real things and to the ego.[39] It may even be said that the cultural objects also have a genetic, but not surely passive constitution; physical objects are passively and genetically constituted but not historical achievements; the ego is constituted by *habitus*, through a sort of auto-genesis, though it never quite becomes an object but at best somewhat like an object. From this we may conclude that not all genetic constitution is passive, though all passive constitution is genetic. Further, it would be fair to add that not all genetic constitution is historical achievement.[40]

The specific sense of horizon intentionality[41] also comes gradually to the forefront in the late twenties. The *Cartesian Meditations* refers to the horizon as the objective sense, implicitly meant and foreshadowed in the actual cogito; the predelineation is never perfect, but in spite of its indeterminateness it does have a determinate structure.[42] The object as a *pole of identity* is meant 'expectantly' through the 'horizon intentionalities'.

The ideas of unconscious and anonymous intentionalities emerge in various contexts. The intentionalities which passively constitute the pre-given world are 'anonymously' there; the experiencing subject knows nothing of them.[43] Phenomenology has to rescue them from this anonymity. It penetrates the anonymous intentional life and uncovers its synthetic processes.[44]

It would be an error to equate the anonymous intentionalities with either the unconscious ones or the intentionalities other than acts. Thus, for example, the horizon intentionalities are not acts but are neither anonymous nor unconscious. Acts may have contributed to the sedimented sense of a pre-given object, and in such a case it is these acts which have become anonymous. Unconscious intentionalities, on their part, may be either acts or not. There are in fact unconscious desires, love and hatred which are acts. The notion of unconscious intentionality makes its appearance in the course of Husserl's attempt to take account of the findings of modern depth psychology.[45]

The concept of operative intentionality (*fungierende Intentionalität*) found only in the form of meagre hints in Husserl's later writings has been made much of by later phenomenologists. In fact, one may say that all the above concepts of intentionality—the concepts of passive synthesis, genetic constitution, horizon intentionality, anonymous intentionality and unconscious intentionality—are brought together in the last papers under the title 'operative intentionality'. Already in the notes to the manuscript of the *Erste Philosophie*, Part II,[46] we are told of the implicit '*Verflochtenheit aller Intentionalität in einem Leben*'. A note of 1925 to the *Phänomenologische Psychologie*[47] speaks of the intentional life as *Weltleben*. The adjective '*fungierende*' is used, along with '*lebending*', perhaps for the first time in the *Formale und Transzendentale Logik*:

Die lebendige Intentionalität trägt mich, zeichnet vor, bestimmt mich praktisch in meinem ganzen Verhalten, auch in meinem natürlich denkenden, ob Sein oder Schein ergebenden, mag sie auch als lebending fungierende unthematisch, unenthüllt und somit meinem Wissen entzogen sein.[48]

The operative intentionality is here said to be that mode of the intentional life which remains unthematic, undisclosed and thus removed beyond my knowledge although it carries me forward in my theoretical as well as practical relationship. To say that operative intentionality '*ist nicht schlechthin, sondern sie fungiert*'[49] is hardly enough, for the same may also be said of all, even act intentionalities.

The operations of the so-called operative intentionalities are anonymous, they are not made thematic except to phenomenological reflection. They are not acts and also not cognitive. Yet they confer sense on the pre-given world, and thus provide the basis for further creation of significance. According to Fink, it is '*die lebendig sinnbildende, sinnleistende, sinnverwaltende Funktion des Bewußtseins, welche zu den einfachen seelischen Einheiten der Akte sich selbst verdeckend zusammenschliesst*'.[50] According to Merleau-Ponty, it is 'that which produces the natural and ante-predicative unity of the world and of our life'.[51]

It appears from the above that the notion of operative intentionality is a logical consequence of the entire trend of thought we have been sketching in the foregoing pages. It is the last ground and source of all meaning and significance. How precisely this notion is related to two other notions appearing and playing a major role in Husserl's later thought, namely the notions of *Lebenswelt* and *Welterfahrendesleben*, is indeed a most difficult problem for an exegesis of the later Husserl.[52]

III

Existential phenomenologists like Heidegger, Sartre and Merleau-Ponty have made much use of the concept of intentionality, but they have subjected Husserl's various theses to searching criticisms and have very often radically altered them. Their main criticisms of Husserl concern several different issues. Some like Sartre have been concerned with the question of the transcendental ego as the *source* of intentional acts; others like Heidegger have sought to rehabilitate intentionality as an ontic or even as an ontic-ontological relation, and consequently do away with the concept of *noema*. Most of them have found fault with the Husserlian concept of the *hyle* and the consequent hylo-morphic scheme, though all these critics surely differ in their attitudes towards the doctrine of constitution in any of its two forms. Another central issue has been the question about the *locus of* intentionality, and finally the problem regarding the relationship between the concepts of transparence and intentionality have been made to bear on all these discussions. Let us take a close look at each of these points of controversy.

1. Sartre, as is well known, rejected Husserl's conception of the transcendental ego and defended the non-egological concept of intentionality of the first edition of the *Logische Untersuchungen*.[53] First,

the ego is not needed to account for the unity of consciousness, intentionality is adequate to unify consciousness as Husserl himself has shown in his lectures on time consciousness. Again, locating the ego *within* consciousness would be to destroy the translucence of consciousness: the 'I' would be an opaque centre which consciousness by its very nature would reject. Furthermore, the unreflective consciousness does not have the form 'I think', though it is surely transparent to itself. The 'I' is an *object of* consciousness, it is *constituted* by reflection, and is not the source of the constituting function.

2. The idea of noetic-noematic correlation is in general abandoned,[54] and intentionality is sought to be understood as an ontic relation. Phenomenological reduction which, as we saw, is a necessary methodological preliminary for the Husserlian notion is rejected, for existentialism is to be a phenomenological *ontology*. Intentionality becomes, as with Heidegger, an openness to Being, but also being-in-the-world of the *Dasein*. The world, Sartre tells us, is not a *noema* but the in-itself.[55] Intentionality is characterized as transcendence,[56] which Husserl's intentionality—according to Sartre—is not.[57] It is transcendence in a two-fold sense: it refers to a being outside of itself, and it transcends the ontic being towards the ontological, i.e. the meaning of being. For Merleau-Ponty also the primary intentionality is the body's motility and so is an ontic relation directed towards the world, and not towards an *irreal noema*.

3. The concept of *hyle*, as is to be expected, comes in for sharp criticism. Sartre has argued that though Husserl came to the recognition of the hyletic component of consciousness in order to account for the element of passivity in knowledge, yet the doctrine itself creates more difficulties than it solves. 'The *hyle* in fact could not be consciousness, for it would disappear in translucency and could not offer that resisting basis of impressions which must be surpassed towards the object.'[58] This objection is genuine, provided only that we accept Sartre's basic thesis that consciousness is always and wholly transparent. Again, even if we do admit the *hyle*, it does not facilitate the self-transcending function of consciousness, we still fail to understand how this subjective layer points towards objectivity. Following Heidegger, Landgrebe[59] has attempted to get rid of the atomistic and sensationalistic conception of sensation common to both Kant and Husserl by construing 'sensing' as 'a structure of the Being-in-the-world'. The many facts to which Landgrebe appeals (for example the fact that sensation is closely connected with movement)

are undeniable, but it is still very doubtful if the general notion of being-in-the-world is adequate to account for the particularity and variety of sensuous data. It has also been pointed out that sensations have properties, like the spatial properties, which make them unfit for being components of consciousness; they, in fact, are intimately connected with body.[60] We seem to be back with the central issue of the status of the body in Husserl's thought. So far as Merleau-Ponty is concerned, it is only to be expected that he will also join with these critics of the doctrine of the *hyle*. We have to remember his original criticisms of the very concept of sensation in the opening chapters of the *Phenomenology of Perception*. But what is more, all sense experience is for him already intentional and charged with significance. Thus he writes:

Every sensation is already pregnant with a meaning inserted into a configuration, and there is no sense-datum which remains unchanged from illusion to truth.[61]

4. Husserl's doctrine of constitution has aroused quite different responses amongst the existentialist phenomenologists. In Heidegger, with the increasing emphasis on the concept of *openness* of *Dasein* to Being, the notion of constitution$_2$ almost drops out; though the notion of constitution$_1$ dimly survives in so far as the project of *Dasein*, its *Verstehen* understood as the prospective dimension of being-in-the-world—which is Heidegger's reconstruction of the Husserlian notion of the noetic act[62]—confers meaning and significance on the other, and also in so far as *Befindlichkeit*—again Heidegger's reconstruction of the Husserlian *hyle*—reveals the pre-given accomplished facticity of *Dasein*, the original situation of having been 'thrown' into the world. Sartre more explicitly rejects the formulation of intentionality as a constituting function,[63] and gives two reasons why this should not be so. In the first place, for consciousness to be of something is to be confronted with a concrete and full presence which is not consciousness. But also, the supposed constitution of the object would involve an infinity which could not possibly be given, whereas there could be nothing in consciousness that is not immediately transparent to it.[64] It is in Merleau-Ponty that the doctrine of constitution is rehabilitated but fully freed from the idealistic overtones of Husserl's thought. As we have already said, he rejects the notion of the *hyle*, but the notion of constitution$_1$ nevertheless survives. For, now the *Sinngebung* is assigned to the body which performs the function of Husserl's noetic act. The body confers

meaning on the world, but this is not arbitrary but reveals, as it were, a body-world pact[65] so that the body's worldfinding activity grounds the general structure of the world. The Husserlian conception of an irreal *noema* is not there, but the idea of correlation and the reciprocity of the elements entering into the structure of intentionality is given a new interpretation. The doctrine of constitution has to take care of the fact that 'the unity of the world, before being posited by knowledge in a specific act of identification, is "lived" as ready-made or already there';[66] as well as of the fact that if the world were constituted in an absolute self-consciousness then the world would have been totally transparent to consciousness, there would have been no error, no illusion, no opacity in the world as well as in consciousness. Consciousness therefore does not embrace or possess the world, but itself a project of the world, is yet perpetually directed towards the world, giving it sense and significance. The latter Husserlian notion of operative intentionality is used to take care of the first of the above-mentioned two facts; and a doctrine of degrees of transparence[67] as well as of degrees of intentionality, combined with the thesis that it is the body which exercises the basic constituting function, enables Merleau-Ponty to take care of the latter fact. But this giving of sense is a continuous process. We give sense, not a ready-made sense from a transcendental pedestal (as with Kant or Husserl) but always in degrees through our continuous explorations. The fully determinate object with completed sense and the absolutely transparent constituting consciousness are both rejected: a consequence of taking time and history seriously! The notion of operative intentionality with its anonymous mode of working leads to the notion of forgetfulness: the task of phenomenology is to make explicit this 'crypto-mechanism', to catch it in the very process of conferring sense and so 'to foil its trick'[68] by capturing the process of emergence of definiteness and meaningfulness. All this hinges, as should be obvious, on three basic propositions:

(a) Intentionality is always a matter of degree;
(b) Transparence is always a matter of degree;
(c) The basic intentionality is that of the body,[69] which gives lie to the absolute opposition set up by Sartre between the for-itself and the in-itself: the body is intentional, and is not yet fully transparent.

5. The existential phenomenologists also differ from Husserl with regard to the *locus* of intentionality, i.e. with regard to the question, 'What sorts of things are intentional?' As we have noted before,

the Brentano thesis about the alleged criterion of the mental has been left far behind. For Husserl, nevertheless, consciousness is a locus of intentionality; if it is the only thing which possesses intentionality remains yet to be seen. Sartre in this respect is an orthodox Husserlian, for with him too consciousness alone is intentional. The great dualism between the for-itself with its complete self-transcendence and total transparence—both entailing its nothingness—and the in-itself dominates his ontology, and the status of the body remains a problem. Heidegger explicitly rejects the primacy of the concept of consciousness; the dualism of consciousness and Being, a Cartesian ghost haunting the *Ideas I*, is sought to be exorcized. Intentionality, whether in the sense of openness to Being or in the sense of being-in-the-world characterizes *Dasein*, not consciousness. While this change persists in the later works, the primacy accorded to intentionality in the *Sein und Zeit* is soon recanted: it is sought to be derived from the rather metaphysical notion of historicity and destiny of Being and its world-project. Intentionality is *made possible*, we are now told,[70] by transcendence and not *vice versa*. It is understandable that Sartre should have found Heidegger's concept of *Dasein* unsatisfactory in so far as it excludes consciousness:[71] Sartre's for-itself is consciousness and not *Dasein*. While Sartre goes back to the early Husserlian thesis that intentionality belongs to consciousness and consciousness alone, Merleau-Ponty's entire philosophy marks a return from the pure for-itself to concrete human existence; but unlike Heidegger, intentionality is located in the body, in that ambiguous region which refuses to be subsumed under any member of the Sartrean pair.

In all these philosophers there is a tendency towards what may be called a monistic conception of intentionality, according to which intentionality *originally* belongs to one and only one sort of things, and if there are other sorts of things which also exhibit it, their intentionality must be derivative from that one original intentionality. In other words, there is only *one original* ascription of intentionality (whether to consciousness, or for-itself, or *Dasein*, or body); and of course all other ascriptions are derivative from, and presuppose, this one. This monistic tendency is relieved by Merleau-Ponty's insistence on the degrees of intentional function, and it is well worth consideration if this clue may be utilized to overcome the monistic tendency and to accord recognition to *radically different* types of intentionality.

6. An issue which emerges out of the foregoing discussion may be formulated as follows: how are the two features of consciousness, namely its transparence and its intentionality, related? Is there a sort of opposition between them, so that in fact consciousness can only possess one of these two and not both? Or, in case there is no such opposition, should we say that any one of the two is primary and the other derivative?

Now, that the transparence of consciousness—or, what the Indian philosophers called its 'svayaṃprakāśatva'—is incompatible with its supposed intentionality is most forcefully defended by the great Indian idealist Saṃkara: for him, the self-illuminating consciousness cannot be *really* of an object, so that the intentional reference is only apparent—the product of a metaphysical ignorance! Now this is not the place to enter into a detailed examination of this view. But Indian thought also contains an exactly opposed answer, namely that since consciousness is always intentional, i.e. is of an object, it cannot at the same time be *of* itself. It would then follow—as was in fact held by the school of the Nayiyaiykas—that the intentional consciousness is never transparent, it becomes aware of itself only through a subsequent act of introspection. At the same time, there is a third trend of thought—upheld by Ramanuja—according to which consciousness is always both: it is immediately aware of itself at the same time as it is also of an object. Now this precisely is what would seem to be the view of Sartre. But ascribing to consciousness total transparence, total coincidence with itself would rule out the possibility of all error, illusion and self-deception. One may even suspect that even for Merleau-Ponty there is an opposition between total transparence and total intentional absorption. Consequently he is led to deny both: neither the *cogito* nor the *cogitatum* is grasped fully. There are in fact, as we have already emphasized, only degrees of both.

While Merleau-Ponty's concept of degrees of intentionality and transparence is highly valuable and almost indispensable for any phenomenology of consciousness, we must nevertheless say that the supposed incompatibility between the two functions does not hold good. The two do not vary in inverse proportion. On the contrary, as Paul Ricoeur has so aptly shown, sometimes the reverse may well be the case: there are acts in which greater self-awareness is attained with increasing absorption in the intentional object, as in the case of acts of decision and resolution.[72]

If there is no opposition between the two, one may ask, as we have done above, is any one of the two more primitive, is any one dependent on the other? Now, it would seem that if we have to make room for the supposed unconscious intentionalities we must have to recognize that intentionality is independent of transparence. But then it would seem that the transparence of consciousness depends on its intentionality. This may seem to have been the view of Sartre: consciousness, on this view, is translucent only in so far as its total intentionality leaves nothing within it, empties it of all contents, and reduces it to nothing as it were. It is this emptied consciousness which is wholly transparent. True, as the Nayiyaiykas contend, if consciousness be wholly directed towards an other it cannot at the same time be directed towards itself. But this self-givenness without being directed towards itself, this non-positing, pre-reflective self-givenness of consciousness is exactly what we have called its transparence; and it could be said that intentionality constitutes a necessary, if not a sufficient condition, of its possibility.

IV

In the preceding section we have briefly touched upon the main issues emerging out of the criticism of Husserl's concept of intentionality by the existential phenomenologists. It remains to be seen to what extent these points may be taken care of from the point of view of Husserlian phenomenology, especially in view of Husserl's later writings.

1. Sartre's criticism of Husserl's concept of the transcendental ego as the source of intentionality may be met in either of two ways. One may argue[73] that Sartre is right in insisting that the ego is not empirically given and that the *mine* is capable of being accounted for within the framework of a non-egological theory of consciousness, but at the same time one may contend that this empirically given intentional structure *presupposes* the transcendental ego. Now this solution, it seems to me, is not Husserlian. The ego that is merely the presupposition is 'transcendental' in the Kantian sense but not in Husserl's sense of that word. Husserl, however, did get beyond the particular version of the doctrine of the ego which Sartre criticized. For, he came to recognize that even the transcendental ego is constituted, though in a manner radically different from the way objects are constituted. In the *Ideen, II*, Husserl says that the pure ego is not in need of constitution,[74] but in a *Beilage* to it[75] he adds that '*schon vorher muß die Lehre vom reinen Ich—zunächst als Pol—revidiert(?) werden*'; and expresses the view that though the ego is a pole of identity, it is

an 'unselbständiges Zentrum für Affektionen und Aktionen'. Of course, the ego is not to be found in the stream of experiences—and so far Sartre's point is not disputed.[76] We are even told immediately after that 'Die absolute Identität erkene ich in der Reflexion'. However, it is in the Cartesian Meditations that we come to the explicit formulation of the doctrine of the self-constitution of the pure ego through habitualities.[77] In fact, it is important to remember the distinction between transcendental ego and transcendental subjectivity.[78] The latter alone is premundane, pre-objective, meaning-giving consciousness; the former is a constituted unity, though its mode of constitution is radically different from the mode of constitution of objects. However, this development of Husserl's thought renders the whole thrust of Sartre's criticism pointless.

2. The central core of the second set of objections also is based on a misunderstanding of Husserl. By positing the irreal noema, Husserl did not want to deny that intentionality relates to beings, or even to Being (whatever that may mean). As we have emphasized in course of our exposition of Husserl's concept of intentionality, he was clearly aware of the fact that the noetic-noematic correlation was not the same as—nor could it be construed as a phenomenological reconstruction of—the intentional reference to object. The noema is not the intended object. But such is human consciousness, one could say, that its intention posits the noema and through it as it were reaches out to the object beyond. But even this way of putting the matter is misleading. For the noema and the object belong to two radically different dimensions—linguistically to two totally different universes of discourse, phenomenologically to two radically different modes of givenness. The possibility of turning away from the object-oriented attitude to the subsequent noema-oriented attitude is an inherent possibility of consciousness. But the introduction of the noema should not be regarded as shutting the door for ontological encounter. It may be supposed that Husserl is introducing a form of the content theory. Possibly he is doing that. But a content theory should take into account two facts. For one, the content is never given together with the object: the two are given in two radically different attitudes. This radical difference in their modes of givenness bears testimony to the radical difference in their modes of being. For another, the content is not another object standing in between the mind and the object, obstructing the reference by its opacity. It is rather a transparent medium which makes intentional reference possible. In defending the doctrine of

the *noema* we have said that perhaps human consciousness is such that its intentionality posits such an irreal medium of reference. Hasn't Merleau-Ponty said that we are condemned to meanings? And yet we are in rapport with the world! It is true that the intentionality thesis requires us to reject the conception of a representative consciousness. But the *noema* is not a representative, not a Lockean Idea, not a copy of the transcendent object. Sartre's for-itself, the totally empty consciousness, fully open to Being but emptied of all contents, the consciousness that is out and out nothing—this precisely is not the human consciousness. A theory of consciousness that would be adequate and fair to human consciousness should of course (i) take into account its intentionality and therefore the fact that it is not a representative consciousness; but (ii) it should also recognize that man is nevertheless condemned to meaning, that it is not passive openness but also active *Sinngebung*. The concept of *noema* is an attempt to take both these facts into consideration.

3. The much belaboured doctrine of the *hyle* had very few defenders amongst Husserl's followers. It is also true that Husserl himself has disowned the version of the *Ideas I* as having been due to the influence of a sensualistic empiricism. But it cannot also be straightaway denied that some form of the doctrine has to be recognized by any phenomenology of consciousness. Sartre's fear that to locate the *hyle* within consciousness would amount to inserting into the all-transparent consciousness a 'centre of opacity' would be justified only if we assume that consciousness is in fact all-transparent. But this is an assumption which one may very well question. The points raised by Merleau-Ponty and Gurwitsch are on surer footing: but they are directed against an atomistic and sensualistic conception of *hyle*. The supposed discrete sensation is quite possibly a myth—a product of theory and not a datum of consciousness. The most elementary data may exhibit intentional structures of various sorts. Nevertheless, the basic thesis that there is some kind of impressional matter does not stand or fall with the conception of sensation; and it is in the former form that the doctrine of *hyle* may still survive.[79] Furthermore, as Ricoeur has shown,[80] this doctrine may be indispensable for those phenomenologists who would like to take the psycho-analytical concept of the unconscious more seriously.

Husserl however came to emphasize the connection between the hyletic stratum of our experience with the body. In the *Ideas I*, where the *hyle* is regarded as a real component of consciousness, the body is regarded merely as the connecting link between pure consciousness—which is by itself an absolute—and the real world.[81] He does recognize there, however, that states like a state of pleasurable feeling have an intentional reference to the 'Menschen-Ich' and the human body, but adds that when abstraction is made from this reference, the state concerned undergoes an alteration such that it finds place in the pure consciousness and loses all natural significance.[82] It is this abstraction from what would otherwise seem to be an essential bodily reference which leads him to locate all *hyle* directly within pure consciousness as its real component. The *Ideas II* contains Husserl's first systematic phenomenology of body.[83] We need not consider here all the different levels of understanding body which Husserl elaborates: body as the 'zero-point of orientation',[84] body as the field of localization,[85] body as the organ of will[86], etc. What interests us here is the clear realization on the part of Husserl that a large part of the hyletic stratum (e.g. touch) is directly founded in the body and that, through it, the intentional component (e.g. the touching) also receives an indirect localization.[87] This localization entails for Husserl[88] that the body is already more than a material thing and possesses a psychic layer (*'es hat schon eine zum "Seelischen' gehörige Schicht'''*)—so that when we speak of the physical body we are abstracting from the total body. He even comes to call the body *'das subjektive Objekt'*.[89]

We may therefore conclude (i) that the concept of *hyle* is indispensable to account for the concrete fullness of the content of our human conscious life; (ii) that it may and should be freed from the atomistic–sensualistic form which the *Ideas I* gave it; (iii) that the conception is also needed to take into account the psycho-analytic concept of the unconscious within the framework of phenomenology; and (iv) that the concept needs to be founded on an adequate phenomenology of body and its psychic stratum. In all these respects, the later writings of Husserl contain valuable suggestions.

4. Some of the criticisms made against the interpretation of intentionality as a constituting function are not sustainable. That the supposed constitution involves an infinity will indeed be admitted by Husserl:[90] there is always a presumption, an element of hypothesis, an 'I can go on . . .' involved in it. The constitution of real things is characterized precisely by this presumptive character. Sartre complains that if this infinity were there it would have been transparent.

Here again he is assuming that total transparence is an accomplished fact. Were it so, reflection would have been rendered superfluous. It is reflection which discovers this 'I can go on', this infinity involved in the synthesis of an endless multiplicity of perspectives. The infinite series need not be completed. A phenomenology of constitution does not *fully* lay bare the constitution: it, on the other hand, courts the tragedy of its own failure to complete the infinite series. But this subjective failure has its correlate in the objective essence of the constituted thing as well. Once we understand this, Merleau-Ponty's charge that a world constituted in consciousness would stand fully revealed loses its biting force. The charge cannot be sustained on the basis of Merleau-Ponty's own concept of consciousness as ever possessing only a degree of transparence.

Whereas the *Ideas* I restricts the constituting function to the pure consciousness and its intentionalities, the two other volumes of the *Ideas* mark an advance in this respect. With the growing awareness of the importance of the body and with the growing liberation of his conception of body from the naturalistic framework, Husserl also comes to realize that the constitution of both nature and psyche is essentially bound up with the constitution of the body. The *Phänomenologische Psychologie* carries this a step further ahead: here Husserl, possibly for the first time, speaks of 'bodily intentionality', and says that the intentionalities in which things come to be given cannot be investigated without investigating the intentionalities of one's own body (*'eine verantwortliche wissenschaftliche Aufwicklung der beiderseitig aufeinander bezogenen Intentionalitäten'*).[91]

5. We have just noted that Husserl came to speak of bodily intentionalities. However, we do not notice in him either of the two possible monistic moves which are likely at this stage. He does not say that bodily intentionality is but a pale reflection of the intentionality of consciousness, that the body only appears to be intentional owing to the intentional consciousness which inhabits it. He also does not say that the basic intentionalitity is that of the body, and that the intentionality of consciousness is only an epiphenomenon of it. That he does not take to any of these two likely monistic moves shows that descriptive phenomenology does not yield ground even in his later writings to speculative system building. We are thus led to the recognition of radically different sorts of intentionality: the precise relationship between these is a matter of descriptive investigation rather than of *a priori* metaphysical speculation. In any case the body-mind dualism reduces to a dualism of intentional function.

6. As we have emphasized before, the issues we have been discussing lead us to the question of the transparence of consciousness. Husserl never held the view that consciousness is totally transparent. On the other hand, he did believe that reflection can bring to givenness what is there in a conscious act. There is something deceptive about this view, no doubt. It has been held by many philosophers (by the Nayiyāyikas, for example, amongst Indian philosophers) that just as the table in front of me is apprehended by an outer perception, so a conscious state within me is for the first time apprehended by an inner perception. I do not think Husserl ever held such a view which is obviously mistaken in relaying too heavily on the analogy between the givenness of outer objects and the mode of givenness of consciousness. Husserl of course did have the tendency to construe the latter as another higher order intentional act directed towards the unreflective act, but he was also aware that the talk of 'inner perception' in this connection might mislead.[92] All experiences, he says, especially all intentional acts are conscious not only in the sense that they are *of* something but also in the sense that they are in a sense, which does not apply to external objects, *wahrnehmungsbereit:* so that when we do apprehend them in reflection we also apprehend them as always having been there. Now even this concession does not suffice to bring out that peculiar mode of givenness of an *Erlebnis* prior to its being reflected upon which Sartre calls its prereflective transparence. In fact, Husserl never came to distinguish between reflection (which is a higher order intentional act directed towards the act being reflected upon) and reflexivity (which is the peculiar mode in which every conscious state is given to itself even prior to its being reflected upon). Every *Erlebnis*, one may say, is reflexive but not reflected upon. Every intentional act is not an 'I think', true; but every one of these is surely reflexive in the sense of having some degree of self-awareness not amounting to reflection. Thus, the reflexivity of consciousness (which the Indian philosophers called its *svayaṃprakāśatva*) cannot be reduced to its intentionality. But one may very well argue, *a la* Sartre, that *only because* consciousness is intentional and in *so far* is free from any opaque content within it, it is transparent.

If this be so, we may try to give some sense to locutions like 'degrees of transparency' or 'degrees of intentionality', and we may also in the same connection give some justification for some form of the doctrine of *hyle*. The argument may be formulated as follows. One may suppose that the translucency of consciousness varies in inverse proportion to the presence of the hyletic element. In states that contain more of unformed matter (which binds them all the more intimately to the bodily substratum) there is less of translucency; in states that contain less of hyletic matter there is more of the same. The so-called unconscious states are from this point of view the nearest approximations to the pure hyletic stuff, and in so far they are the least reflexive. As Ricoeur has so well argued, to speak of unconscious desires and hatreds is misleading in so far as it may lead one to imagine that there are in the unconscious fully formed desires or hatreds only lacking in the quality of consciousness.[93] While thus one should avoid what Ricoeur has called the Realism of the Unconscious, one should also avoid the other extreme view according to which the unconscious is the 'mere impressional matter not yet brought to life by an intentional aim', the view namely that the unconscious is not yet intentional, not yet *of* . . . In the latter view, defended by Ricoeur himself, the socalled unconscious desire, for example, is what the 'impressional matter' *would be* when it is made animated by an intention and thereby made conscious. This view leaves it unexplained why, if there is no unconscious intentionality and if it is the psycho-analyst who helps to transform the indeterminate matter into a desire or a hatred, does the patient 'recall' from the depths of his memory and identify the disturbing element as a desire or a hatred which *was* there in his mind? Further, why should the disturbing matter be interpreted as a hatred and not as a suspicion, why as a love and not as a fondness? Is the intentional form which the psycho-analyst confers entirely arbitrary? We are therefore led to the hypothesis that the unconscious is already intentional, that it is already *of* . . .; yet the intentional formation is vague, the mere pattern is laid down but not its definite meaning. The hyletic stuff predominates over the intentional meaning. The lack of transparency is accounted for by the presence of the hyletic stuff. But it is not entirely opaque, as no intentional act can be. For why otherwise does the patient 'recognize' and 'recall' it?

We may thus speak of degrees of intentionality: the bodily, the preconscious, the horizon intentionalities, the intentionalities of emotional and affective life and the intentionality of knowledge. Those intentionalities which are most transparent, i.e. in whose case to have the act is also to be aware fully that one has it, are precisely those in whose case the hyletic stuff is almost absent. In knowledge in the strict sense the intention stands fulfilled, there is no content which obstructs the reference, no representation. The cognitive consciousness is the nearest approximation to the empty consciousness, for here the entire emphasis is on the object side: this is the element of truth in the modern theory that knowledge is not a mental state and that to describe one's knowledge is to describe the object one knows and not one's own mental state. For in knowledge consciousness is so fully absorbed in the object that the act has been emptied of all contents and approximates to the ideal of a pure consciousness that is nothing. And for that very reason we have here the highest degree of transparency: one cannot fail to be aware as and when one knows.

Our thesis then is this: intentionality is a necessary condition of reflexivity. But the more that is needed to constitute the necessary and sufficient condition is the relative absence of unformed hyletic stuff in consciousness.

This doctrine of degrees of intentionality and degrees of transparency of consciousness is consistent with Husserl's later doctrine that even transcendental self-experience is not entirely adequate.[94] He never accepted a total coincidence of consciousness with itself, just as he never accepted a total opacity in it. As Fink points out in his note to the *Krisis* book, the intentional analysis of phenomenology destroys the appearance of *'unmittelbarer Gegebenheit des Bewusstseins'*.[95]

NOTES

1. Special references may be made to: H. Spiegelberg, 'Der Begriff der Intentionalität in der Scholastik, bei Brentano und bei Husserl', *Philosophische Hefte* 5 (1936), pp. 75–91; L. Landgrebe, *Phänomenologie und Metaphysik*, (Schröder, Hamburg, 1949), pp. 59–69; A. Gurwitsch, 'On the Intentionality of Consciousness', in *Philosophical Essays in Memory of Edmund Husserl*, ed. M. Farber (Harvard University Press, Cambridge, Mass., 1940); A. De Waelhens, 'L' idée phénoménologique d'intentionnalité', in *Husserl et la Pensée Moderne*, ed. H.L. Van Breda and J. Taminiaux (Martinus Nijhoff, The Hague, 1959).

2. In fact, Chisholm regards this as the ontological part of the Brentano thesis. Cf. Chisholm's essay on 'Intentionality' , in *Encyclopedia of Philosophy*, ed. P. Edwards (Colliers & Macmillan, New York, 1967).

3. F. Brentano, *The True and the Evident*, English translation by R.M. Chisholm et al. (Routledge & Kegan Paul, London), p. 78.

4. F. Brentano, *Psychologie vom empirischen Standpunkt*, vol. II (Felix Meiner, Hamburg, 1971), pp. 133–8.

5. Ibid.

6. E. Husserl, *Logische Untersuchungen*, 4th edn., (Max Niemeyer, Halle, 1928) (to be henceforth referred to as *LU*), II.1., pp. 370ff.

32 • EXPLORATIONS IN PHILOSOPHY

7. Ibid., p. 369.
8. Cf. E. Husserl, *Phänomenologische Psychologie, Husserliana*, vol. IX (Martinus Nijhoff, The Hague, 1962) (to be henceforth referred to as *P. Ps.*), p. 268; *Erste Philosophie*, I (Martinus Nijhoff, The Hague, 1956) (to be henceforth referred to as *EP*), p. 349; *Die Krisis der Europäischen Wissenschaften und die Transzendentale Phänomenologie* (Martinus Nijhoff, The Hague, 1954) (to be henceforth referred to as *Krisis*), p. 236.
9. *P.Ps.*, pp. 260–66, 314.
10. According to G. Berger, the category of *noema* is more fundamental than that of being or of non-being. Cf. G. Berger, *Le cogito dans la philosophie de Husserl* (Paris 1941), p. 54.
11. A. Gurwitsch, *Studies in Phenomenology and Psychology* (Northwestern University Press, 1966).
12. R.M. Chisholm, 'Sentences about Believing', in *Proceedings of the Aristotelian Society*, vol. LVI, 1955–56, pp. 125–47; 'On some Psychological Concepts and the "Logic" of Intentionality', in *Intentionality, Minds, and Perception*, ed. H.N. Castañeda (Wayne State University, Michigan, 1967), pp. 11–35; also his Encyclopedia article.
13. L. Landgrebe, *Phänomenologie und Metaphysik*.
14. H. Spiegelberg, *'Der Begriff der Intentionalitat'*, p. 86.
15. Contrast Quinton, 'Mind and Matter', in *Brain and Mind, Modern Concepts of the Nature of Mind*, ed. J.R. Smythies (Humanities Press, New York, 1965). Quinton argues (p. 224) that the Brentano thesis rules out behaviourism. It surely does, if intentionality is regarded, as was done by Brentano himself, as a criterion of the mental, and if behaviour is understood in a mechanistic way, not otherwise.
16. A. Diemer, *Edmund Husserl, Versuch einer systematischen Darstellung seiner Phänomenologie* (Meisenheim, 1956).
17. Cf. J.N. Mohanty, *Edmund Husserl's Theory of Meaning* (Martinus Nijhoff, The Hague, 1964), pp. 80–86.
18. Cf. P. Ricoeur, *Freedom and Nature. The Voluntary and the Involuntary*, transl. by E.V. Kohak (Northwestern University Press, Evanston, 1966), pp. 205ff.
19. Cf. P. Ricoeur, *Husserl, An Analysis of his Phenomenology*, transl. E.G. Ballard and L.E. Embree (Northwestern University Press, 1967), p. 192.
20. T.W. Adorno, *Zur Metakritik der Erkenntnistheorie, Studien über Husserl und die phänomenologische Antinomien* (Kohlhammer, Stuttgart, 1956), p. 171.
21. E. Husserl, *Ideas* I (references will be made to the Boyce Gibson translation in the paperback edition which will be henceforth referred to as *Ideas* I), p. 250.

22. A. Gurwitsch, *Studies*, pp. 138–9.

23. *Ideas I*, p. 267.

24. For elaboration of this point, see J.N. Mohanty, 'Notas a las lecciones de Husserl sobre la conciencia del tiempo', Dianoia, Anuario de Filosofia (Mexico, 1968), pp. 82–95.

25. R. Sokolowski, *The Formation of Husserl's Concept of Constitution* (Martinus Nijhoff, The Hague, 1964), pp. 92–3, 100, 114–15.

26. *Ideas I*, p. 226.

27. Gaston Berger, bearing witness Husserl's later thought in this matter, refers to 'how much the word "construction" could irritate Husserl' (Gurwitsch, *Studies*, p. 160). For an account of the different stages of Husserl's attitude towards the notion of productive synthesis, see Iso Kern, *Husserl und Kant* (Martinus Nijhoff, The Hague, 1964), pp. 249ff.

28. P. Ricoeur, *Husserl*, p. 41.

29. E. Husserl, *Ideen*, I (Husserliana edition), p. 100. (This edition will be referred to as *Ideen* I.)

30. *Ideen* I, § 82.

31. *Ideen* I, § 95.

32. *Ideen* I, § 117.

33. *Ideen* II (Husserliana, vol. IV) (Martinus Nijhoff, The Hague, 1951), § 4.

34. E. Husserl, *Analysen zur Passiven Synthesis* (1918–26) (Martinus Nijhoff, The Hague), p. 196.

35. *Cartesian Meditations*, translated by D. Cairns (Martinus Nijhoff, The Hague, 1960), § 38 (to be henceforth referred to as *CM*).

36. *P.Ps.*, pp. 98–9.

37. *Formale und Transzendentale Logik* (to be henceforth referred to as *FuTL*) (Max Niemeyer, Halle. 1929), p. 184.

38. R. Sokolowski, *The Formation of Husserl's Concept of Constitution*, p. 172.

39. G. Funke, *Zur transzendentalen Phänomenologie* (Bonn 1957), pp. 12–13; CM § 32.

40. Thus T. Seebohm, *Die Bedingungen der Möglichkeit der Transzendental-Philosophie* (Bouvier, Bonn, 1962): '. . . ist die genetische Intentionalanalyse auf die Zusammenhänge dieser Typen in der Einheit des Buwuβtseinsstromes selbst gerichtet.' This surely is not *eo ipso* a historically oriented programme.

41. For example, in *P.Ps.*, p. 431.

42. *CM*, p. 19.

43. *CM*, p. 64.

44. *CM*, p. 47.

45. *Krisis*, p. 240.

46. *EP*, II, pp. 318–19.

47. *P.Ps.*, p. 428.

48. *FuTL*, p. 208; § 94.

49. G. Brand, *Welt, Ich und Zeit, nach unveröffentlichten Manuskripten E. Husserls* (Martinus Nijhoff, The Hague, 1955), p. 23.

50. E. Fink, *Studien zur Phänomenologie* (Martinus Nijhoff, The Hague, 1966), p. 219.

51. M. Merleau-Ponty, *Phenomenology of Perception* (Routledge & Kegan Paul, London, 1962), Introduction.

52. J.J. Kockelmans, *Phenomenology and Physical Science. An Introduction to the Philosophy of Physical Science* (Duquesne University Press, Pittsburgh, 1966), pp. 53ff.

53. J.-P. Sartre, *The Transcendence of the Ego. An Existentialist Theory of Consciousness*, trans. by F. Williams and R. Kirkpatrick (Noonday, New York, 1957).

54. J.-P. Sartre, *Being and Nothingness. An Essay on Phenomenological Ontology*, trans. by H.E. Barnes (henceforth referred to as *BN*) (Methuen, London, 1957), p. lxi.

55. *BN*, p. 4.

56. *BN*, p. lxiii.

57. *BN*, p. 109.

58. *BN*, p. lix.

59. L. Landgrebe, 'Prinzipien der Lehre vom Empfinden', in *Zeitschrift für philosophische Forschung*, 8 (1954), 193–209.

60. H.U. Asemissen, *Strukturanalytische Probleme der Wahrnehmung in der Phänomenologie Husserls*, Kant-Studien Ergänzungshefte 73, 26–34 (Kölner Universitätsverlag, 1957).

61. M. Merleau-Ponty, *Phenomenology of Perception*, p. 243. Also see the same work, pp. 213, 267, 405.

62. This is so according to Diemer.

63. *BN*, p. lx.

64. *BN*, p. lxi.

65. T. Langan, *Merleau-Ponty's Critique of Reason* (Yale University Press, New Haven, 1966), p. 23f.

66. M. Merleau-Ponty, *Phenomenology of Perception*, p. xvii.

67. Cf. ibid., pp. 124–125.

68. Cf. ibid., pp. 57, 58–9, Also, M. Merleau-Ponty, *Signs*, transl. McCleary (Northwestern University Press, 1964), p. 173.

69. M. Merleau-Ponty, *Phenomenology of Perception*, p. 137.

70. M. Heidegger, *Vom Wesen des Grundes* (Klostermann, Frankfurt, 1949), pp. 15, 44.

71. *BN*, p. 85.

72. P. Ricoeur, *Freedom and Nature*, p. 61.

73. This is the argument of Natanson in his 'The Empirical and Transcendental Ego', in *For Roman Ingarden. Nine Essays in Phenomenology*, ed. A.T. Tymieniecka (Martinus Nijhoff, The Hague, 1959).

74. *Ideen* II, § 28; but the doctrine of the autogenesis of the ego is surely suggested in the same work, p. 102.

75. Ibid., p. 310f.

76. *P.Ps.*, pp. 207–8.

77. *CM*, § 32. On 'habitualities', see P. Ricoeur, *Husserl*, pp. 54–5.

78. G. Funke, *Zur transzendentalen . . .*, pp. 22–3.

79. Seebohm, e.g., holds that the concept of *hyle* may be non-sensualistically interpreted within the framework of the intentionality thesis. See *Die Bedingungen*. p. 97 fn. 18.

80. P. Ricoeur, *Freedom and Nature*, pp. 373–409.

81. *Ideas I*, § 53.

82. Ibid., § 53.

83. *Ideas II*, Section 2, Chapter 3.

84. *Ideen* II, pp. 56, 158f.

85. Ibid., p. 151.

86. Ibid., p. 151f.

87. Ibid., p. 153.

88. *Ideen* III, p. 118.

89. Ibid., p. 124. From this point of view, Ricoeur's statement (in his *Husserl*, p. 61) that the distinction between existence and objectivity is not known to Husserl may only be conditionally accepted.

90. *CM*, § 28.

91. *P.Ps.*, p. 197.

92. *Ideen* I, § 38.

93. P. Ricoeur, *Freedom and Nature*, pp. 387–9.

94. *CM*, esp. § 9.

95. *Krisis*, p. 474.

chapter

two

Can Intentionality be Explained Away?*

I t may generally be said that the main trend of philosophical
thinking runs counter to the thesis of intentionality, viz the thesis
that the mental states and possibly some bodily behaviour
exhibit a peculiar, not further analysable, directedness towards an
object. Idealists have maintained that consciousness, in its inmost
essence, is free from reference to objects. They speak of a 'pure'
consciousness, of subjectivity as freedom from attachments to the
world of objects. They suspect that the intentionality thesis would
amount to a kind of denial of such freedom to consciousness.
Idealists of a different kind, namely the subjective idealists, recognize
objective consciousness but locate the object within consciousness
as an idea or representation, as an *ākāra* of consciousness itself. This
is also tantamount to a denial of intentionality.

The thesis of intentionality is opposed also by the realists for whom
the alleged peculiar reference of consciousness to its object is simply
not there. Within the framework of a realistic ontology there can only
be a real relatedness of consciousness to its object—both the relata
being equally real, their qualitative differences notwithstanding.
Intentional directedness is replaced either by a neutral compresence
(Alexander), or by a causal relation (as in some Nyaya systems) or, at
its best by some not to be further analysed relation (*svarupasambandha*)
which is surely a real relation after all.

*Indian Review of Philosophy, Vol. 2, No. 2, April 1971, pp. 167–76.

In this essay I will not undertake to defend the intentionality thesis as against these idealistic and realistic distortions of the phenomena concerned. I wish to consider primarily a powerful trend of thought which, under the guiding ideologies of physicalism, unity of the sciences, and extensionalist philosophy of language, seeks to do away with everything psychological, indeed with all non-extensional discourse. This thesis is professedly confined to a merely linguistic commitment, but its philosophical consequences reach out beyond a reformation of scientific discourse.

I

To start with, let us recall certain attempts to reduce intentional sentences to non-intentional ones which have been well taken care of by Chisholm in his 'Sentences about Believing.'[1] I think Chisholm has been able to show most convincingly that such translations into non-intentional language owe their plausibility to the fact that they at some stage covertly use intentional terms. There are two ways of maintaining this position. One may, as Chisholm does, show that any attempt to translate belief sentences into non-intentional language (of specific response, or of appropriate behaviour, or of disposition to act, or to expect, etc.) is either inadequate or, if true, will be found on closer examination to be making covert use of the concepts of belief, 'springs of action', 'fulfilment', etc., all of which are intentional. But I think, one can even go further. Even if one does not find any mental concept in the alleged translation, one may still be using intentional concepts, for many of our concepts of bodily behaviour are intentional. The intentionality thesis as such is not opposed to behaviourism though it surely is opposed to a mechanistic concept of behaviour. Thus suppose there is a mental verb m with an intentional object o, and suppose its behaviouristic translation into the language of response is $r(o)$. Let us grant also that the translation is adequate, in other words that the mental word 'm' is dispensable. But $r(o)$ is no less intentional. The truth of the statement 'S makes the response r (o)' logically entails neither the existence nor the non-existence of o. The response r is directed towards o, and the sense of this directedness is closer to the directedness of a mental act towards its object, and is radically different from the relation of 'being caused by'. To bring in the concept of 'being stimulated by o' is of no help, for a stimulus qua stimulus is not a cause. The concept of 'being a stimulus of a response' is an intentional concept.[2]

II

Carnap in *The Logical Structure of the World and Pseudoproblems in Philosophy* denies any uniqueness to the intentional relation, and reduces it to a relation that obtains also amongst terms which are far from being intentional. The latter is the *sort* of relation which holds good between an element and a relational structure of a certain sort. Other such relations, according to Carnap, are: the relation of a given plant to the botanical system of plants; the relation of a given hue to the system of colours; the relation of a person to his family, his state or his occupational hierarchy. It is not at the first sight quite clear how the relation of an experience to its intentional object is of the same sort as the above mentioned relations. Carnap's explanation however is as follows. Take the thought of a tree. From the point of view of Carnap's constructionism, the intended tree is 'a certain, already very complicated ordering of experiences, namely of those experiences of which we say that the tree is their intended object.'[3] The experience which at present intends the tree belongs to the same order of experiences out of which the tree is constructed. Thus Carnap requires two conditions to be fulfilled so that the intention relation may hold good between an experience and an order of experience (which for him is the intended object): for one thing, the former must belong to the latter; for another, 'this order must be one of those constructional forms in which real-typical objects are constructed'.[4] Unless each object essentially belongs to a certain order of experiences it could not be constructed, it could not be intended.[5]

Now it should be obvious on closer examination that Carnap's reduction of the concept of intentionality in fact presupposes that concept. The intended object is sought to be constructed out of, or analysed into, an order of experiences, 'namely of those experiences of which we say that the tree is their intended object.' Thus the intended object o is analysed into an order of experiences $e_1, e_2, e_3, e_4, \ldots$ such that each of these *es* intends the same o. Only if this is so can the proposed construction be meaningful. In fact, as we saw earlier, the order, Carnap stipulates, must be such that real objects could be constructed in it; and this requirement is nothing but this that each member of the order should itself be intentional. Carnap thus fails to eliminate intentionality. The analogy he draws with the relation of a given plant to a botanical system is farfetched, and does not bring out the essential feature of the very scheme he presents. In his own scheme the relation:

$$e \longrightarrow o$$

may be restarted as:

$$e \text{ is a member of } [e_1(o), e_2(o), e_3(o), \ldots\ldots\ldots\ldots]$$

The intentionality *reappears* within each member of the series, and so the intentionality of *e* which is a member of it remains unimpaired. Understood in this way, Carnap's constructionism looks surprisingly like Husserl's later theory of intentionality as constitutive, or of the intended object *qua* intended, i.e. the *noema* as being constituted in the *noetic* acts. This would not be a denial of intentionality but giving it a new extension.

III

The view that the objects of intentional attitudes are linguistic entities so that intentional sentences may be replaced by sentences relating people to linguistic entities has been advocated by Carnap at some places,[6] also by Quine[7] and Sheffer.[8] We may here make two observations on such a view so obviously repugnant to facts.[9] In the first place, it does not as such eliminate intentionality, it shows concern about how to avoid admitting the intended objects with their claim to a curious sort of being. As emphasized before, the concern is understandable but avoidable. You do not improve matters by introducing a linguistic entity—the word 'unicorn' for example in the case of one's thought of a unicorn—as the object of the mental act. The underlying assumption is that there should be something *real* towards which a mental act could be directed; if it is not a real unicorn, if it is not to be a curiously subsistent unicorn, it can only be the word 'unicorn'! The whole point about intentionality is thereby lost, the fact namely that the real existence or non-existence of the intended object is not entailed by the fact that it is an intended object of an act. Further, as Chisholm has pointed out, the validity of this view depends upon the availability of certain semantic sentences corresponding to each intentional sentence, which is indeed hard to substantiate.[10]

Quine repudiates mental entities, and prefers to construe consciousness as 'a faculty of responding to one's responses' whereby responses are regarded as physical behaviour.[11] But even this is not to eliminate intentionality, for—as we have emphasized before—the concepts of response and behaviour are incurably intentional. Sellars formulates a more cautious position.[12] He conceives of a possible situation where men think but do not know that they think, where their use of language is meaningful because it expresses their thoughts but they do not know that it is the expression of their thoughts. In such a situation, they would have no concept of inner mental episodes though there are in fact such episodes: there would consequently be no concept of intentionality. The purpose of this argument is not at all clear to me. Surely every user of language, though expressing his thoughts and other mental acts, does not have a fully explicit concept of intentionality. But this fact, does not show—even if we grant the situation conceived by Sellars—that the intentionality of linguistic and other forms of human behaviour can be theoretically dispensed with, or even that the intentionality of mental acts is to be denied. Sellars of course contends that 'the categories of intentionality are nothing more nor less than the metalinguistic categories in terms of which we talk epistemically about overt speech as they appear in the framework of thoughts construed on the model of overt speech.'[13] What he means thereby seems to be this: In the ordinary object language where we talk about things, persons and places, events and episodes, inner or outer, we do not use the categories of intentionality. Of course we have beliefs and we express them, we have thoughts and we communicate them. It is only when we talk about our overt speech, and further do so epistemically that the categories of intentionality arise. One may of course talk about overt speech in other ways. One may, for example talk about its syntax, its grammar and so on without making use of the concept of intentionality. But one can also talk about overt speech epistemically: thus of an expression '1' one may say that '1' expresses a thought t, and t is about p. The 'about' introduces intentionality. Thus the concept of intentionality is meta-linguistic.

That the categories of intentionality are metalinguistic in origin need not be disputed: this fact is only the linguistic counterpart of the fact that the concept of intentionality—not the intentional directedness itself—is a product of reflection on the first-order experiences. That it is further a product of an epistemically-oriented metalanguage only restates in the formal mode of speech the fact that the reflection which reveals intentionality (and so generates the concept of it) is a *phenomenological* reflection, and not an objectively-oriented reflection.

IV

I wish now to turn from the linguistic critics of the intentionality thesis to some more orthodox critics. The thesis that mental phenomena are characterized by intentionality has been taken by many as entailing a distinction between act and content. Consequently, some critics of the intentionlaity thesis take their stand against the concept of a mental act, some others seek to demolish the mental act: both groups of critics think that if they succeeded in their attacks they would be in effect refuting the thesis of intentionality.

Russell in his *Analysis of Mind* (1921) recants his earlier sympathy with the Brentano thesis on the ground that the act seems to him unnecessary and fictitious. 'The occurrence of the content of a thought', he writes, 'constitutes the occurrence of the thought. Empirically, I cannot discover anything corresponding to the supposed act; and theoretically I cannot see that it is indispensable.'[14] Now Russell seems to be thinking that the concept of intentionality is defined in terms of the concept of act, and consequently if there are no acts the intentionality thesis will have to be rejected. Russell is wrong, for in fact it is the concept of act that is defined in terms of that of intentionality, and not *vice versa*. An act is anything which exhibits intentionality, and if empirically it may not be possible to detect anything like a mental *activity* it surely is possible to discern the directedness, the of-ness, the peculiar aboutness which characterizes our thoughts and beliefs, desires and wishes, loves and hatred. If Russell is willing to admit mental contents, and if they possess such directedness then they precisely are to be called 'acts'. The act and the content may be one, as with the Bauddhas, and this one thing, call it 'act' or 'content', may be intentional.

Bosanquet in his *Three Chapters on the Nature of Mind* complains that the Brentano–Meinong view does not permit the real world 'to enter by virtue of identity into the world of knowledge',[15] and takes the supposed obviousness of the mental content, of the 'psychical matter' to be the basis of that view. But the thesis that mental phenomena are characterized by intentionality entails neither that there are mental acts *in the sense* in which Russell says there are none, nor that all the characters of the object are to be transferred to the content. If some phenomenologists did subscribe to the act-content-object distinction, that is on grounds other than the mere intentionality thesis and that has to be judged on its own merits. The Naiyāyikas accepted intentional directedness but rejected all content of consciousness (which they regarded as being entirely *nirākāra*); the Buddhists accepted content of consciousness (which for them is *śakāra*) but denied—if they happened to be idealists—intentionality. Brentano started with a statement of the thesis which suggests, with its notion of 'intentional inexistence', a conception of mental content having a mode of being 'that is short of actuality but more than nothingness'.[16] But later on he seems to have retained the intentionality thesis but outright rejected any suggestion of a duplication of the object in the content.[17] Husserl in the *Logische Untersuchungen* II.1. attacks the theory of content interpreted as a *Bildtheorie* and as a theory of the 'immanent object of the act',[18] though one should allow that there is an important element of truth in Oskar Kraus's diagnosis that 'the older doctrine still haunts the *Ideen* (sections 88, 91) and appears in the correlation fictions of *noema* and *noese*'.[19] What is intended to be emphasized by these remarks is not that the content theory is to be outright rejected, but only that the intentionality thesis as such need not commit us to an act-content-object analysis: it states a minimum phenomenological finding which leaves room for further decisions on their own merits.

The critics of the intentionality thesis are bothered by several different things. Some like Quine (in 1966) are concerned about the notion of the mental in general, others like Russell (in 1921) worry not about the mental as such but about the notion of mental *acts*. Others are bothered by the prospect of having to admit into their ontologies curious entities which are intended in those acts. Now the concept of intentionality does not stand or fall—though it is severely affected thereby—with the concept of the mental in general, it surely is not committed to a philosophy of the ghost in the machine. It is committed neither to a dualism between body and mind, nor to a mentalism (contrary to what Popper maintains).[20] In fact, as Quinton has argued,[21] it is compatible with an identity theory according to which the identity between bodily and mental states is not logical but contingent. Which of these theories one is willing to accept will be chosen on its own independent merit, and not merely on the basis of one's acceptance of the Brentano thesis; though having accepted the Brentano thesis one cannot revert to a mechanistic-naturalistic type of thinking about the mind or even about the body.

The concern about the curious entities that one may have to admit into one's ontology should one recognize the irreducibility of intentionality is also unfounded. As we have emphasized, the intentionality thesis is neutral as between realism and idealism, and its true nature cannot be grasped unless one stubbornly refuses to ontologize, i.e. unless one takes up the strictly phenomenological attitude which indeed commits one to tread on a razor's edge.

NOTES

1. In *Proceedings of the Aristotelian Society*, LVI (1955–56), pp. 125–47.

2. Contrast Quinton ('Mind and Matter', in Smythes [ed], *Brain and Mind, Modern Concepts of the Nature of Mind*, [New York: the Humanities Press, 1965] who argues (p. 224) that the Brentano thesis rules out behaviour-ism. It surely does if intentionality is regarded, as was done by Brentano himself, as a criterion of the mental. In our view this is not so, and so intentionality thesis does not rule out, analytically, behaviourism.

3. Carnap, *The Logical Structure of the World and Pseudoproblems in Philosophy*, E.tr. by Rolf A. George (London: Routledge & Kegan Paul, 1967), p. 262.

4. Ibid., p. 262.

5. Ibid., p. 263.

6. See Chisholm, 'Intentionality', in *The Encyclopedia of Philosophy*, edited by Paul Edwards, (NY: The Macmillan Co. & The Free Press: 1967), Vol. 4, pp. 200–4.

7. Ibid.

8. Ibid.

9. Ibid.

10. Chisholm, ibid.

11. Quine, *The Ways of Paradox and Other Essays*, (New York: Random House, 1966), especially pp. 213–14.

12. In Feigl, Scriven, and Maxwell (eds), *Minnesota Studies in the Philosophy of Science*, vol. II (Minneapolis: University of Minnesota Press, 1958), pp. 521–39.

13. Ibid., p. 522.

14. In G.N.A. Vasey (ed.), *Body and Mind*, Reading's in Philosophy (London: George Allen & Unwin, 1964), p. 268.

15. Bosanquet, *Three Chapters on the Nature of Mind*, (Macmillan, London, 1923), pp. 43–4.

16. Chisholm in *Encyclopedia*, pp. 200–1.

17. Compare, for example, his letter of 1905 in Brentano, *Truth and Evidence*, E.tr. by Chisholm *et al.* (London: Routledge & Kegan Paul, 1965).

18. E. Husserl, *Logische Untersuchungen II.1.*, pp. 421–5.

19. Brentano, *Truth and Evidence*, p. 159.

20. Popper, in *Conjectures and Refutations* (Harper and Rao, New York, 1965), p. 298.

21. Quinton, in Smythes (ed.), *Brain and Mind*, (Humanities Press, New York, 1965), p. 225.

chapter

three

On Husserl's Theory of Meaning*

I n this essay, I want to examine some recent criticisms and interpretations of Husserl's theory of meaning. First of all, it is necessary to comment briefly on this occasion on the widely held view that Husserl took over *from* Frege the crucial distinction between 'meaning' and 'reference' (with only a change of terminology) and extended it beyond the domain of linguistic expressions to acts of consciousness. That this view (as also the widely prevalent opinion that it is Frege's review of his *Philosophie der Arithmetik* which led Husserl to overcome his psychologism) is not tenable, I have argued in another paper.[1] As I have argued there, it rather seems more plausible, on the basis of evidences from Husserl's writings prior to the publication of Frege's 'Sinne und Bedeutung' (1892) and prior to his review of Husserl's *Philosophie der Arithmetik* (1894), that Husserl had already overcome psychologism, to the extent that he ever did, before Frege's review and that he had arrived at his own distinction between 'meaning' and 'reference' independently of Frege's.

II

Leaving this historical issue aside, for my present purpose I shall next draw attention also to the misleading character of any tendency to collapse the distinction between Husserlian 'essences' and Husserlian

*The Southwestern Journal of Philosophy, Vol. V, No. 3, Nov. 1974, pp. 229–44.

'meanings' (*Sinne*). Solomon has recently tried to elucidate Husserl's notion of 'essence' with the help of the Fregean notion of '*Sinne*'.[2] Two questions must be asked in this connection: First, are Husserlian meanings essences? Second, are all Husserlian essences also meanings? Now, in order to answer these two questions, we have to recall the function of *Sinne* or *noemata* in Husserl's philosophy. If N_A be the *noema* of an act A, then N_A is not also the object, the *Gegenstand*, or the reference of A. The act A, irrespective of its quality, is directed toward its object O_A, but not toward its *noema* N_A. An act of reflection may be directed, no doubt, toward N_A, but then again we have to distinguish between the object of that reflective glance and its *noema*. One of the functions of a *noema* or *Sinne*, *quâ noema* or *Sinne*, is to serve as the *medium* of reference: to say this is only to indicate a whole area of problems such as identification, reidentification, and individuation of that object. Now it would seem that Husserl had an incipient ontology, at least in the *Logical Investigations* and in the *Ideas*, according to which all things that are may be divided into two fundamentally distinct domains: the real and the ideal.[3] The real is characterized by temporality and individuality.[4] The ideal is timeless (though the precise sense of this 'timelessness' needs to be explicated). The ideal entities, further, are of two kinds: the singular (like the number 2) and the universal ('man').[5] Both are often characterized by Husserl as 'species'. Now there is no doubt that Husserl does often speak of meanings as 'species'.[6] In fact, he often classifies ideal objects into 'meanings' and those that are not meanings. The following text should make his point clear. Seeking to unravel the various meanings of the words 'concept' and 'species', Husserl writes:

General objects and general presentations or meanings, *i.e.*, *direct* presentations of general objects, are alike called concepts, but equivocally so. The concept of Redness is either Redness itself—as when its manifold objects, *i.e.*, red things, are opposed to this concept—or it is the meaning of the name 'redness'. Both plainly stand in the same relation to one another as do the meaning *Socrates* and Socrates himself.[7]

Thus, although Husserl in the *Logical Investigations* speaks of meanings as species,[8] yet he again warns us[9] that the concepts 'meaning' and 'concept' (in the sense of 'species') do not coincide:

Meanings, we said, constitute a *class* of 'universal objects' or species. Each species, if we wish to speak of it, presupposes a meaning, in which it is presented, and this meaning is itself a species. But the meaning in which an object is thought, and its object, the species itself, are not one and the same

. . . . The universality *that* we think of does not therefore resolve itself into the universality of the meanings *in which* we think of it. Meanings, although as such they are universal objects, fall, *in respect of the objects to which they refer, into individual and specific meanings* . . . .[10]

Husserl's answer then to our first question is that meanings do exhibit an ideality, nontemporality, and independence of real occasions which they share with those other ideal entities which more appropriately should be called 'essences'. Although this does entitle us to say that meanings are essences, it is important to bear in mind the distinction between the meaning of 'redness' and the essence redness, or the meaning of '$\sqrt{4}$' and the number 2. Perhaps the distinction may be stated thus: an essence *is*, as much as real things, persons, processes, and events are. The concept of 'essence' is an ontological concept. But again to say of a thing (real or ideal) that it *is*, is to say that it can be referred to, that it is the *Gegenstand* of an act, especially of an act of expression (propositional or nominal). But a meaning *qua* meaning is not such an object of reference, not a *Gegenstand*, but the medium of reference. When it becomes, in a reflective act, an object of reference, it is, to that extent, not functioning as a meaning. A meaning *qua* meaning then is not an entity. Essences are entities, as much as real things are. Our second question—are all Husserlian essences meanings?—has then to be denied. They all are certainly objects of possible reference. Just as one and the same real thing may be referred to through different meanings, so one and the same essence (the number 2, for example) may be referred to through different meanings (for example, the meanings of '$\sqrt{4}$' and '$\sqrt[3]{8}$').

Thus, Husserlian essences are not Fregean *Sinne*. What are closest to Fregean *Sinne* are the Husserlian *noemata*, and Husserl never ceased to emphasize the difference between *noemata* and essences. Consider, for example, the following text:

One need not confuse noema (correlate) and essence . . . . The apprehension of one is not that of the other, although here a change of attitude and direction of apprehension is essentially possible, through which the apprehension of the noema can transform into that of the corresponding ontic essence.[11]

The concern with *noemata*, Husserl goes on to tell us, is possible in a phenomenological attitude, the concern with essences in an onto-logical attitude.[12]

1. Husserl, as has been mentioned before, does speak of meanings

as species. The decisive text for this view is the following: 'Meaning is related to varied acts of meaning . . . just as Redness *in specie* is to the slips of paper which lie here, and which all 'have' the same redness.[13] Now there is no doubt that this is a highly dissatisfying comparison. Of each of those slips of paper which 'have' the same redness, one can say 'It *is* red', but there seems to be no way of saying likewise of each act of meaning that 'It *is* . . . .' Naturally, therefore, Husserl came explicitly to reject this particular thesis (though not the thesis of the ideality of meanings). In *Experience and Judgement*, this rejection is stated thus:

The irreality of objectivities of understanding must not be confused with generic universality . . . It is a great temptation to think that the proposition belongs to the various acts of which it is the sense by virtue of its generic universality, as, for example, many red things belong to the generic essence 'redness' . . .

But one must say in opposition to this: certainly, the proposition is general insofar as it refers to an infinite number of positional acts in which it is precisely what is intended; but it is not general in the sense of generic universality, i.e., *the generality of an 'extension'*, which belongs specifically to the generality of a species, to a kind of genus, and, at the lowest level, to a concrete quiddity. . .[14]

2. I have said that it is not the Husserlian essences but the Husserlian *noemata* that are close to the Fregean *Sinne*. However, we should not overlook three major differences between even these two conceptions. In the first place, the Husserlian *noemata* are conceived at first as *ideal contents* and only subsequently as intentional *correlates* of subjective acts; whereas the Fregean *Sinne* stand in no such relationship to the acts apprehending them. Both Husserl and Frege emphasized the objectivity of meanings as distinguished from the subjectivity, variability, and privacy of mental states. For Husserl, the objectivity of meanings rules out being a real component of mental acts but not being an intentional correlate. In fact, all objectivity, for Husserl, consists in complicated structures of such intentional correlations. Since Frege did not have Husserl's full-blown concept of intentionality, and since he thought of mental acts as nothing but immanent, private states, for Frege, to be objective is to be independent of such states in the strongest possible sense. Frege's sense of objectivity of the *Sinne*, then, is more *naïvely* ontological, and Husserl's is critically phenomenological. This difference is reflected in what I

would call the second major difference between Fregean *Sinne* and the Husserlian *noemata*: the Fregean *Sinne* are the meanings of linguistic expressions themselves, whereas the Husserlian *noemata* are meanings not of expressions but of acts (including speech acts).

It is usually held that Husserl took over the Fregean concept and extended it to all acts. Quite apart from the question whether he got his basic conception from Frege or not, his *Bedeutung* (which, in the *Investigations,* is the counterpart of Frege's *Sinne*) is the meaning of expressive *acts* (*ausdrückende Akte*), of speech acts, and not of words or sentences taken as such. Therefore, even prior to Husserl's generalization of this notion over the entire domain of acts, his concept of meaning is closely related to his concept of intentionality. His interest in the *First Logical Investigation* is not in words or sentences, but in the acts constituting them into meaningful expressions. The ideal, objective meaning of the First Investigation is the intentional correlate of a real, meaning-intending act of expressing. It is this notion, and not the Fregean concept, that could then, in the *Ideas* I, be extended to all acts. The ontological nature of Frege's theory regarding his *Sinne* is further clear—and this is the third point of difference I wanted to emphasize—in Frege's thesis that in oblique and intentional contexts, it is the customary *Sinne* that become objects of reference; but Husserl does not regard the *noemata* as objects of reference of expression in intentional or act contexts. Thus, the Fregean *Sinne* enter into Frege's ontology; the Husserlian *noemata* do not find a place in Husserl's ontology.[15]

III

The legitimacy of Husserl's extension of his concept of *Bedeutung* (of the *First Investigation*) to all intentional acts has recently been very forcefully challenged by Hubert Dreyfus.[16] Dreyfus is especially concerned with perceptual acts which are fulfilling acts *par excellence,* and one of his main contentions is that Husserl's Fregean concept of meaning, appropriate as it is for 'signitive' acts, cannot legitimately be applied to perceptual acts. In effect, Dreyfus is challenging the validity of Husserl's concept of 'fulfilling sense' or 'perceptual noema'. Thus, writes Dreyfus,

. . . in the *First Logical Investigation* acts were divided into signifying and fulfilling acts. Then the perceptual act, which one would suppose to be a fulfilling act par excellence, was in turn analysed into *its* signifying and intuitive components . . . Thus a regress develops in which sense coincides with sense indefinitely. At each stage we arrive at a fulfilling meaning for an intending meaning, but at no stage does the fulfilling meaning imply a sensuous filling.[17]

In other words, if part of the reason for the distinction between Fregean *Sinne* and reference lies in the fact that one may perform an act in which an object is 'emptily', merely 'signitively' intended, referred to as being such and such without such intention being fulfilled, without the object itself being bodily given, *then* to make the same distinction again in the case of perceptual acts would require that even in perception the object is not bodily presented, that the perceptual intention is in need of further fulfillment. But this would only contradict the very sense of perception which, *per definition*, presents its object bodily and directly. In Dreyfus' words, the perceptual meaning has to be an 'incarnate meaning', an *Anschauungssinn* and not an interpretative meaning, *Auffassungssinn* (which the Fregean *Sinne* has to be); it has to be 'an entirely new sort of sense whose existence would be essentially inseparable from the intuitive content of the object whose sense it was.'[18]

Dreyfus' criticism, if valid, would not only need a total revision of Husserl's philosophy of perception, but would also need a turning away from transcendental phenomenology to existential phenomenology. I will not comment on this latter claim in this essay. What I want to do is try to understand why it is that Husserl introduced the concept of 'fulfilling sense' or 'perceptual noema' when he did explicitly recognize both the fulfilling character of perception and the necessary separation between the 'noema' and its 'filling'. In fact, it would seem that the notion of a fulfilling sense is a self-contradictory notion, and how could Husserl have been led to it?

Now, it is not the programme of transcendental phenomenology, but that of eidetic phenomenology that is at the root of Husserl's conception. Of course, each particular perceptual act presents its object bodily; it is an experience of concrete 'filling'. In an obvious sense, no two acts of perceiving are identical. They are, to say the least, numerically distinct. So also, no two acts of judging are identical. The same applies to other kinds of acts as well. However, one does speak of the same judgement, the same belief, the same doubt. One may also speak of the same perception. One may, in an important sense, say 'I have now the same perception as you had then.' In the *Logical Investigations*, Husserl sought to explicate this sense of 'sameness', to give a criterion of identity, of *acts*. Two acts may be said to be identical, in this sense, when they have the same 'quality' and the same 'matter':

Talk about the same presentation, judgement etc. points to no individual sameness of acts, as if my consciousness were in some way conjoined with someone else's. It also means no relation of perfect likeness, of indiscernibility as regard constituents, as if the one act merely duplicated the other.[19]

This unity of matter and quality is what Husserl calls the intentional essence of an act, and he explicitly recognizes that the intentional essence does not exhaust the act phenomenologically.[20] If this concept of identity applies—Husserl in fact calls it a 'conceptual ruling'[21]— not merely to signitive acts but also to perception, then one can speak of the 'intentional essence' of a perceptual act. A perceptual act may then have the same 'matter' as another; however, they may differ from one another otherwise. It is this concept of 'matter' which becomes the *Sinne* of *The Ideas*, hence, the need of a perceptual *Sinne* or *noema*.

We have, then, to keep in mind two things. First, the perceptual *Sinne* does not contain the entire 'fullness" (*Fülle*) of perceptual experience:

. . . all differences of fulness [sic] which go beyond mere identification, and which variously determine peculiarities of fulfilment [sic] and increase of fulfilment, [sic] have no relevance in the formation of this conception.[22]

. . . the 'fulfilling sense' carries no implication of fulness [sic], that it does not accordingly include the total content of the intuitive act, to the extent that this is relevant for the theory of knowledge.[23]

Identity of percept in the above defined sense is compatible with differences in the descriptive contents of the expressions. Second, the perceptual *Sinne* is not the same as the meaning, *Bedeutung*, of the corresponding linguistic expression. With regard to this point, it is well known that Husserl, in the *Ideas*, did recognize a close relation between the *Sinne* of an act and the *Bedeutung* of the 'corresponding' linguistic expression. But he also did not want to identify them. *Ideas* §124 lays down the thesis that every meaning of every act can be expressed conceptually through *Bedeutungen*, but Husserl also points out that 'expression' indicates 'a special act-stratum' to which all other acts must adjust themselves in their own way and with which they must blend remarkably in such a way that every noematic act-meaning, and consequently the relation to objectivity which lies in it, stamps itself 'conceptually' in the noematic phase of the 'expressing'.[24]

Making allowances for the inadequacies of the metaphors he uses here (stamping', 'copying', 'mirroring'), we can say that the meaning (*Bedeutung*) of a perceptual statement like 'This is white' is a conceptualization of the *Sinne* of the perceptual experience which that statement expresses. The perceptual *Sinne*, then, is not conceptual; the *Bedeutung* of the perceptual statement is, and the two are not identical. Besides, as Husserl also points out, in spite of a certain 'congruence' between the two, 'the upper layer need not extend its expressing function over the entire lower layer.'[25] Furthermore,

The stratum of the meaning-function is not, and in principle is not, a sort of duplication of the lower stratum. Many directions of variability in the latter do not appear at all in the meaning whose function it is to express; they and their correlates do not 'express themselves' at all; so it is with the modifications of relative clearness and distinctness, the attentional modifications, and so forth.[26]

I had earlier said that Husserl's *Bedeutung* is not the same as 'Frege's *Sinne*. For, Husserl's *Bedeutung* is the meaning of an *act* of expression, Frege's *Sinne* is the meaning of the expression as a physical object. Now, we may add that although Husserl's *Bedeutung* is ideal and conceptual (like Frege's *Sinne*), not all noemata for Husserl are conceptual. The Husserlian *Sinne* of nonlinguistic acts, though expressible (within limitations), is nonconceptual; and when it is 'expressed', the meaning of the expression and the *Sinne* are 'congruent' but not identical. The *Sinne* or *noema* is always ideal. 'Ideality' and 'conceptuality' are not the same. Much of Dreyfus' criticism of Husserl's 'perceptual noema' rests upon an interpretation according to which all Husserlian *Sinne*, like the Fregean, are conceptual—which, as we have just seen, is not the case.

Let us now return to Dreyfus' main argument against Husserl: namely, the argument that the Husserlian concept of perceptual noema leads to an infinite regress. This argument has its positive side: the point that perception is an immediate and direct encounter with its object. Now, Dreyfus concedes that in the case of seeing *that*, there needs to be something like a Husserlian *Sinne*: seeing *that* . . . is not referentially transparent, it does not go direct to the object, it is mediated by conceptual meanings. Thus Husserl writes:

Mere sense, however, never fulfils [*sic*] categorical acts, or intentions which include categorical forms: fulfilment [*sic*] lies rather, in every case, in a sensibility structured by categorical acts.[27]

The cases of direct seeing, as contradistinguished from cases of seeing that . . ., are referentially transparent and free from conceptual mediation; it is in these cases that the Husserlian—and Fregean—*Sinne* are, according to Dreyfus, uncalled for. Restricting ourselves to these, then, we find that two Husserlian theses are pertinent. First, the thesis that perception is perspectival: this thesis requires that perceptual adumbrations point beyond themselves to other possible ones, so that although the overriding intention is nevertheless directed to the object perceived, the object as such is nothing but the 'Idea of the completely fulfilled sense.'[28] The dialectic, then, of the presented and the appresented, which underlies the perceptual situation, is utterly different from the dialectic of the intuitively given and the emptily intended. The latter dialectic underlies the Fregean distinction between conceptual *Sinne* and reference; the former underlies Husserl's theory of perception. Within the total horizon of a fulfilling act (which fulfills a prior empty intention of the object now being perceived), there nevertheless are unfulfilled intentions which point towards further possibilities of fulfillment, further determinations of the 'inner horizon' of the object. By abolishing this possibility, we can have a philosophy of perception in which the object is directly perceived all at once, so that perception achieves a satiety and points to nothing beyond it, but which would not be a phenomenoloically satisfactory position.

The second point is the presence of the 'now'-component in the perceptual sense, which serves to distinguish the object as such from the perceptual sense and provides an added justification for the talk of *Sinne* in this context.[29]

Further justifications are provided by the following considerations: When an act of perceiving of mine does fulfill a prior meaning intention, it is not every detail of the act, every *hic et nunc*, that plays that role or that is necessary for the total act's playing that role. Furthermore, it is not *qua* this act and *qua* mine that it plays the fulfilling role. Rather *any such act* (my perception at some other time as well as someone else's perception now) could have played the same role. Hence, within a fulfilling experience, one may single out a central core by virtue of which alone, the act fulfills *that* intention and none other.

Again, the same perception may serve to fulfill or verify different intentions (e.g., 'This is white', 'This is not red'). Here again, we need to recognize that the same perception's differing role requires a different 'slice' of its body to serve as its fulfilling sense.

Thus, it would seem that Husserl's notion of perceptual *noema* is phenomenologically well founded, and the extension of *his* concept of *Bedeutung* to perceptual acts is indeed a sound philosophical achievement. A theory of perception which dispenses with the *noema* and seeks to rehabilitate a direct realism has to fall back on the classical, not the Husserlian, transcendental consciousness. The counterpart of the purely objective is the pure transcendental consciousness. If human subjectivity, both in its bodily and its intellectual dimensions, is 'condemned to meaning', as Merleau-Ponty says, it is not clear how by replacing the noetic act by the bodily 'set', we can hope to get rid of the mediating '*Sinne*', when the body, phenomenologically considered, is not a physical object but an intentional movement. If the body is intentional, a bodily 'set' cannot logically guarantee real existence of that towards which it is directed, and the object would be *intended* by the bodily movement and there would always be a gap between the object as such and the object as intended.

IV

The most powerful, subtle, and thorough criticism of Husserl's theory of meaning is to be found in Jacques Derrida's *Speech and Phenomena*.[30] Derrida's avowed purpose, founded in the Heideggerean ideal of overcoming western metaphysics, is to bring out the underlying metaphysical presuppositions of Husserl's phenomenology. This metaphysical presupposition is found in the 'systematic interdependence' in Husserl's thought, between his theory of meaning, his intuitionism, the primacy of consciousness, and the emphasis on the 'now' in his analysis of time consciousness. They all are taken to constitute different aspects of what Derrida, following Heidegger, calls the metaphysics of presence.[31] In this essay, I will not comment either on this diagnosis or on the general notion of 'metaphysics of presence' save by way of raising certain doubts. I will, rather, restrict my comments to some other details of Derrida's exceptionally fine analysis of Husserl's First Investigation.

First of all, let us recall Derrida's criticism that Husserl's theory of meaning, developed in the *First Logical Investigation*, is based on a separation of expression from the indicative sign. The indicative function by which a sign points to or motivates belief in the *existence* of the signified is not what, for Husserl, constitutes an expression *qua* expression. An expression, Husserl does not deny, does serve as an indication in communicative speech. The speech of the utterer indicates to the hearer that the speaker is having such and such mental states. But, as is well known, Husserl turns away from communicative speech to solitary monologue in order to find the essence of expressions *qua* expression. Here in solitary monologue, he argues, there is no point in ascribing to the expressions any indicative function, for the inner mental states are the speaker's own and are being directly lived through by him. Therefore, what for Husserl constitutes an expression *qua* expression is not its indicative function as a sign, but its meaning-function. According to Derrida, here is 'reduction' to begin with:

Having its 'origin' in the phenomena of association, and always connecting empirical existents in the world, indicative signification in language will cover everything that falls subject to the 'reductions': factuality, worldly existence, essential non-necessity, nonevidence, etc.[32]

Not only does Husserl abstract from the indicative function of expressions and so from their connections with empirical existence, he also abstracts from the concrete physical event, the written or the spoken word. Thereby, he reduces it to the phantisized inner speech, the 'voice' (as Derrida calls it) which, again, is immediately present to the speaker within the solitude of his mental life. Thus, the expression, for the *First Logical Investigation*, is the pure inner speech endowed with the meaning function, both being directly present within his conscious life. An expression can only indicate what is not present (e.g., the speaker's mental states for the hearer).[33] When reduced to elements that are present, the inner speech and the meaning intention are all that are there.[34]

Now Derrida's otherwise fine and perceptive study suffers from one grave oversight which must be pointed out. In the *First Logical Investigation*, Husserl distinguishes between three functions of an expression: meaning, referring, and announcing (*Kundgebung*). All three are present in communicative speech: the words uttered by the speaker express their meanings, refer to their objects, and announce to the hearer the appropriate mental state or states of the speaker. It is this last which, for Husserl, is a sort of indication, since the mental states of the speaker are *not* given to the hearer. In solitary monologue, the last is redundant and so falls away. But even here, the other two, and not merely the first, are present. Even in solitary monologue, speech refers to the world. It is then not true to say, as Derrida does, that for Husserl the indicative function covers all that falls subject to the reductions—factuality, worldly existence, essential non-necessity, non-evidence, and so on. All these, rather, fall within what language *refers* to even in solitary inner speech. If Derrida's diagnosis is to be valid, then it should be true that for Husserl the referring function, together with the announcing, would belong to the generic function of indicating. However, it seems to me that this is not the case. That the object referred to is not to be regarded as also the indicated is borne out by the fact that for Husserl both the sign indicating and that which is indicated must be believed to be existent. The referent of a word used in inner, or even in overt speech, may be nonexistent and may be known to be so. The referring function is thus not contingent to an expression: 'To use an expression significantly and to refer expressively to an object (to form a presentation of it) are one and the same.'[35] Nevertheless, for reasons that are well known, Husserl, like Frege, distinguished between meaning and reference.

If then, Derrida wants to say that by abstracting from communicative speech and therefore from the indicative function, Husserl is also, in effect, applying the *epoché* and excludes all reference to the contingent, factual world, then he is mistaken.[36] However, for quite other reasons, I partly agree with Derrida inasmuch as it has always seemed to me that Husserl's abstracting from communicative speech was an unnecessary, and even for his own purposes, a misleading move. This is what I wrote in 1964:

> ... if the contrast is the same as that between public thinking and private thinking, then Husserl would seem to be defending the view that it is in private thinking that one catches hold of the meaning function in its purity ... [But then] the risk that we run is psychologism and the consequent relativism. The true nature of thought, it might be argued, manifests itself in reflection upon its communicative function; for here in communicative speech, subjectivity is overcome and thought exhibits itself as an objective, over–individual process.[37]

Husserl's general theory of the ideality of meanings, then, does not need his reduction of speech to 'inner monologue'. On the contrary, it would seem to need 'sharability' and 'communicability'.

Derrida's elaborate critical appraisal seeks to connect the Husserlian reduction to inner monologue to the implicit metaphysics of presence: both the inner voice and the meaning intention are present to the speaker (while the speaker's mental states are non-present to the hearer and so need to be indicated). Now as said earlier, I cannot, in the present context, enter into a detailed examination of what Derrida means by 'metaphysics of presence'; and even if the thesis about Husserl's implicit metaphysics be valid, I cannot here pursue the question, why a 'metaphysics of difference' should be preferred to a metaphysics of presence. One needs also to ask, even if it be true that western metaphysics has been dominated by the metaphysics of presence, that fact by itself does not show this metaphysics to be false or in need of overcoming or that it should yield place to a metaphysics of nonpresence. These are larger issues beyond the scope of this essay. However, in the present context, I would like to make two points. In the first place, although Husserl did, in the *Investigations* and the *Ideas*, generally speaking, regard one's own mental life to be immediately, adequately, and apodictically present to oneself, he came to modify this position considerably, without abandoning his basic theory of meaning. He comes to recognize that caught as one's mental life is in the flux of temporality, we have in fact to 'swim after it'.[38] Inner perception is also far from being adequate, as he recognizes in the *Cartesian Meditations*[39]—even if he still ascribes to it a sort of apodicticity. However, the point is that if the speaker's mental state and meaning intention are present to him and not to the hearer, it is also Husserl's thesis that the constituted meaning, as an ideal unity, is inter-subjective, is 'grasped' by the other, no less directly than by the speaker. In the second place, the mental state of the speaker which is nonpresent for the hearer and so is 'announced' is also—Husserl tells us—intuitively apprehended by the hearer. He, 'as we certainly can say, *perceives* him as such.' Husserl then continues:

When I listen to someone, I perceive him as a speaker, I hear him recounting, demonstrating, doubting, wishing, etc. The hearer perceives the intimation in the same sense in which he perceives the intimating person—even though the mental phenomena which make him a person cannot fall, for what they are, in the intuitive grasp of another.[40]

Again:

The hearer perceives the speaker as manifesting certain inner experiences, and to that extent he also perceives these experiences themselves: he does not, however, himself experience them.[41]

Thus, the distinction between presence and nonpresence is not as sharp as Derrida makes it out to be. There are, in fact, two modes of being present: the presence of my own lived experiences to myself and the presence of the other to me. There are again various shades of gradations in between these. In fact, it is this that led me to suggest that Husserl's assimilation of the 'announcing' (*Kundgebung*) function of speech to the indicating function of signs is misleading. This is what I wrote:

A mark never makes us *see*, or even apprehend, the signified; at its best, the presence of the mark makes us believe in the presence of the signified. But the expression makes the hearer see, or even apprehend the speaker as having certain mental experiences: expressions therefore are not just marks of the experiences, but announce them and reveal them to the other.[42]

Derrida goes further: in a somewhat enigmatic analysis he seeks to lay bare what he calls 'the complicity' between voice and ideality.[43] It is as though the Husserlian theory of the ideality of meanings and the reduction of language to inner speech were connected by a secret tie. Is this what one *prima facie* would expect the situation to be? On the contrary, one would have thought that with the emphasis shifting from written language to the spoken, from the spoken to the *act* of speaking, the decisive step had been taken that would place meaning back in the living context of that act. But curiously enough, Derrida speaks of the 'unfailing complicity here between idealization and speech'.[44] Possibly, the complicity he is referring to exists not between overt speech and ideality, but between inner voice and ideality. It is most plausible that this is what he means, although he is also advocating a much broader thesis according to which 'speech is possible only because a certain kind of "writing" precedes it'.[45] In a broader context, Derrida is against the primacy of speech, of the vocal medium;[46] in a narrower context, he is, of course, exposing the consequences of the Husserlian reduction to inner speech.

Now it is not for me to comment here on the thesis of the primacy of 'writing' over speech. I can only refer (without feeling very sure that this would be relevant to the issue which in any case is obscure) to the fact that the most ancient Sanskrit scriptures, the *Vedas*, are known throughout the age-long tradition as having been heard and transmitted through the spoken words, as *śruti* as contrasted with the written. I would suppose this may be the case with many other traditions as well.

But Derrida's point about 'the complicity between voice and ideality' is what is directly pertinent for us. What does he mean by this complicity? The argument runs somewhat like this: ideality of the object needs that the consciousness of it should be nonempirical.[47] The supposed inner voice, not being the concrete physical utterance, is precisely this nonempirical consciousness. The purity of this dis-embodied voice, occurring in absolute 'self-proximity', 'makes it fit for universality'.[48] Since it is not a worldly occurrence, it can be re-produced:[49] hence the possibility of ideal objects. As Derrida puts it, 'absolute ideality is the correlate of a possibility of indefinite rep-etition'.[50]

In this remarkable argumentation, what I wish to deny is *not* the just cited statement about ideality, but the initial premise that ideal-ity of meaning needs that the correlative act of consciousness should be nonempirical. The novelty of the Husserlian thesis is not that there is a necessary correlation between ideal meaning and nonem-pirical consciousness, but that *real*, temporal acts of consciousness belonging to the real mental life of real persons are correlated to ideal meanings or noemata.[51] What is repeatable is not the same voice, but the same meaning. Each utterance, explicit, subvocal or purely phantasized, is a *real* occurrence: the purely inner is also a *real* event and in the strictest sense cannot be repeated. What is re-peatable is its 'ideal content', the meaning. The 'purity' of inner speech makes it no less real and no more repeatable than the 'impure' phys-ical utterance. There also lurks in this argument of Derrida's deep misunderstanding of what the relation is between empirical and transcendental consciousness in Husserl's philosophy—a relation, a 'parallelism', which Husserl often characterized as the wonder of all wonders.[52] But that is a theme to which we need not return for the present.

NOTES

1. 'Husserl and Frege: A New Look at their Relationship' (read at the Husserl Circle meeting, Duquesne University, 1974; forthcoming in *Research in Phenomenology*).

2. Robert Solomon, 'Sense and Essence: Frege and Husserl', *International Philosophical Quarterly*, 10, (1970), pp. 378–401.

3. Husserl, *Logical Investigations*, Eng. tr. by J.N. Findlay (New York: Humanities Press, 1970; henceforth to be referred to as *LI*). Vol. I, p. 353.

4. *LI*, I, p. 351.

5. Ibid., I, p. 341.

6. Ibid., I, p. 341; also pp. 323, 330, 331.

7. Ibid., p. 431.

8. Ibid., I, p. 323.

9. Ibid., I, p. 331.
10. Ibid., I, pp. 331-2.
11. Husserl, *Ideen* III (*Husserliana* Bd. V), p. 85.
12. Ibid., p. 86.
13. *LI*, I, p. 330.
14. Husserl, *Experience and Judgement*, Eng. tr. by J.S. Churchill and K. Ameriks (Evanston: Northwestern University Press, 1973), pp. 261-2.
15. The relation as well as the distinction between Frege's *Sinne* and Husserl's *Noema* has been well worked out in two unpublished Stanford dissertations: R.T. McIntyre, 'Husserl and Referentiality: The Role of Noema as an Intentional Entity' (1971) and D.W. Smith, 'Intentionality, Noemata and Individuation: The Role of Individuation' (1971).
16. H. Dreyfus, in L. Embree (ed.), *Life-World and Consciousness* (Evanston: Northwestern University Press, 1972), pp. 135-70.
17. Ibid., pp. 146-7.
18. Ibid., p. 147.
19. *LI*, II, p. 591.
20. Ibid., p. 591.
21. Ibid., p. 590.
22. Ibid., p. 738.
23. Ibid., p. 744.
24. Husserl, *Ideas* I, Eng. tr. by Boyce Gibson (Collier Books edition), p. 320.
25. Ibid., p. 324.
26. Ibid., p. 325.
27. *LI*, II, p. 670.
28. Husserl, *Analysen zur passiven Synthesis* (*Husserliana* Bd. XI), p. 364.
29. Ibid., pp. 311-12, 330.
30. Jacques Derrida, *Speech and Phenomena*, Eng. tr. by David Allison (Evanston: Northwestern University Press, 1973).
31. The same point, though in a somewhat different manner, is made by K.H. Vollkmann-Schluck, in his 'Husserls Lehre von der Idealität der Bedeutung als metaphysisches Problem', H.L. Van Breda and J. Taminiaux (eds), *Husserl und das Denken der Neuzeit* (The Hague: Martinus Nijhoff, 1959), pp. 230-41.
32. *Speech and Phenomena*, p. 30.
33. Ibid., p. 40.
34. Thus Derrida: 'The meaning is therefore *present to the self* in the life of a present that has not yet gone forth from itself into the world, space or nature', (p. 40).

35. *LI*, I, p. 293.
36. Derrida's confusion between 'indicating' and 'referring' is shared by Newton Garver. In his Introduction to *Speech and Phenomena*, Garver takes Husserl's indication to be the same as Frege's 'reference' (p. xv).
37. J.N. Mohanty, *Edmund Husserl's Theory of Meaning* (The Hague: Martinus Nijhoff, 2nd edn, 1969), pp. 15–16.
38. For example, *Ideas* I, p. 127.
39. Husserl, *Cartesian Meditations*, Eng. tr. by Dorion Cairns (The Hague: Martinus Nijhoff, 1960), pp. 22–23.
40. *LI*, I, p. 277.
41. Ibid., p. 278.
42. *Edmund Husserl's Theory of Meaning*, p. 11.
43. *Speech and Phenomena*, p. 77.
44. Ibid., p. 75.
45. David Allison, in his Translator's Introduction to *Speech and Phenomena*, p. xl, fn.
46. Contrast Newton Garver: 'Derrida falls squarely within the movement which regards the role of utterances in actual discourse as the essence of language and meanings . . .' (*Speech and Phenomena*, p. xxii). This would seem to be a misunderstanding.
47. *Speech and Phenomena*, p. 76.
48. Ibid., p. 79.
49. Ibid., p. 80.
50. Ibid., p. 52
51. *Cf.* Aron Gurwitsch, *Studies in Phenomenology and Psychology* (Evanston: Northwestern University Press, 1966), pp. 156–7.
52. I have dealt with this in my paper, 'Life-World and Consciousness', read at the Gurwitsch Memorial Symposium held at the New School for Social Research, New York, March, 1974, and to be published in a special issue of *Social Research*.

chapter

four

*Husserl and Frege: A New Look at their Relationship**

H usserl's explicit rejection of psychologism as a theory of the origin of the logico-mathematical entities and his advocacy of a conception of pure logic as a science of objective meanings were first expounded in the *Prolegomena to Pure Logic* (1900), and Husserl tells us that the *Prolegomena*, in its essentials, is a reworking of lectures he had given at Halle in the year 1896.[1] Føllesdal, in his careful study of the relation between Frege and Husserl during these years, asks the question, at what point of time between 1890 (the year of publication of the *Philosophie der Arithmetik*) and 1896 did this change in Husserl's mode of thinking take place?[2] The papers published during 1891–93 do not, according to Føllesdal, bear testimony to any such change. In the paper 'Psychologische Studien zur Elementaren Logik' of the year 1894, Husserl is still found to believe that the foundations of logic can be clarified with the help of psychology. Accordingly, the change must have occurred between the years 1894 and 1896. Frege's famed review of the *Philosophie der Arithmetik* appeared in the year 1894. Føllesdal therefore conjectures that it is Frege's review which must have led Husserl to a complete revision of his prior mode of thinking.[3] This view about the Frege–Husserl relationship is shared by many writers. A recent writer even speaks of Husserl's 'traumatic encounter with Frege'.[4]

*First appeared in *Research in Phenomenology*, Vol. V, 1975. Reprinted here with permission J.N.M.

In this chapter I wish to argue that the basic change in Husserl's mode of thinking which by itself could have led to the *Prolegomena* conception of pure logic had already taken place by 1891. This change may be discerned in Husserl's review of Schröder's *Vorlesungen über die Algebra der Logik*.[5] It also underlies the programme of *Inhaltslogik* worked out in 'Der Folgerungs-kalkül und die Inhaltslogik' of the same year.[6] If pure logic is defined in the *Prolegomena* in terms of the concept of ideal objective meanings,[7] then already the 1891 review of Schröder's work contains this concept. If the major burden of Frege's 1894 review of the *Philosophie der Arithmetik* is the lack of distinction, in that work, between the subjective and the objective,[8] between *Vorstellung and Begriff* and between both and the object, then Husserl already had come to distinguish between *Vorstellung*, meaning and object in his 1891 review. If this be so, then another historical judgement—connected with the above—needs to be revised. It has been held by many authors that Husserl's distinction, in the *Logische Untersuchungen*, between meaning and object of an expression is Fregean in origin. Thus, for example, Hubert Dreyfus writes: 'Husserl simply accepted and applied Frege's distinctions . . . The only change Husserl made in Frege's analysis was terminological.'[9] Now, if Husserl's review of Schröder already contains that distinction, then it surely antedates the publication of Frege's celebrated paper 'Über Sinn and Bedeutung' of 1892, and Husserl must have arrived at it independently of Frege.

I

Referring to Schröder's distinction between univocal and equivocal names, Husserl writes:

. . . he lacks the true concept of the meaning of a name. That requirement of univocity is also expressed in the form: 'The name shall be of a . . . constant meaning.' (48) However, according to the relevant discussions on pages 47–48, the author identifies the meaning of the name with the representation (*Vorstellung*) of the object named by the name, from which the striking consequence follows, to be sure, that all common names are equivocal. It is not as if the author had overlooked the distinction between equivocal and common names—and besides, who could overlook it! But to see a distinction and to apprehend its essence are two different things. Moreover, he uses the term 'meaning' (*Bedeutung*) itself equivocally, and that in an already intolerable degree. In the above quotation, in spite of mutually opposed and false explanations, what is intended is the ordinary sense. On another occasion, however, what is actually meant is the object named by the name; how otherwise, e.g., could, in verbal contradiction with the above mentioned requirement, the common names be as such characterized as being such that 'several meanings are true of them with the same right and justification!' (69) And even that is not enough; the class corresponding to the common name is also called its meaning (69 fn.). It is therefore understandable that the author is not able to formulate the essence of equivocation precisely . . . It is further connected with unclarity in the concept of meaning that Schröder regards names such as 'round square' as meaningless (*unsinnige*) and sets them apart from univocal and equivocal names. Obviously he confuses here between two different questions: (1) whether there belongs to a name a meaning (*ein 'Sinn'*); and (2) whether an object corresponding to a name exists or not.[10]

This paragraph clearly shows that Husserl did distinguish, already in 1891, between:
1. the sense or meaning of a term (for which he is using both *Bedeutung* and *Sinn*, though in the *Logische Untersuchungen* he will prefer '*Bedeutung*');
2. the object (*Gegenstand*) which the name may designate in case the object exists; and
3. the presentation (*Vorstellung*) of such an object.

Representations may vary, but the meaning or *Sinn* may remain the same. Further, there may be no object that is designated, and yet a name may have meaning. Even when there are objects that are designated, the multiplicity of objects does not imply multiplicity of meanings. He therefore has a clear distinction between *Vorstellung, Gegenstand* and *Bedeutung* or *Sinn*.

It is true that these remarks do not contain the thesis of the *ideal* objectivity of meanings, but they certainly do not confuse meaning with *Vorstellung* and therefore testify to an awareness of the *objectivity* of meanings as contrasted with the subjectivity of the *Vorstellungen*.

Could Husserl have derived this threefold distinction from any of Frege's earlier writings? If anywhere in Frege's writings before 1891, we are to look for it in *Die Grundlagen der Arithmetik* (1884). But Frege writes in his letter to Husserl of 24 May, 1891 that he had not yet in the *Grundlagen* drawn the distinction between meaning and reference.[11] It is unlikely then that Husserl took it from him. It is more likely then that both arrived at the distinction independently, as Husserl writes back to Frege: 'I also notice, that in spite of essential points of divergence, our points of view have many things in common. Many observations which forced themselves on me, I find had been expressed by you many years earlier.' That seems in principle to be a true account of their relationship at this stage, though it would seem that on this point, i.e. the distinction between meaning and reference, Husserl and Frege must have arrived at it about the same time and independently of each other.

What is of importance for our present purpose, however, is that Husserl's overcoming of subjectivism in favour of an objective theory of meaning and the consequent theory of logic is already foreshadowed in the 1891 review of Schröder's work and three years prior to Frege's review of the *Philosophie der Arithmetik*. The other (1891) paper, i.e. the one on *Inhaltslogik* more clearly brings this out.

II

Amongst the major theses which Husserl puts forward, in so far as his conception of logic at this point is concerned, we may mention the following:

1. A calculus *qua* calculus is not a language: 'the two concepts are fundamentally different. Language is not a method of systematic-symbolic inference, calculus is not a method of systematic-symbolic expression of psychic phenomena.'[12]
2. A logic *qua* logic is not a calculus. A calculus is a technic, a *Zeichentechnik*. Logic is concerned, not with mere signs, but with conceptual contents.[13]
3. Deductive logic is not the same as a technic of inference, nor is it exhausted by a theory of inference. There are deductive operations other than inferring. A deductive science does not consist only in inferences. It may involve, for example, the operation 'computing' (*Rechnen*) which is not inferring.[14]
4. It is not true that only an extensional calculus of classes is possible. A calculus of conceptual contents, or intensions, is also possible.[15]
5. An *autonomous* extensional logic of classes is not possible, for every extensional judgement (*Umfangsurteil*) is, in truth, an intensional judgement (*Inhaltsurteil*). The concept of class presupposes the concepts of 'conceptual content' and 'object of a concept'.[16]
6. Every judgement has two aspects: logical content and 'algorithmic content.'[17] The logical content is the judged content (*Urteilsgehalt*), i.e. that which it states (*das, was sie behauptet*). When a categorical judgement is reduced to relation of subsumption amongst classes, this brings out its *algorithmic content*. The two are equivalent, but

not always identical. They are identical when the judgement is a judgement about classes.

7. A judgement by itself is directed not towards classes or conceptual contents, but towards objects of concepts (*Begriffsgegenstände*).[18]

8. Geometrical thinking is not operation with signs or figures. The signs are mere 'supports' for the 'conception of the truly intended operations with concepts and with respective objects of those concepts.'[19]

Most of these theses are retained, with modifications and shifts in emphasis no doubt, in the *Prolegomena* and the *Investigations*. Pure logic is the science of meanings. 'Everything that is logical falls under the two correlated categories of meaning and object.'[20] Algorithmic methods spare us genuine deductive mental work by 'artificially arranged mechanical operations on sensible signs'[21] and 'their sense and justification depend on validatory thought.'[22] Certainly, Husserl has now, in the *Prolegomena*, much more sympathetic understanding of the 'mathematicising theories of logic' and he has come to regard the mathematical form of treatment as the only scientific one which alone offers us 'systematic closure and completeness.'[23] But he is still cautioning us that 'the mathematician is not really the pure theoretician, but only the ingenious technician, the constructer, as it were, who looking merely to formal interconnections, builds up his theory like a technical work of art.'[24] But this note of warning is mollified by the assurance that what makes science possible is not essential insight but 'scientific instinct and method',"[25] and that philosophical investigation should not meddle in the work of the specialist but should seek to 'achieve insight in regard to the sense and essence of his achievements as regards method and manner'.[26] The thesis that extension of a concept presupposes its intension is developed in the Second Investigation, though there is more explicit emphasis on the ideal objectivity of meanings and there is the talk of the *Inhalt* as a *species*.

III

Husserl sent copies of his 1891 papers to Frege. We know of this from the correspondence between the two men. It is worthwhile therefore to find out what Frege's responses to the Husserl papers were. In his letter of 24 May, 1891, after acknowledging receipt of Husserl's *Philosophie der Arithmetik* and the papers on Schröder and

Inhaltslogik, Frege emphasizes that the two have many ideas in common, and renews his own decision to write down his own thoughts on Schröder's book.[27] He agrees with some of Husserl's criticism of Schröder, for example of Schröder's definitions of '0', '1', 'a + b' and 'a − b'. Referring to the *Philosophie der Arithmetik*, Frege hopes that sometime in the future, time permitting, he may reply to Husserl's criticisms of his own theory of number. He draws attention to one major difference between them, and that concerns how a common name relates to its objects. Frege illustrates his own view with the help of the following scheme:

Sentence	Proper name	Common name
↓	↓	↓
Sinn of the sentence (*Gedanke* = Thought)	*Sinn* of the proper name	*Sinn* of the common name
↓	↓	↓
Bedeutung of the sentence (its truth-value)	*Bedeutung* of the proper name (*Gegenstand*)	*Bedeutung* of the common name (= concept) → object which falls under the concept

In the case of common names, one step more is needed—according to Frege—to reach the object than in the case of proper names. Further, in the case of common names, the concept may be empty, i.e. there may be no object without its ceasing thereby to be scientifically useful. In the case of proper names, however, if a name does not name anything, i.e. lacks an object, it is scientifically useless. This refers to Frege's well-known and controversial thesis that concepts constitute the reference, not the *Sinn*, of common names. Frege contrasts with this Husserl's view that the *Sinn*, (or, in Husserl's language, the *Bedeutung*) of a common name is the concept expressed by it and its reference is constituted by the object or objects falling under the concept. The letter makes it clear that Frege does recognize that Husserl had the distinction between *Sinn* and *Gegenstand*, only he does *not* ascribe here to Husserl a distinction between *Vorstellung* and *Sinn*.

Husserl writes back to Frege on 18 July, 1891. He admits the great intellectual stimulus he had received from Frege's theories, and he goes on to express his views about the many points of agreement between them—to which reference has been made earlier. Amongst these points of agreement, Husserl refers to his own distinction between 'language' (*Sprache*) and 'calculus' which he now finds in Frege's

1883 paper on 'Über den Zweck der Begriffsschrift'[28] where he distinguishes between the concept of 'calculus ratiocinator' and the concept of 'lingua characteristica'. It appears to him that the *Begriffsschrift* is intended to be a lingua characteristica and not a 'sign language constructed in imitation of the arithmetical'. He concludes the letter by expressing agreement with Frege's rejection of 'formal arithmetic' as a *theory* of arithmetic, however important it may be as an extension of the arithmetical technic. Husserl is referring to Frege's 'Über formale Theorien der Arithmetik'[29] whose copy Frege had just sent him. The sense of 'formalism' in which Frege rejects it as a theory of arithmetic is that according to which the signs for numbers like '1/2', '2/3', 'π' are empty, meaningless signs (*leere Zeichen*). According to this theory, as Frege understands it, these empty signs themselves are numbers and they constitute the proper subject matter of arithmetic.[30] That Husserl should concur fully with Frege's total rejection of such a theory of arithmetic should be obvious from the foregoing summary of his views. The *Prolegomena* however shows much greater understanding of the significance of formalism, but even there his philosophy of arithmetic is not formalistic. His formal logic is the correlate of formal ontology, and in large parts of the work he is concerned not with a specific formal science but with the form of theory in general.

From the above survey of the Frege-Husserl correspondence of 1891[31] it becomes clear that Frege did not quite show any recognition of the presence of the *Vorstellung-Sinn* distinction in Husserl's Schröder review. However, as we have already seen, this distinction is there, which suggests that Husserl was already on his way, independently of Frege's 1894 review, towards, the objective conception of logic of the *Prolegomena*.

IV

Let us now look at other comments by Frege on the Husserl papers of 1891. We know that in his 24 May 1891 letter to Husserl, Frege writes that Husserl's Schröder review had made him decide to publish his own thoughts on Schröder's book and that his comments on it may appear in the *Zeitschrift für Philosophie und philosophische Kritik*. However, Frege's 'Kritische Beleuchtung einiger Punkte in E. Schröders Vorlesunen über die Algebra der Logik' finally appeared four years after in the *Archiv für systematische Philosophie*.[32] In this review, Frege, amongst other things, brings out the essential points of difference between Schröder's concept of *'Gebiet'* (domain) and the logical concept of class, and points out how Schröder unknowingly oscillates between the two. In so far as the logical concept of class is concerned, Frege considers it entirely mistaken to take a class as consisting in individual things, as a collection of individuals—a mistake which, according to him, derives from Schröder's attempt to extend his *Gebietekalkül* to the logic of classes.[33] And yet, asks Frege, how else is a class constituted if one abstracts from common properties? 'Only through the fact that the classes are determined by the properties which their individuals should have, only through the fact that one uses expressions such as "the class of objects which are b", is it possible to express general thoughts when one states relations amongst classes; only through this that one comes to logic.'[34] Thus Frege agrees with Husserl's comments: the extension of a concept presupposes the intension of the concept. In Frege's own words: 'In reality I hold the view that the concept logically precedes its extension, and I consider it a mistake to attempt to found the class, as extension of a concept, not on the concept itself but on the individual things.'[35] However, despite this agreement with Husserl's point of view, Frege refuses to side with *Inhaltslogik* as against the so-called *Umfangslogik*, and adds: 'Nevertheless, I am in many respects possibly closer to the author (i.e. to Schröder) than to those whom one could call, in opposition to him, logicians of content (*Inhalt*).'[36] He has obviously Husserl in mind. The question naturally arises: why does Frege reject the conception of an *Inhaltslogik* even though he does not agree with a purely extensional analysis of classes?

The reasons become partly clear when one considers his remarks on *Inhaltslogik* in the 'Ausführungen über Sinn und Bedeutung'[37] which possibly belongs to the period 1892–95. Frege writes:

Even if one has to concede to the *Inhalts*-logicians that the concept itself, as contrasted with its extension, is the foundational, nevertheless it should not for that reason be understood as the meaning (*Sinn*) of the concept-word, but as its reference, and the *Umfangs*-logicians are nearer the truth in so far as they locate in the extension (*Umfang*) an essential meaning (*Bedeutung*) which, though not itself the concept, is yet very closely connected with it.[38]

We have already found that the *Inhaltslogik* is a logic of meanings. Although Frege regards the concept as primary and extension as derivative, he also considers the concept itself to be the *reference* of a concept-word. A logic of concepts then would be a logic, not of *Sinne* but of *Bedeutungen* (in Frege's senses of those words) and hence closer to an extensional logic. The following paragraph further clarifies Frege's argument:

They (i.e. the *Umfangs*-logicians) are right when, because of their preference for the extension of a concept to its intension, they admit that they regard the reference of words, and not their meaning, to be essential for logic. The *Inhalts*-logicians only remain too happily with the meaning, for what they call 'Inhalt', if it is not quite the same as *Vorstellung*, is certainly the meaning (*Sinn*). They do not consider the fact that in logic it is not a question of how thoughts come from thoughts without regard to truth-value, that, more generally speaking, the progress from meanings (*Sinne*) to reference (*Bedeutung*), must be made; that the logical laws are first laws in the realm of references and only then mediately relate to meaning (*Sinn*).[39]

Also in the same 'Ausführungen', Frege makes reference to Husserl's distinction between whether a name has a *Sinn* and whether an object corresponding to it exists or not. But he finds this distinction insufficient, for Husserl does not distinguish between proper names and concept-words and, as we saw earlier, Frege differs widely from Husserl on this point. Again, there is no reference to Husserl's distinction between *Vorstellung* and *Sinn*. The one likely recognition of this is the covert statement that the *Inhalt* of the *Inhalts*-logicians, if it is not *Vorstellung*, must be the *Sinn*.[40]

V

We may sum up our conclusions in so far as the Frege–Husserl relationship about the years 1891–94 is concerned:

1. The two men arrived at the *Vorstellung–Sinn*–reference distinction independently of each other.

2. Husserl's overcoming of psychologism and acceptance of a theory of objective pure logic was fundamentally independent of Frege's 1894 review of the *Philosophie der Arithmetik*. The basic change had occurred in 1891. That this should have occurred in the very year of publication of the *Philosophie der Arithmetik* is made all the more plausible by the following note by Husserl, belonging to a much later date:

Ich las viel in der "Philosophie der Arithmetik." Wie unreif, wie naiv und fast kindlich erschien mir dieses Werk. Nun, nicht umsonst peinigte mich bei der Publikation das Gewissen. *Eigentlich war ich darüber schon hinaus, als ich es publizierte.* Es stammte ja im wesentlichen aus den Jahren 86/87.[41]

3. (a) Frege agrees with Husserl that the concept of a class presupposes the concept of concept, that the extension of a concept presupposes the intension.

(b) Nevertheless, while Husserl went on to develop the idea of an *Inhaltslogik* and subsequently a logic of meanings (though he did not quite reject *Umfangslogik*, to be sure, but wavered between (i) asserting a bare equivalence between the two logics and (ii) asserting the primacy of the *Inhaltslogik*, Frege sides with *Umfangslogik* and that for two reasons: (a) his belief that logic is concerned not with mere consistency of thoughts but with their truth-value, and (b) his theory that the reference of concept-words is the concept itself (as contrasted with Husserl's view, which may also be said to be the standard, view, that the concept is the *Sinn* of the concept-word.)

We cannot here discuss whether these two Fregean theses are acceptable or not. But we know now where exactly the two men stood in relation to each other between the years 1891 and 1894.

NOTES

1. E. Husserl, *Logical Investigations*, Eng.tr. by J.N. Findlay, Vol. I, (New York: Humanities Press, 1970), p. 47.

2. D. Føllesdal, *Husserl und Frege*, (Oslo: I Kommisjon Hos H. Aschehoug & Co., 1958), p. 23.

3. Ibid., p. 25.

4. R.C. Solomon, 'Sense and Essence: Frege and Husserl', *International Philosophical Quarterly*, 10, 1970, p. 380.

5. Published in *Göttingische gelehrte Anzeigen*, 1, (1891), pp. 243–87.

6. Published in *Vierteljahrsschrift für wissenschaftliche Philosophie*, 15, (1891), pp. 168–89, 351–6.

7. *Logical Investigations*, Vol. I, p. 322.

8. Thus writes Frege: 'First of all, everything becomes presentation. The references of words are presentations . . . Objects are presentations . . . concepts, too, are presentations.' A little later on: 'Everything is shunted off into the subjective.' (G. Frege, 'Review of Dr. E. Husserl's *Philosophy of Arithmetic*', Eng.tr. by E.E.W. Kluge, *Mind*, LXXXI, (1972), pp. 321–37; esp. 323–4.

9. Lester E. Embree, *Life-World and Consciousness, Essays for Aron Gurwitsch*, (Evanston: Northwester University Press, 1972), pp. 139–40 (in H. Dreyfus, 'The Perceptual Noema: Gurwitsch's Crucial Contribution'). In a footnote on p. 140, Dreyfus rejects Gurwitsch's claim that Husserl discovered the distinction between real mental states and ideal

meanings and refers to 'Husserl's explicit attribution of this distinction to Frege' in the *Logical Investigations*, I (Findlay edition), p. 292. This reference however is misleading. First, this is not the place where Husserl first introduces the distinction. The distinction is introduced, first, in the 1891 Schröder review as this chapter will argue. Second, at this place, Husserl is only referring to Frege's different terminology.

10. *Göttingische gelehrte Anzeigen*, I, (1891), p. 250.

11. Thiel considers the terminology of 'sense' and 'reference' obligatory for all Frege works after 1890. Cf. Christian Thiel, *Sense and Reference in Frege's Logic* (Dordrecht-Holland: D. Reidel, 1968), p. 44. Angelelli finds the distinction already in the *Begriffsschrift* ('only the famous terminology . . . is lacking here') and in the *Grundlagen*, § 67. Cf. Ignacio Angelelli, *Studies on Gottlob Frege and Traditional Philosophy* (Dordrecht-Holland: D. Reidel, 1967).

12. *Göt. gel. Anz.*, I, (1891), pp. 258–9.

13. Ibid., p. 247.

14. *Op.cit.*, p. 246.

15. *Vierteljahrsschrift f. wiss. Phil.*, 15, (1891), pp. 169, 171.

16. *Gött. gel. Anz.*, I, (1891), p. 257.

17. Ibid., p. 262.

18. *Viert. f. wiss. Phil.*, 15, (1891), p. 178.

19. *Gött. gel. Anz.*, I, (1891), p. 249.

20. *Logical Investigations*, I, pp. 322–5.

21. Ibid., p. 69.

22. Ibid., p. 69.

23. Ibid., p. 244.

24. Ibid., p. 244.

25. Ibid., p. 245.

26. Ibid., p. 245.

27. G. Frege, 'Kritische Beleuchtung einiger Punkte in E. Schröders Vorlesungen über die Algebra der Logik', *Archiv für systematische Philosophie*, I, (1895), pp. 433–6.

28. In *Jenaische Zeitschrift für Naturwissenschaft*, 1883, XVI, Supplement, pp. 1–10.

29. In *Sitzungsberichte der Jenaischen Gesellschaft für Medizin und Naturwissenschaft für das Jahr 1885*, (Jena: Fischer, 1885–86), pp. 94–104 (now reprinted in Ignacio Angelelli [ed.], *Freges Kleine Schriften*, [Hildesheim: Georg Olms, 1967], pp. 103–111).

30. Frege, *Kleine Schriften*, p. 105.

31. I am indebted to Professor F. Kambartel of the University of Konstanz, director of the Frege-Archiv, for making these available to me.

32. See fn. 27 above.
33. Frege, *Kleine Schriften*, p. 207.
34. Ibid., p. 208,
35. Ibid., p. 209.
36. Ibid., p. 209–10.
37. In G. Frege, *Nachgelassene Schriften* (Hamburg: Felix Meiner, 1969), pp. 128–36.
38. Ibid., p. 134.
39. Ibid., p. 133.
40. Ibid., p. 133.
41. Husserl, 'Persönliche Aufzeichnungen', ed. W. Biemel, in *Philosophy and Phenomenological Research*, XVI, (1956), 293–302, esp. p. 294 (Italics mine).

chapter

five

The Relevance of Husserl Today*

We are remembering Husserl's passing away fifty years after the event. When one celebrates the birthday of a philosopher, or the date of publication of his major work, it is appropriate to recall what new ideas he brought into existence. On the contrary, when one remembers the passing away of such a philosopher, it is most appropriate to reflect upon the question: how has time, in our present case half-a-century, dealt with his thought? We, of course, expect quite naturally that the death of the philosopher does not imply the demise of his ideas. There seem to be good reasons to expect that the philosopher's demise releases his ideas from his personal authority and custodianship and onto the public domain for interpretation, appropriation and judgement. Here in the competitive marketplace of the western world of thought, where fashions and styles change and along with them the standards that philosophy as a vocation imposes on its practitioners, the fortunes of ideas face an uncertain future. Let us first take stock of how Husserl's philosophy has fared in this regard. But my taking stock of it cannot be separated from my own personal experience.

I began reading Husserl in 1950. Having been trained in an Indian University where Oxford still exercised the major influence, everything I read in Husserl's *Ideas* seemed to run counter to the reigning

Husserlian Studies, Vol. V, 1975.

philosophical orthodoxy. Its essentialism was opposed to the prevailing nominalism aided by the idea of family resemblance. Its mentalism seemed to have been already rendered unworkable by the linguistic criticisms of the ideas of 'privileged access' and 'private language'. Its theory of the ideality of meanings seemed quaint in comparison with the verifiability (or falsifiability) theories. The theory of 'eidetic intuition', if not mystical, stood opposed to the prevailing empiricism. Everything weighed in favour of why I should not read Husserl. Precisely for those reasons, the rebellious in me persisted—encouraged by certain familiar-sounding overtones from the Indian philosophical literature.

That was in the early fifties. Now in the late eighties, how do precisely those theses of *Ideas* fare? The reigning canons as well as fashions have changed. Logical positivism (of various brands) is a forgotten thing of the past. No one wishes to use verifiability (or falsifiability) as a mark of cognitive meaningfulness. Ordinary language analysis is not practised by any significant group of philosophers. Even in Oxford Austin is not much talked about. Far from being set aside as meaningless, metaphysics is thriving. Wittgenstein is still a force to reckon with, but were he alive he would have been amused by the company—now hoisted upon him—of Dewey and Heidegger. In this philosophical climate of the English-speaking world, Husserlian ideas are no longer perceived as quaint. Essentialism is in vogue. The locution of possible worlds is not far from the idea of imaginative variation. Meanings as abstract entities *à la* Frege are again respectable. Prejudices, however, die hard. When some years ago at the Donald Davidson conference at Rutgers University, Michael Dummett, in his key note address, said that the origins of analytical philosophy lay, not in Carnap (as so many Americans think) but in Eastern Europe in Frege and Husserl, that created considerable ripples of surprise and consternation. When, on the other hand, Hans Sluga pointed out that when analytic philosophy traces its origin back to Frege, that is a Frege whom it has sundered from the intellectual milieu of neo-Kantianism, one begins to realize how unstable and fragile are our attempts to set up barriers amongst philosophical ideas which rather tend, even by their very oppositions, to join together to form one intellectual horizon.

Husserl thus fares well in the world of so-called analytic philosophy. Whether you are doing possible world semantics or cognitive science, theory of perception or theory of meaning—Husserlian ideas are very much alive, competing and proving their fertility. But how is Husserl faring on the European continent?

Every movement of thought currently reigning on the continent owes something to Husserl. We know that Husserlian ideas contributed to the development of structuralism as well as to that of hermeneutics, that the new readings of Marx and Freud owe some of the seminal ideas to Husserl. Even many deconstructionist programmes were incited by perceived tensions in Husserl's thought. But it is from these progenies—that can trace their lineage via Heidegger to Husserl—that Husserlian phenomenology receives at present its bitterest attacks—not surprisingly, for no quarrel is more bitter than family strife. Here too, taking Husserl more seriously would contribute to greater sanity, self-restraint and intelligibility that are sadly so much needed.

II

In this essay I will first draw attention to the concern with the 'content' of consciousness and bring a Husserlian perspective to bear on it. Then I will likewise turn to continental thought and provide a critique of it from a Husserlian perspective.

Interpreting Frege's idea of sense, Michael Dummett writes:

There is no room for any doubt that, for Frege, sense is the content of understanding, or, rather, the principal ingredient of that content; it is that which one who knows the language apprehends as objectively associated with the expression; and that apprehension is an instance of knowledge.[1]

However, he distinguishes this Fregean sense from the literal significance that an expression has, i.e. its linguistic meaning, as well as from 'a speaker's private understanding of it'. All three, i.e. (i) the objectively existent sense, (ii) the linguistic meaning, and (iii) the content of the speaker's private understanding, need to be distinguished from (iv) the mode of presentation of the referent.

It is this last which Gareth Evans identified with the Fregean sense. It is a way of thinking of the object or the referent. Even a perceptual experience, Evans writes, 'has a certain *content*—the world is represented in a certain way.'[2]

Likewise, in their introduction to the volume *Subject, Thought and Context*, Pettit and McDowell propose to understand by 'content' 'what is specified in a "that" clause in the attribution of, say, a belief or an intention', and then proceed to discuss to what extent the content of a person's state is determined by physical and/or social context.[3] In his own contribution to that volume, McDowell defends the idea of subjective propositional content that is yet intrinsically object-dependent, the idea that intentionality is compatible with genuine object-dependence. The reason for this position is that 'the materials otherwise available for intentional determination of the object of a thought seem incapable of generally getting the answer right'.[4] This is the way to (i) recognize the Fregean thoughts as contents of subjectivity, and (ii) yet to avoid that loss of connection between thought and object that is a consequence of allowing the thoughts complete autonomy. What McDowell means is that if we allow thoughts complete autonomy, then the intentional nature of a thought, the content of one's consciousness cannot determine which object it is that makes one's thought true or false, and so cannot determine what it is that the subject is thinking about.

Gareth Evans makes a similar point when he distinguishes between 'descriptive thoughts' and 'information based thoughts'.[5] However rich and detailed the descriptive content of one's belief may be, it cannot amount to that sort of identifying thought which is based on some informational link with the object of the thought: the information must originate in episodes involving that object and so must have a causal history. In the case of a merely descriptive content, such a link is missing.

Christopher Peacocke his book *Sense and Content,*[6] is concerned with the contents of psychological states whose descriptions contain expressions such as 'table' and 'to write on', which refer to objects in the world. The content of an experience is 'representational', and is distinguished as much from the object as from the 'sensational properties' of that experience.[7] Peacocke also distinguishes the content of an experience from the content of a judgement caused by that experience, as also from the informational content which refers back to what 'causally explains' some features of the experience. In the representational content, the object is presented in a certain mode. This mode of presentation need not be a property of the object: 'only the properties themselves, and not properties under modes of presentation, enter causal explanations'.[8] Peacocke's contention that every experience has some sensational properties parallels Husserl's thesis that every intentional act has a hyletic component. The representational content has two features: for one thing, it concerns the external world, and at the same time is also an intrinsic feature of the experience itself.

For the limited purposes of this essay, I will neither expound nor examine in any details the theories of Dummett, Evans, McDowell and Peacocke. I want only to draw attention to one clearly Husserlian feature of these *concerns:* the concern with what may be the content of an experience, where the content is distinguished from the object it represents and where the notion of content does not *eo ipso* contain the idea of a causal link. It is also important that meanings are now beginning to be seen not merely as linguistic, but also as contents of consciousness. There are however three issues that arise out of the foregoing sketch, which I want to comment upon: (i) Is the meaning as content nothing but a way of thinking (as Evans wants to take it to be), or is it to be taken as a much richer concept? (ii) How strongly should one construe the distinction between content and object? (iii) How is one to take the alleged object-dependence of the content? Upon our answers to these questions shall depend the ability of Husserlian thinking to come to terms with the problems that recent philosophy has been discussing.

A Husserlian will fruitfully and with confidence take up each of these issues. With regard to (i) he will distinguish between contents that are Fregean thoughts and contents that are not, the latter being the perceptual contents; as to (ii) he will defend the Fregean distinction (on the Dummett reading) between content and object on all counts as against the Russell–Evans–McDowell strategy of making the object—at least in the case of singular thoughts—a constituent of the content itself; and as to (iii) he will embed stories about causal links within theories (that are themselves thought-contents) and insert all contextual considerations into the external horizon of contents instead of treating them as determining the latter *ab extra*. The Husserlian will regard the contents of consciousness as publicly shareable and linguistically expressible meanings (and not as private and ineffable). The study of consciousness in all its modalities (perceptual, scientific, religious—to name a few) and their contents will provide the foundation for all ontology. But in this project, no privileged access by any of these modalities, no privileged picture of the world will be presupposed, as the Newtonian was for Kantian thinking.

From the point of view of Husserl, the most pertinent and unacceptable feature of the revival of Russell (via a Russellian interpretation of Frege!) is making the object out there a component of thought about it—especially when that thought is singular and demonstrative. While I agree with Dummett's criticisms of this view (which ascribed to the mature Frege the view that in the absence of a referent there is no sense either), criticisms which I will not repeat, I want to draw attention to an emerging Husserl interpretation that is not very far from this new Frege interpretation. According to this interpretation, proposed by Sokolowski,[9] the noema is the object qua intended and so not an abstract entity different from the object. It is ironical that when Sokolowski's explicit aim is to set aside the so-called Fregean reading of Husserl, what he is doing is in agreement with the Frege interpretation of Evans and McDowell. Again we begin to see how philosophical interpretations, despite their intentions, tend to exhibit meetings of extremes in philosophy. The relevance of Husserl was never more clear for Oxford philosophy—not even when Gilbert Ryle returned from his meetings with Husserl and set out to map the eidetic structure of the region delimited by the concept of mind.

III

Let me now return to Husserl's contemporary critics on the European continent. While philosophers in Oxford are thinking about problems which directly concerned Husserl so that a dialogue with Husserl may be in the offing, philosophers across the Channel, even if they stand in the direct lineage of the master, reject him as espousing foundationalism, as being insensitive to the hermeneutic point of view, as imprisoned within the Cartesian ego cogito, and above all as still bewitched by that allegedly original sin of western metaphysics, i.e. the so-called metaphysics of presence. Should I even make an attempt to show that Husserl's thinking survives these onslaughts? I am not asking a rhetorical question. In a most serious vein, I am wondering how does one respond to critics who neither want to give nor believe in giving arguments for their positions—for arguments presuppose what is called logo-centrism—and who will not adduce evidence or phenomena in support, for on their view there are no given phenomena. However, even at the risk of being accused of being unfair, I will single out a few of the more forceful arguments, or seeming-arguments that I consider pertinent.

First is an argument from history. Human knowledge and experience—including ontological claims about essences of things as well as semantic claims about what words mean—are all subject to inexorable historical change. The world changes, so also do our modes of self-understanding. This universal historicity contradicts all claims to apodictic, atemporal insight into allegedly foundational structures.

Every philosophical interpretation, including the foundationalistic, is a product of its own historical milieu. One confronts a bottomless pit of foundationless historicity.

Now, this familiar argument should be correctly understood, for it may cut both ways—that is to say, historicism may prove to be an ally of foundationalism, indeed of transcendental philosophy. Historicism began in the nineteenth century, with Herder and Hegel, by conceiving of history as a manifestation of universal spirit (Geist). Even in its 'materialist' form, as in Marx, it remained tied to an essentialism (with regard to man's species-nature) and a scientificity that looked for rigorous laws of historical development.

Anti-foundationalism needs to abjure essences as well as rigorous laws of history, it needs to be able to say that the scientificity that holds up the ideal of Newtonian physics, for example, derives from a historical accomplishment, and could not claim unlimited sway over all time and all fields of enquiry. Essences need to be historicized, as much as the norm of scientificity itself. Recent researches in history of science have seemed to many to be moving in this direction.

But the foundationalist may want to retort: what after all is this 'history' whose ubiquitousness is supposed to yield such radical consequences for thought? Is not the idea of 'history' itself a high-level construction? First of all, there are histories—not merely histories of countries, regions, provinces, counties, towns, villages, families and individual lives, but also histories of literature, music, science, etc. Make combinations of these two kinds of histories, and you get further differentiations which we need not have to pursue further. The point that I want to highlight is that not only the idea of History (with a capital 'H'), but even such low-level concepts as emerge from filling in the blanks in 'history of—', require a great deal of abstraction, selection and collection of facts not, prima facie, belonging together. For example, history of music will have to contain histories of European, Indian and Chinese music (each one of these subhistories may likewise involve the same processes). One consequence of looking at the matter in this way is that an idea of history comes to be perceived as *constituted* by the historian's fundamental project. The ontological and epistemological burden that such an idea could carry has then to be remarkably light.

Consider an example from a well-known work: Richard Rorty's *Philosophy and the Mirror of Nature*. The author of this book wants to set aside the traditional philosophy 'as an attempt to escape history—

an attempt to find non-historical conditions of any possible historical development'. The positive moral of the book, he goes on to tell us, is 'historicist'. It puts the three notions of 'mind', 'knowledge' and 'philosophy' in the historical perspective, i.e. shows that each of these has a historical origin. But what Rorty does in order to 'deconstruct' such powerful notions as 'the Glassy Essence' of man is to show how, historically, they are rooted in other concepts, such as the idea that we have the ability to apprehend abstract universals. Now, the story, as it is told, draws upon a selected domain of history of philosophy, i.e. history of western philosophy. Even if that sequence and that order of dependence which Rorty unfolds is true, it certainly is not true when one enlarges the domain of enquiry to include, for example, Indian philosophy—where the concept of the 'inner' as distinguished from the 'outer' is found to be conceptually, as well as historically, independent of some of the other concepts which, for Rorty, are its historical presuppositions, namely the theory of abstract universals, the Aristotelian epistemology and the Cartesian body-mind dualism.[10] One finds history useful for deconstruction, and finds in history a suitable tale to tell in support of that philosophical motive, only by suitably restricting the domain of 'history' (and suitably selecting one's relevant facts). The only way this sort of fundamental objection can be set aside is by insisting that in totally different cultures (with their own histories), one should not look for the same concepts. Relativism thus provides a safe haven to historicism, and yet historicism is brought in to bolster up relativism.

The anti-foundationalist may concede my point, and may, in fact, insist that any account of historicism which ties together various disjointed epochs (disjointed in time and space) into one history, and then proceeds to establish law-like generalizations across the entire domain of history—actual and possible—would be, despite its historicism, yielding to foundationalism. What is needed is to free 'historicism' from the temptation in favour of monism and making law-like generalizations. In other words, an anti-foundationalist, if he is to use the idea of history in his own support, must emphasize the radical *contingency* of history, even when history is restricted to one's favoured region. In more recent thought, this needed contingency has been sought to be assured by the emphasis on 'discontinuity'. First introduced by Gaston Bachelard into philosophy of science with a view to ward off an idealistic philosophy, it has been effectively used by Foucault in his work on the history of ideas and institutions. Discontinuities and 'ruptures' prevent looking for a common norm, a common set of rules (of discourse and of practice), a common overarching conceptual framework, and so a common foundation (for example, in a reflecting subjectivity which claims to comprehend them all). Whereas traditional history denied or annulled discontinuities by taking recourse to an all-encompassing unity (such as the Hegelian Geist), this 'total history' presupposed, as Foucault tells us, that all the events, even of a well-defined spatio-temporal region, are subject to 'a system of homogenous relations', that 'one and the same form of historicity operates upon all economic structures, social institutions and customs, mental attitudes, technological practice, political behaviour, and subjects them all to the same type of transformation, and that history itself may be described in terms of internally cohesive great unities.[11] As against this total history the thesis of discontinuity emphasizes discontinuities, ruptures, thresholds, limits and transformations, and rejects the ideas of 'tradition', 'influence', 'development', 'evolution', and 'spirit'. Instead of the use of the idea of 'synthesis', one uses the more methodologically rigorous idea of 'dispersed events'.[12]

It is not my purpose to examine this historiography in details. My earlier criticism of the historicist agreed implicitly with some of the moves of the new historian of ideas. But one cannot but raise the following problems:

(i) Demarcating an epoch (or a discourse) as a discontinuous unity, and so separated from what went before and what comes after by an epistemological rupture, is to unify an entire group of disparate events under one common description, and so must involve an arbitrary selection of events *in so far* as they can be brought under that description. One could have chosen a different guiding description, and demarcated as a discontinuous totality an area that very well intersects or overlaps two neighbouring discontinuous totalities of the first plan. One can, in this manner, think of several discontinuous series, with the ruptures falling at different places (see Fig. 1). Is there eventually any non-arbitrary way of coming up with such a series? Can there be even in principle a justification of the series that Foucault gives?

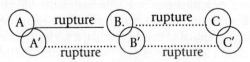

Figure 1

Since no a *priori* justification is called for, one has to appeal to empirical evidence, but the very idea of what is to count as empirical evidence is, in this theory, determined by the rules of discourse obtaining within a discourse.

(ii) Since for each discourse, there is no preexistent theme (such as 'madness') which it takes up, and since, on the contrary, it is rather 'the interplay of rules that make possible the appearance of objects during a given period of time',[13] there is indeed a doctrine of transcendental constitution of the large themes or 'objects'—to be sure, not constitution by a transcendental subjectivity, but by 'discourse'. To insist that what appears is a series, interspersed by gaps, interplays of differences, distances, substitutions and transformations, is not to assuage that anxiety, for it is no less the case, in Husserlian transcendental phenomenology, that a constituted objectivity is a series of different perspectives collected together under a presumptive unity.

(iii) The decisive difference between transcendental phenomenological constitution and constitution by discontinuous systems of discourse may lie elsewhere: in the grand monism of an overarching reflective grasp which the former presupposes and the pluralism of many, discontinuous systems of discourse of the latter. But that is only seemingly so, for the historian of ideas—even when he rejects continuity in favour of discontinuity—surveys the entire series; his work is based on a grasp that comprehends several 'breaks' or 'ruptures'. His history provides a totality within which discontinuities and contingencies erupt. He claims to be able to comprehend them all—even if he has no explanation of why the contingencies arise. It is not very different in perception. Perception presents things that are discontinuous. Each one is a contingency, yet perceptual consciousness places them against an overall background—the horizon of the world which yet lets each contingency to stand by itself. The point I am making is that historical contingency provides no more a resistance to foundationalist philosophy than does perceptual contingency.

Histories are constructions. They are constituted by the historian's interest, project, methodology and overall goal. The grand history—the one history of mankind—is a still higher-level construction, be it a 'total history' or a fractured one. The foundationalist may then hope to be able to comprehend how histories or History arise—not historically, but conceptually. In other words, it is a legitimate enquiry to look for the methodological and purposive activities (and categories) that go into the constitution of a history. The histories then cannot provide a strong ground for anti-foundationalist arguments.

The foundationalist may proceed to argue, in positive defense of his own point of view, that history as a science or as laid out in books on history presupposes at least two fundamental features of human existence and consciousness: temporality and historicity. Under a certain construction, the distinction between the two disappears. 'Temporality' in this view (deriving from Husserl), is not being *in* time, but rather being caught up in a stream of its own flowing in which every 'now' carries around it a horizon of past and future, i.e. of retention of what has just been and protention of what is just about to be, such that as a 'now' recedes into the past together with its entire horizon, new 'nows' emerge, not as discrete points but, by virtue of internal referrings back and forth, constituting a continuous flow. Temporality in this sense is not a feature of physical events, of sciences as enquiries or as bodies of knowledge, or of institutions such as the British Parliament. Let me call these latter—lumping together physical time and historical time—*objective* time as distinguished from the subjective, lived temporality of one's inner consciousness. (From the present, i.e. phenomenological perspective, Kant was right in locating original time in the 'inner sense' as an inner self-intuition, but wrong in construing this inner time as being the same as the outer, physical time.) While this subjective time has a Cartesian ring, its correlate, i.e. the historicity of human existence, does not arouse that suspicion. But historicity of human existence, in its original nature—as distinguished from the derived historical features of human cultural products and social institutions—is as little a matter of public, 'outer' observation as is the inner, lived temporality of consciousness. The two are better construed as two sides of the same coin: to arrive at either we need to put all conceptions and experiences of objective time under brackets (to use a Husserlian locution) and be able to reflect on time as lived within or as a feature of my being-in-the-world (the 'world' construed, not as the external world of things and events, but as that world-*horizon* which is a structural feature of our consciousness and existence). As characterized by this historicity, existence is carrying the burden of the past (in the form of tradition) and moving ahead towards the ultimate end (i.e. death).

Faced with the spectre of foundationalism in thus identifying temporality/historicity as essential features of consciousness/existence, the anti-foundationalist introduces a curiously obfuscating *use* of the pair of concepts: continuity-discontinuity, presence-absence. Since time, even the inner phenomenological time, in Husserl's account, is constituted by the now with the retention and protention surrounding it, there is—now it is argued—no pure undifferentiated immediacy, no total selfpresence of consciousness to itself. But rather, within the texture of the 'living present', the now, there is the 'interplay' of presence and absence, of continuity and discontinuity—so that temporality cannot provide an absolute foundation even for one's own inner subjective life—not to speak of history and the world experience. To answer this, one needs to examine anew what precisely is the nature of a transcendental-phenomenological foundationalism.

It is also implicitly presupposed, in much criticism of Husserl, that transcendental philosophy looks for an apodictic foundation. Husserl's essentialism certainly did look for apodictic truths, but the same is taken, wrongly in my view, to be true of his transcendental philosophy. If we consider the Kantian transcendental philosophy, it should dawn upon us that the Kantian foundational constituting subjectivity cannot be characterized as an apodictic ground. The reason for this is simple, although it has often been missed by the critics: 'necessity' is one of the categories of the understanding which, in the Kantian thesis, has its origin in the nature of human reason. That nature then cannot itself be said to be 'necessary'. It is not logically necessary that the human mind has the structure Kant says it has. The opposite of the Kantian thesis is possible and conceivable. The necessity is at most a transcendental necessity—which is related to the concept of the possibility of our experience's being what it is. The alleged apodictic foundation—the target of much criticism—is simply not there in any variety of transcendental foundationalism, not in Husserlian thinking on the matter, to be sure, despite Husserl's misleading locutions to the contrary. How a phenomenological transcendental philosophy can dispense with the notion of apodicticity is beyond the scope of this essay.

I will conclude by making a few remarks on that relativism which seems most assuredly to go against Husserlian transcendental philosophy. Not only does relativism not go against Husserlian thinking, but, I would insist, relativism itself presupposes an absolutistic standpoint. Not unlike the naïve perceiver and the naïve interpreter, one who lives within his own culture or his own world does not consider himself to be inhabiting one amongst many possible worlds. As a matter of fact, he regards himself to be in the only world that is there. In this respect, Davidson's conclusion, after his critique of alternate conceptual frameworks, exactly captures this naïvity.[14] Who then is a relativist? Where should one position oneself so as to be able to have any number of possible worlds, radically incommensurable with each other, laid out before one's gaze? The conclusion is inevitable: from the reflective stance of a transcendental ego, from the stance of one who is not subject to relativism but is able to objectify and reflect upon the relativistic situation—consequently from the standpoint of one who is already positioned to 'overcome' relativism.

There are other arguments—if arguments they are—of those who claim to have 'deconstructed' Husserl. They find, for example, in the idea of constitution, more particularly in that 'immer weiter' that Husserl detects in every constitution, testimony that constitution is being endlessly 'deferred', that there is an admitted failure to accomplish the goal that one set out to reach. This is a perverse account of constitution. Things *are* constituted. Reflectively lay bare the constitution, and you have an infinity. The infinity belongs to the constitution, nothing is being postponed. One hears that Husserl, while admitting the flux character of time consciousness, sought to arrest this flux in order to reach stability in ideal meaning unities.. Deconstruction would then exhibit the instability of the stable meanings, it would return to the uninhibited flux. But what justifies the premise that all is flux? The rhetoric uses this thesis of flux as though it was a self-evident, indisputable truth. If Husserl recognizes the flux character of consciousness, experience and the world, he also saw that the flux has an abiding structure. He rightly saw also that the flux of experience 'throws out' stable formations, unities of meaning, complex meaning structures called theories, objectivities of various orders: they are neither apodictic nor contingent. The only wisdom is not to see Heraclitean flux everywhere. One also needs to understand how stable structures emerge out of the Heraclitean flux—some, as with logical and mathematical entities, claiming to be timelessly 'valid'. It is to Husserl's lasting credit that he perceived both the flux and the abiding.

I cannot at the end help expressing a feeling: it is deeply distressing to note the concern one finds today amongst philosophers about the 'end' of philosophy. People who talk endlessly about meta-philosophical questions, including if philosophy is not breathing its last, do little philosophizing themselves. The sensitivity to philosophical problems and receptivity to modalities of experience are being condemned as belonging to that modernism which, we are told, has now been transcended. Whence does contemporary culture derive this legislative authority so as to rule out of existence the problems of reason? From history, we shall be told. But which history? Whose history? We need the courage to face serious problems—some timeless and ahistorical, some arising out of our situation—and do philosophy conscientiously and seriously, with a true radicalness and not with that illusory radicalness that begins by handing over to time and history the inevitable dissolution of what one does not have the courage to think through. We were never in greater need of returning to the early Husserl than now.

NOTES

1. M. Dummett, *The Interpretations of Frege's Philosophy* (London: Duckworth, 1981), p. 82.
2. G. Evans, *The Varieties of Reference,* (ed.) J. McDowell (Oxford: Clarendon Press, 1981), p. 226.
3. P. Pettit and J. McDowell (eds), *Subject, Thought and Context* (Oxford: Clarendon Press, 1986), p. 13.
4. Ibid., p. 164.
5. The *Varieties of Reference*, pp. 307–8.
6. C. Peacocke, *Sense and Content* (Oxford: Clarendon Press, 1983).
7. Ibid., p. 4.
8. Ibid., p. 7.
9. R. Sokolowski, 'Intentional Analysis and the Noema', *Dialectica* 38 (1984), pp. 114–29.
10. Cf. B.K. Matilal, *Perception. An Essay on Classical Indian Theories of Knowledge* (Oxford: Clarendon Press, 1986).
11. M. Foucault, *The Archaeology of Knowledge* (New York: Pantheon Books, 1971), p. 10.
12. Ibid., part II, ch. 1.
13. Ibid., pp. 32–3.
14. D. Davidson, 'On the very Idea of Conceptual Scheme', in *Proceedings of the American Philosophical Association* 17 (1973/74), pp. 5–20.

chapter

six

Husserl on Relativism in the Late Manuscripts*

Husserl's attempts to *refute* certain forms of relativism, especially psychologism, historicism, biological specism, all of which he regarded as relativistic, in the *Logische Untersuchungen* and in the *Logos* essay of 1910 are well-known,[1] and I will not discuss them here. In general, from the very inception phenomenology has been anti-relativistic. Husserl thought he had conclusively refuted relativism, by refuting some varieties of it. Paradoxically enough, Husserl's thinking had elements which gave rise to relativism from within phenomenology. The task therefore which he tried to face up to was: how to overcome relativism, if refutation was not possible? One can make a strong argument to the effect that relativism cannot be refuted, for refutation would make use of a logic and the relativism may not accept the validity of that logic.

In general, in the early attempts to refute relativism, Husserl appealed to the fact that the relativist asserts a thesis which he would want the others to accept, which would be inconsistent on his part to do. But the relativist may reply that he has no thesis even if he had one; or, that he has no first level thesis, only he has a second level meta-thesis that he has none; or that the alleged inconsistency is not logical but pragmatic, and even if it were logical he does not accept that logic anyway. And so the conversation would go.

*B.C. Hopkins (ed.) *Husserl in contemporary context*, (Kluwer, The Hague, 1997).

Husserl also argued that in so far as the relativist makes truth relative to some entity—a mind, biological organism, society, history, culture, or what have you—he must admit some non-relativistic nature of that entity to which he makes truth relative, so he cannot be wholesale relativistic. But the relativist may concede, at a meta-level, that truth is relative to one's mind; he may refuse to advance a non-relativistic theory of mind so that at the first level the thesis would have many possible formulations, each of which will have a hypothetical antecedent, 'If the mind is . . ., then . . .'. Husserl, perhaps, at the stage of the *Logische Untersuchungen* would have responded to this move by urging that this 'If . . ., then . . .' must itself be objectively true. I am not sure if he insists on this in that work, but this certainly is part of what he insists in a letter to Dilthey: cultural relativity itself presupposes absolute principles, which themselves are not relativistic. But if I have construed what he, at least in part, means in that letter, then the relativist may reply that the 'If, then' has no absolutely valid construal, and how one would construe it depends upon what logic one adopts.

Husserl also uses an argument from the meaning of 'truth', and insists that the relativist departs arbitrarily from what we generally mean by it. (He might as well mean by 'truth' what we mean by 'tree'!) But the relativist would regard it as an easy victory. What does *we* mean? It may be that some cultures have a certain understanding of 'truth', which does not oblige others to conform to it. Husserl may reply—this certainly is one of Frege's arguments against psychologism—that while the relativist only admits the predicate 'taken to be true', this predicate *contains* the word 'true' which must be non-relativistically construed, otherwise there would be an infinite regress. But the relativist may want to insist that for him 'taken-to-be-true' is one indivisible predicate, not further analysable, from whose context 'true' cannot be separated and then absolutized.

I will recall only one more criticism of relativism, advanced by Husserl in the *Logos* essay. From facts, he writes, only facts can follow, from historical facts, other historical facts. But from facts one cannot draw any conclusions which would entail either confirming or refuting an idea. Absolutely objective truth is an idea, so no amount of historical, psychological or ethnological facts could refute the idea that truth in itself is true for every man. An idea is not a subjective representation. Neither does the fact that it has not yet been possible to reach such absolute truth prove that the idea is invalid in the sense that it is, in principle, impossible to be actualized. However, the relativist—accepting Husserl's claim that European science and philosophy have been guided by this idea—may argue, again making use of Husserl's own principle that facts can only entail facts, that that fact cannot be used to prove that all of mankind ought to pursue that idea.

Husserl finds in naturalism, as also in historicism, attempts to explain away ideas by facts, to reduce all reality and all life to an unintelligible heap of facts bereft of ideas—all guided by '*der Aberglaube der Tatsache*'. Now, even if such a prejudice must be rejected, it is not immediately clear that all relativism suffers from it. It is quite possible that the relativist would recognize that different cultures and historical epochs have entertained and let themselves be guided by different ideas. What, however, he would deny is that there is an idea, the idea of absolute truth—add to it ideas of absolute goodness and absolute beauty—which either does, or should, guide all mankind's cognitive, ethical and aesthetic pursuits.

Now, what does Husserl mean by 'idea'? Often, when he speaks of 'idea', he means 'essence'. But in our present context, he means something like the Kantian Idea which, for knowledge, is not constitutive but regulative. Husserl appears to be caught in a teleological mode of thinking, according to which human cognitive process, in whatever historical epoch or in whichever cultural set up, always is guided by the Idea of absolute truth. In effect, he appears to have assigned a constitutive role to a regulative idea. As he maintains in the *Ideas*, to every truly existing object there corresponds, in principle, i.e. a *priori* and with unconditioned, universal generality, the idea of a possible consciousness in which that object itself is originarily (*originär*), and therefore completely adequately apprehensible. This idea is constitutive, for this correlation is an essential necessity.

II

Later in his life, Husserl, as is well known, questioned the ideas of apodictic and adequate evidence, and he became increasingly conscious of the difficulty of finally and decisively overcoming relativism. A simple, direct refutation of the sort stated above is not found any longer. On the other hand, as he thematized the life-world at the beginning and at the centre of his thinking, he was led to recognize other dimensions of the problem of relativism. At first it appears as if the life-world, as the *Sinnesfundament* of the sciences, provided exactly that which we need in order to overcome relativism—

namely a fixed ground on which all men, in practical everyday context, are leading their lives. But this hope was shattered. For there is not one life-world, there are many life-worlds.[2] The most forceful statement of this recognition is the following paragraph from 1927.

So sind für den Zulu das, was wir Wissenschaftler, Wissenschaftliche Werke, Literatur als Bücher, Zeitigungen etc., kennen und erfahren, einfach nicht da, obschon die Bücher als Dinge und ev. als mit den und jenen Zaubereien behafteten Dingen da sind—mit welchen Interpretationen sie eben wieder nicht für uns da sind . . . . Jede solche Menschheit habe eine andere konkrete Welt (A V 9).

[Thus, the stuff we scholars experience and are familiar with—scientific works, literature in the form of books, newspapers, etc.,—is simply not present for the Zulus, even though the books as mere things are present, possibly as things endowed with some kind of magical powers—with which interpretation they are, in turn, not present for us . . . . Every social group has a different concrete world.]

In that case, the question is: whether a proposition which is true in one life-world can be false in another? Perhaps, a more important question is: whether a sentence which is meaningful in one life-world, i.e. expresses a thought, can be utterly meaningless in another, i.e. cannot be expressing a thought? The relativistic skepticism may concern the question of truth, or it may concern the question of meaning. Husserl has the latter question in mind, when, for example, he says that sentences about Michaelangelo's David are, for the Bantu, neither true nor false, they are totally *sinnlos* so that,

. . . über Wahrheit und Falschheit, über Sein und Nichtsein in unserer Welt können wir miteinander streiten, nicht aber mit dem Bantu, da er als einzelner seines 'Wir' eine andere Umwelt hat (A V 10).

[concerning truth and falsehood, being and non-being, in our world we can take issue with one another; not however with the Bantu, since he has in accord with his unique 'we' another surrounding world.]

In the manuscripts from the thirties, Husserl comes to be concerned very much with the idea of 'situational truth' ('*Situations-Wahrheit*'). But even before that, in 1924, in a manuscript on the Idea of Science (A 1 25), he writes about what is practically satisfactory in pre-theoretical, practical life, and goes on to assert that different practices have different standards of exactness and inexactness. (Compare the standard of exactness in supermarkets with the standard of exactness in the pharmacy.) He wonders if the ideal of complete adequacy is not, in principle, unattainable, and also not *gefährlich*. However, he still falls back on idealization as the process by which a common homogenous, non-relative world is constituted. In a manuscript from 1932 (A IV 1) the idea of 'situation' plays a dominant role. Pre- and extra-scientific judgements are said to be situational judgements. The scientist obviously is not satisfied with them and wants to abstract from all situation-bound praxis. Situational truth, again, is related to our 'normality' concept, to *our* normality, which is common to different similar situations we encounter, we who belong to the same cultural group. In A VI 2 he speaks of 'occasional, relative, subjective *Sein*' and of 'occasional text'.

Der praktische Wahre ist relativ auf der praktischen Zweck, der nur auf eine gewisse Nahsituation abgestimmt ist—der Relativismus der jeweiligen Nähen und Fernen der Situation gehört zum Wesen der Erfahungswelt als solcher.
[Practical truth is relative to the practical aim, which is only attuned to a certain local situation. The relativism ensuing from proximity or distance from this situation belongs to the essence of the experiential world as such.]

Again, the problem is, how to overcome this relativism of situations? The general answers is: by idealization.

This last quotation brings out a relativity which, in these manuscripts, is taken to permeate all experience: namely the relativity of the near and the far (of which the pair 'homeworld' and 'foreign world' are specific cases). In one particularly interesting manuscript (A IV 3), Husserl goes on to distinguish between different degrees of nearness. The first domain of nearness, for a child, is the child's own room, then the home, the part of the street with which he gets familiar, and so on. Within the appropriate domain, at any time, there is 'reliability', 'trustworthiness', 'continuous confirmation of experience'; beyond it, there is extension through 'induction' of the personal *Umkreis*.

Interestingly enough, this relativity only opens up a structurally eidetic feature of everyone's world which is characterized by the distinction between the old and the familiar and the new. The new is not only the new individual under the old and familiar type, but the new type, the *Neuartige* and the *Fremdartige*, which again as experience goes on, is appropriated into the old type. In the home, nothing is foreign. The home has the character of thoroughgoing normality.

The foreign, *der Fremde*, is what is not 'home'. But the *Fremde* one can get to know and so make familiar, and therewith, under suitable conditions, an extension of the 'home'.

One should note that while drawing attention to a relativity with which every child, and every cultural community, begins, Husserl is also, for one thing, showing a necessary structure of every life-world, and, for another, showing how the relativity is to be overcome (by making what is strange, foreign, unfamiliar gradually familiar). The latter process requires 'understanding the other'.

The manuscript A IV 3 continues to deal with the last question, and begins by casting doubt on the possibility of a complete understanding of the other. A complete knowledge of the other is not, in principle, possible, for the other has his own individual historicity, his own genetic self-constitution, which I cannot fully lay bare. I cannot even fully uncover my own genetic constitution, Husserl adds. I cannot fully reinstate my own transcendental constitution by the help of memory, but only through reconstruction of its general type. How can I 'win over' the horizon of the other's experiences, his purposes, his interests etc., in their determinate predelineations? There is a basic structure which I can apperceptively ascribe to the other: the *type* 'I', bodily structure (*Leiblichkeit*), that in his world there are things, persons, environment, foreign things and persons; he too has the type 'home', the type 'foreign world'. It is in this context that Husserl points out, even the most 'foreign' has a core of commonality and his world has earth and heaven, day and night, stones and trees, mountains and valleys, animals and birds—all understood analogically in the most general types, even if as strange. The gap between the far and the near is closed by analogizing apperception of the far, 'as if' it were near (for example apperception of the earth as a star and of the star as earth)!

In A IV 7, dating from 1931, Husserl states that relativity characterize finiteness, and wants to bring all kinds of relativism under the title of *Situationsrelativität*. The world is said to be the 'universal situation'. The present world is said to be itself given in its situation of present and past worlds.

A certain relativity even affects the very meaning of 'science' (A IV II of 1934). I have my own idea of science, others have theirs. The peasant has his own idea of science. And yet, science aims at determining the nature of the world in itself, as it is for 'everyone'. Who is this everyone? And whose conception of science is it that aims at being in itself? If it is the modern European conception of science, what privilege has it over other possible conceptions of science?

III

Given these various sorts of relativism, the task Husserl sets upon himself is: how is the concept of a world-in-itself, world for everyone, determinable by a body of absolute and objective truths, a world that is '*unendlich*'—in space as well as in time—at all possible? My impression is that Husserl never really rejected this Idea, but he still had to make sense of it, that is to say in his own phenomenological context, to show its constitution.

Without going into details in this essay, I will only present some of the attempts—the various *Ansätze*—he makes towards solving this problem, without deciding if any of these would be his final answer. We can however venture one suggestion: he never took back the answer in terms of idealization. But that is a very general concept. The task is to show what specific processes are involved. Some of the suggestions are as follows:

1. The different life-worlds—howsoever different they may be—have a common structure: spatio-temporality, birth and death, 'generative history', heaven and earth, 'far' and 'near', and, of course, the things, animals, men, in fine, the perceptual world (howsoever differently they may be perceived). This common structure makes it possible to make a beginning towards understanding another life-world.

2. The most foreign world, the unknown and the unfamiliar, has always a core of familiarity, a typicality which inevitably comes to our aid.

3. To the question, how is the *Sinn* of the 'other world' constituted in mine? Let us suppose, the Zulu has not, in his world, the sense 'book'. But there is nevertheless a common stratum of sensory data. We strip our world of all 'our' cultural meanings until we reach this common sensory data. Then we can step-by-step constitute the meanings which constitute the Zulu's world. But the problem with such a method of *Abbau* and *Aufbau* is that we need to know precisely the meanings which constitute the Zulu's world, and we cannot assume we already know them.

4. The different ego-subjects with all their different life-experiences and cultural points of view have, nevertheless, common structures—including structures of corporeality and of consciousness.

5. If one considers the various worlds as world-noemata, then one can apply Husserl's earlier doctrine of the constitution of the identity of an object through the overlapping synthesis of the noemata, to the present problem, and say that the identity of a world is constituted through the overlapping world-noemata.

6. This abstract schema Husserl concretizes, on various occasions, by adding that it is only through communication (in linguistic context, by translation) that a common world comes to be gradually constituted.

7. Husserl even concedes that scientific judgements are also situation-bound, bound to the specific horizon determined by the scientific tradition, its practical goals and methods. So he tries to show why this tradition is able to comprehend other traditions, and not vice versa.

8. One of the sub-problems is the constitution of infinite space and infinite time. He asks, what could *motivate* the idea of endlessness—when both space and time of the everyday world are indeed finite. In one of the texts (text no. 14) included in *Husserliana* vol. XV, Husserl reflects on the idea of 'generation'—that everyone has parents, the essential human property of 'natality' ('*Gebürtigkeit*') as motivating the idea of time stretching endlessly into the past, but that still leaves the question of time stretching endlessly into the future. But there is also the feature of 'iterability' which belongs to every experience. This *iterability* is at the root of every idealization. In the *Krisis*, we have an account of how Euclidean geometry arises through idealization of everyday experience. That is only the beginning of the story, the rest of which would include algebraization, and formalization of geometry into a theory of manifolds. Thus in A I 25, we are told that everyday experience is characterized by horizon-anticipation, the original basis of induction, as that what is not directly experienceable is regarded as an extension of experience. The first step of idealization is then said to be an iterative induction, leading to the idea of an infinite world, but this also entails a certain, homogeneity of the world.

It appears as if Husserl's final concept of truth oscillates between an Idea of absolutely objective truth and the truth which we actually attain and which is not falsely hypostatized but rather always, in each case, holds good within a determinate horizon. He will not throw away either this fact or that Idea, and much of his thinking was concerned with establishing a bridge between the two.

NOTES

1. For this entire question, I am indebted to Gail Soffer's excellent book *Husserl and the Question of Relativism* (The Hague: Kluwer, 1991). I am also thankful to Professor Bernhard Rang and Mr. S. Rombach for help in using the Husserl *Nachlass* in Freiburg.
2. Cf. Soffer, *Husserl and the Question of Relativism*, pp. 149–57. I am grateful to Gail Soffer for drawing attention to this.

chapter

seven

Time: Linear or Cyclic, and Husserl's Phenomenology of Inner Time Consciousness*

There is one pervasive feature of Husserl's thinking which is deeply unsatisfactory even from the strictly phenomenological perspective and even for one like me who is largely sympathetic to his transcendental philosophical project. Let us accept for the purpose of this essay the project that phenomenological constitution analysis must begin with the constituted sense structure as its guiding clue (*Leitfaden*), and then, following its lead, must return to the explicit or implicit, overt or anonymous constitutive performances which, within the life of transcendental subjectivity as laid bare through transcendental reduction, bring about, constitute or make possible that sense structure. Since constituted senses are given not as isolated entities but rather as structured and sedimented in layers in the world as we experience it, it is very important that these senses are comprehended, to begin with, in the precise manner of their position in the world. Any prejudice or preference in choosing, isolating and describing these constituted senses will show up in the resulting constitution analysis. A very likely source of this sort of prejudice is in according *priority* to a certain level of sense structure to another. It is in this last sort of work that I find a deeply dissatisfying feature of Husserlian thinking. I will first illustrate what I have in mind by referring to a case where I think Husserl shows profound

*Philosophia Naturalis, 25, 1985.

insight in this regard, and then argue that with regard to some other cases, including the question of time, his *initial* prejudice might in fact be a source of some inadequacies in his otherwise profound phenomenology of time.

The case where Husserl shows profound insight is with regard to the constitution of scientific objectivities. He sees rightly that scientific theory as a constituted ideality and the objects of physics as theoretical constructs are founded upon the everyday perceptual world. To recall the well-known example from the *Crisis*, the ideal geometrical shape 'circle' is the product of a process of idealization exercised upon the perceived circular shapes which are only more-or-less circular. Once this order of founding–founded relation is recognized in the constituted sense-structure, the analysis of the constituting process will be on the right track. Consider what would have happened if Husserl, in his initial starting point, had given ontological primacy to physics, and had held that it is the world of physics which is the founding order, the 'real' behind the perceived world which is but the world of appearance. As a description of the constituted sense-structure, this 'inverted' picture (which is the ontology of many so-called scientific realists) would have led to a very different account of the constituting process than what Husserl has given us.

Let me now return to the question of 'time'. It seems to me that the constituted structure with which Husserl begins is the objective world-time considered as a linear and irreversible flow (or series) in which every event, physical or psychical, is supposed to have a unique place. In a text from 1904, Husserl writes that one of the tasks of phenomenology is to describe 'the given, naive and scientific time consciousness according to its sense (*Sinn*)'.[1] Of course, objective, scientific time will have to be subjected to *epoché*, and phenomenology has to show how this *sense* (i.e. the sense of objective time *as a sense*) is constituted within the phenomenologically, reduced time consciousness. In another text, written around 1908, he anticipates a possible objection:[2] the entire procedure of his phenomenological analysis of time is subject to an empirical presupposition, namely that he takes for granted the objective flow of time and then investigates into the conditions of the possibility of a perception of this objective time. To this objection, Husserl responds by asking: how much of an objective time flow has he really taken for granted? Certainly, he has taken it for granted exactly to the extent one presupposes a thing when one analyses the concept of thing, or to the extent one presupposes something that is perceived when one analyses perception. But, Husserl asserts, he has not taken for granted the truth of a world-time and of a world, or the true existence of any thing or of the duration of a thing. But we certainly can take for granted the *appearing* duration, the *appearing* thing, etc.—which are 'absolute givennesses', to doubt which would be simply meaningless. What then Husserl investigates is not the condition of the possibility of an already presupposed, actually existing world-time and world or of our cognition of them, but of the world-time as such, i.e. as appearing, of duration of things as such, i.e. as appearing. So far, I think, Husserl is on a securely phenomenological ground.

However, the case with 'thing' and 'thing-perception' is, in an important respect, different from that of time. There is an alternative to the conception of linear world-time in a manner in which there is no alternative to the concepts of 'thing' and 'thing-perception'. And this alternative is not a higher order theoretical construct, but—if certain accounts are true—belongs to a more primitive level of the life-world of many communities and traditions. Let me call this alternative conception of time, the concept of time, as cyclic. My argument, taking its start from this alternative conception of time, shall proceed in several stages. First, I will introduce this concept as it is available to us from a well-known phenomenology of religion and ask if Husserlian phenomenology can account for the constitution of such an experience of time. Second, I shall *weaken* the contrast between the two conceptions of time—linear and cyclic—emphasizing the metaphorical nature of both and the interdependence of the two, and then ask how *this* conception of time fares against the background of Husserlian thinking. Finally, I will maintain that there is an element in Husserlian phenomenology which can be of avail to us even here thus vindicating the inner strength of Husserlian thinking about time.

II

Phenomenologists who have sought to describe the structure of religious experience and its world, have noted that the spatial and temporal structure of the religious world show markedly different features than those of the ordinarily perceived (or, conceived), profane world.

First of all, as Van der Leew notes, the sacred time assigns different values to different segments of time, to different seasons of the year, or even to different years.[3] Thus there is the year of salvation, just as spring, summer and winter carry different religious values. Second, mythical religious consciousness tends 'to allow time to stand still', thereby constituting the mode 'in those days' or 'once upon a time', which functions, not as a past, but as a mode of eternity.[4] The festival calendar assigns to each period a specific individuality and potency. What is most important for my present purpose is the determination that religious or sacred time has the structure of 'eternal recurrence', so that in the religious universe every creation recreates its structures, as Eliade puts it.[5] The religious time is not exhausted in its historicity (contrary to Heidegger's thesis). There is rather a recognition that the present repeats the past cycles, that a present ritual or celebration 'opens' on to sacred time and 'repeats' the mythical archetypes.[6] The mythical event, the sacred history, is indefinitely recoverable and repeatable, and in this sense, sacred time is cyclic. In archaic communities, people reproduce, in minutest details, 'the paradigmatic acts of the gods', so that the religious man 'periodically becomes the contemporary of the gods'.[7]

I assume that as a description of the religious experience of time, these are appropriate and point to an experience of time that is more 'primitive' than the experience of 'physical' time as one, irreversible, quantitative, measurable, value-less flow. The question, then, is not how the conception of sacred time constitutes itself on the basis of the one 'physical time', but rather how, by what process of profanization, desacrilization, the conception of one 'physical' time arises out of that sacred time which the primitive mythical consciousness always experienced. But, in this essay, I want to ask: can Husserlian phenomenology with its built-in prejudice in favour of a naturalized world (and so also a consequent prejudice in favour of a physical, irreversible, linear flow of time), can have a theory of the constitution of the sacred, circular time? Or, is the Husserlian insight hopelessly tied to its initial determination of the constituted world-time?

A first consideration of the matter confirms this apprehension. As is well known, after bracketing the world-time Husserl returns to the inner time consciousness and finds there the ubiquitous now-retention-protention structure. As every now-point of consciousness recedes into the past, it carries with it its own retention-protention horizon, just as every emerging now shows up with its own retention-protention structure. Thus the inner time consciousness is as much linear and irreversible in direction as the objective world-time. The major differences between the two lies only in this much that the inner time does not consist in discrete moments, or in a series of bare nows, but rather in a continuous receding back into the past of every now together with its retention-protention horizon. Thus, in inner time consciousness, unlike in the objective world-time, the present, i.e. the now, *opens out* into the immediate past as also into the immediate future, it is not a bare, self-enclosed point shut off from the past and the future. But along with its horizontal structure, it too is linear and constitutes an irreversible flow. It appears, then, that the constituting inner time consciousness cannot constitute the sacred time with its circular and recurrent nature and its qualitative valences and potencies. The constituting and the constituted suit each other, and together form one mode of thinking and experiencing: the linear and the historical.

III

But are there in fact two sharply sundered experiences of (and thoughts about) time: the linear and the cyclic? There is a widely held view, prevalent in such fields as comparative culture and religion, which ascribes the conception of time as cyclic to Greek and Indian thoughts and the conception of time as linear to Judeo-Christian thought. One is not clear whether to these two *conceptions* of time there also correspond two different modes of *experiencing* time. It is also held, along with the above contrast, that the *conception* of time underlying modern science is that of a linear time. One may want to add that under the influence of such a conception, one also *experiences* time as linear.

To examine this cluster of views which have reduced themselves almost to cliches would be a large project. For the present, I want to make only a few general remarks on them. In the first place, the general claim that often an interpretive framework does influence how we experience (or, seem to experience, to say the least—although the distinction between experiencing and seeming to experience is extremely difficult to have one's grips on) is perfectly legitimate, which is not to say that every conception of time yields a new way of experiencing time, or that there is no way of experiencing time *prior to* all interpretive frameworks. In fact, the claim of phenomenology rests on the availability of such a mode of experiencing. In the second place, I wish to make a historical remark: it is not only not obvious, but would seem to be not the case, that the Indian conception of *time* was cyclic.[8] Lots of changes—changes from birth to re-birth, or of natural and human processes—were conceived as cyclic processes, but these cycles—including cosmic and historical epochs, *kalpas* and *yugas*—were themselves inserted into an overall temporal series, succeeding each other, so that the Indian philosophies (*darśanas*) did not quite focus on the alleged circularity of time, but rather on such questions as: is time subjective or objective, conceptual (and language dependent) or experiential, continuous or discontinuous? It appears that those who ascribe to Indian thinking a cyclic conception of time confuse between time and the cycles of changes that take place in time, and furthermore between the locution about 'cycles of change' and the thesis of recurrence of identical events across such cycles. Laying that broad contrast then to rest, I want to call into question also the seemingly obvious view that the conception of time modern science operates with, is that of a linear, one-dimensional, irreversible flow. It is primarily to Kant that we owe such a thesis. I will question this widely held view, again briefly, on this occasion, by appealing to two different sorts of arguments. First, we should not forget the obvious: namely that 'linear' and 'cyclic' are after all metaphors, spatial and geometrical metaphors, and any thinking about time which *rigidly* applies such metaphors must be at some important point, seriously muddled. I do not for a moment wish to claim one should not think of time with these, or such other, metaphors: what I am emphasizing is that we should not forget that these are after all *spatial* metaphors and that, consequently, there must be a surplus of meaning about time that these metaphors may not be able to capture.

It does not follow, then, that we should be thinking of time without spatial metaphors, or that we should be—as Bergson asked us to do—intuiting time and not thinking of it. But it may be that these metaphors—linear and cyclic—may implicate each other, both with regard to how time needs to be *thought* and how time is in fact *experienced*. That in fact this is so, has recently been forcefully argued by Stephen Jay Gould in his *Time's Arrow, Times Cycle: Myth and Metaphor in the Discovery of Geological Time*.[9] Gould emphasizes that the two metaphors—arrow and cycle—have helped man to understand time: the former to express the uniqueness of the order of events and the latter to articulate the lawfulness and predictability of events: the former expressing the uniqueness of history and the latter immanence of law. But the metaphors have to be found in all traditions including the Judeo-Christian (in which the arrow metaphor came to predominate, but the cycle metaphor nevertheless does appear). These two 'eternal metaphors' are also to be found in the geological and biological times intertwined and inseparable. The idea that the scientific view of world-time is simply linear is a naïve over-simplification, as also the view that the Indian is wholly cyclic and the Judeo-Christian is wholly linear. Nor is the idea of irreversibility as canonical for physics. Reversibility is a distinct physical, and not merely logical, possibility.

If the objective world-time is to be thought by an interplay of the cycle and the arrow metaphors, if that interplay gives us the constituted *sense* of time as the framework for objective changes and processes, we can now, again as before, return to Husserl's inner time consciousness and ask, if this enriched sense of time could have its 'origin' in the experiential time of the pure 'reduced' consciousness.

I had earlier expressed doubt if Husserl's description of the constituting inner time consciousness could be useful for accounting for the *origin* of the sense of the cyclic, qualitatively differentiated time of the mythical–religious world, on the ground that that account in terms of the now-points receding into the past along with its retention-protention horizon is exactly suited to yield the constitution of the linear world-time. For in this account, the past is still conceptually tied to memory—to secondary recall in objective time and to primary retention in phenomenological time. It cannot accommodate the idea that the past can be relived in the present, that the past—as in religious experience of a sacred event—can return as a content of one's present experience. We need, then, a very different point of origin, at a depth beyond the flux of immanent experiences.

Now I wish to suggest that Husserl's work on inner time consciousness does lead up to this depth: this is indicated by the concept of the 'living present' ('*der lebendigen Gegenwart'*.) I can only briefly state why I consider this level of inner time consciousness to be the constituting origin of that dynamic interplay of the two metaphors—time's arrow and time's cycle—which characterizes our understanding of the world-time.

IV

First of all, we have to realize that the locution 'flow of inner time consciousness' is a *metaphor* taken from the language of constituted objective time. 'The flow of the modes of consciousness', Husserl writes, 'is not a process (*Vorgang*), the now-consciousness is not itself

(a) now.'[10] It is not something temporal.[11] Second, absolute consciousness is not an immanent act nor a series of immanent acts nor is it a noetic phase conferring sense on a hyletic phase. It is rather the unchanging, abiding consciousness that accompanies all immanent experiences and their components. It is because of it that the immanent flux or experience is aware of itself as a flux. This flux is always given to itself—this givenness itself is the absolute consciousness—as a unity in the living present. Even as the present escapes itself into the just past and the not-yet future, this so escaping itself is also given as the living present. With this Husserl is able to avoid the infinite regress that perpetually haunts thinking about time and consciousness. In the very structure of the living present, the just past, the present, and the not-yet future are *present* as one: the absolute consciousness then is not a linear succession of nows with their temporal horizons, but the abiding self-presence, even as self-escaping, of all experience. My contention is, that with this conception of the original and ultimate foundation for all experience of time, Husserl has grasped a level of awareness of time that is beyond the metaphors of 'arrow' and 'cycle', and so holds out the promise that even if those two metaphors, in their mutual interplay, are indispensable for grasping objective world-time, we can penetrate into a depth of time consciousness where we are beyond those metaphors. It is this level of time consciousness that most probably the Buddhist (and the yoga) 'instant' (kṣaṇa) signified—the ultimate foundation of all empirical consciousness.

NOTES

1. E. Husserl, *Texte zur Phänomenologie des inneren Zeitbewußtseins* (1893–1917), ed. R. Bernet (Felix Meiner, Hamburg, 1985), p. 54.
2. Ibid., p. 180.
3. Van der Leew, *Religion in Essence and Manifestation*, Eng. tr. by J.E. Turner (Peter Smith, Gloucester, 1967), p. 384.
4. Ibid., p. 386.
5. M. Eliade, *The Quest, History and Meaning in Religion* (University of Chicago Press, Chicago, 1969), p. 173.
6. M. Eliade, *Patterns in Comparative Religion* (Sheed & Ward, Cleveland and NY, 1958), 1963, p. 389.
7. M. Eliade, *The Sacred and the Profane: The Nature of Religion* (Harcourt, Brace World Inc., New York, 1959), pp. 91f.

8. Cf. A.N. Balslev, *The Concept of Time in Indian Philosophy* (Otto Hairassowitz, Wiesbaden, 1983).
9. Cambridge, Mass., 1986.
10. Husserl, *Texte zur Phänomenologie des inneren Zeitbewußtseins*, p. 199.
11. Ibid., p. 237.

chapter

eight

Levels of Understanding Intentionality*

Franz Brentano's thesis that the mental is characterized by a peculiar directedness towards an object or by intentionality, has been recognized, in contemporary philosophy, by a large body of philosophers of widely differing persuasions. Those who have come to terms with this phenomenon have found a place for it within their larger philosophical positions: this affects the way they understand the nature and role of intentionality. In this essay, I will distinguish four types of theories of intentionality—each of which is characterized by a certain understanding of its nature and function, an understanding which derives from the overall philosophical framework within which the phenomenon of intentionality is situated. These are the naturalistic-causal, the descriptive-psychological, the existential, and the transcendental-constitutive theories. I review them in that order, as representing four *levels* of our understanding of intentionality. For all four, Brentano's thesis remains the 'neutral' and indispensable starting point.

I

If one is impressed by the irreducible uniqueness of mental life, and yet happens to be a naturalist, or even a physicalist, one would want to carve out a niche within the heart of one's naturalism in order to

*The Monist, Vol. 69, No. 4, Oct. 1986, pp. 505–20.

find a place secure enough for the intentional. It does not matter if you are a metaphysician or not. If you are not, you would still want to find within the larger framework of physicalistic, truth-functionally regimented language, a secure place for intensional discourse. Yet how is this niche, this sanctuary, to be related to the larger structure—the oasis to the surrounding desert?

I will consider three representative opinions—those of Wilfrid Sellars, Fred Dretske and John Searle. Sellars's view is, in the first place, that our concepts about intentionality of thoughts are derived from *concepts* about meaningful speech.[1] This way of putting the matter betrays an effort *not* to reduce thought itself to language. But, in effect, Sellars's position nevertheless is that while in order of knowing language is prior to thought, in order of being what is fundamental is the animal representational system. A representational state is defined as 'a state of an organism' which is 'the manifestation of a system of dispositions and propensities by virtue of which the organism constructs maps of itself in its environment, and locates itself and its behaviour on the map'.[2] Such representative systems can be brought about by natural selection and then transmitted genetically.[3] Furthermore, in every representational system—animal or human—the symbols constituting the system stand for objects which are represented, and there is besides a counterpart character ϕ^* (or a counterpart relation R^*) correlative to the character ϕ (or the relation R) in terms of which that object (or those objects) is being represented.[4] This structural similarity, though necessary, is not however sufficient for making the system into a map in which the animal locates itself and its object. The organism must be a perceiving–remembering–wanting–acting creature, with a strategy for finding the appropriate sorts of objects, so that the representational system is so structured, i.e. is such a complex *system* of representational systems, that these latter together constitute a strategy for finding the appropriate object. With this Sellars succeeds in incorporating intentionality into a biologically and behaviouristically conceived concept of animal representational system which, in the order of being, is first—even if our overt speech acts are first in the order of our knowledge.

Turning now to Dretske, we see that whereas Sellars finds the ontological basis of (human) intentionality in the animal representational system, Dretske extends the notion of intentionality beyond even the biological, to a much larger area of nature, namely to a large number of purely physical systems.[5] For Dretske, 'intentionality, rather than being a "mark of the mental", is a pervasive feature of *all* reality—mental and physical.' He can say this, just because he understands intentionality in terms of the idea of *information*. There is a flow of information from one point to another in his account, if there is a set of conditional probabilities relating events at the two ends. There must be a lawful dependence, statistical or deterministic, between events at those points. Dretske then shows that a nomic relation between two properties F and G is an intentional relationship. If F is lawfully related to G, and 'G' is extensionally equivalent to 'H', F is not necessarily related in a lawful way to H. Therefore statements describing the lawful relations between properties and magnitudes is not extensional. Thus, any physical system whose internal states are lawfully dependent in some statistically significant way is an intentional system. In this sense, a thermometer and a galvanometer have intentional states.

But a thermometer or a galvanometer does not *know* things. Cognitive states are a variety of intentional states. The intentional states of thermometers and galvanometers have their *contents*. The reason they nevertheless do not *know* whatever *information* they carry is that they carry *too much* information, without distinguishing between informations that are *cognitively* different. Thus, the thermometer can only carry the information that the mercury has risen that high *along with* the information that the temperature has increased so much. It cannot distinguish between the two informational contents, and so cannot carry the one information without carrying the other information. In Dretske's words, the instrument is 'insensitive to such cognitive differences'.[6] It is not intentional enough. In order for an intentional state to be sensitive to such cognitive differences, and therefore to be able to *know* in the strict sense, the intentional state must have a content which consists not only of the information it carries but also of the *manner* in which that information is represented.[7] An organism with cognitive powers must have an informational capacity 'that is at least as rich in its representational powers as the language we use to express what is known'.[8] Thus cognitive states possess a *higher degree of intentionality* than the thermometer does, or a rat does. All three, however, can have intentional states having their own contents.

There are interesting differences between Sellars's idea of a representational system and Dretske's idea of an intentional state. Dretske's account is free from that behaviourism which attaches to Sellars's: the content of the intentional state is not simply *extrapolated* from the verbal or non-verbal behaviour, as Sellars would have it. The content, in Dretske's view, really belongs to the state, and the cognitive intentional state is really an *internal* state. But, after all, it is an intentional state built out of systems (physical and biological) that are intentional *to a lesser degree*. Thus, we have higher-order intentionalities built upon lower order ones, but at some point down the road—one may suppose—the lower order ones must be built out of purely extensionally describable building blocks.

One may want to pursue this last line of thinking and arrive, instead, at a position which so totally extends the category of intentionality over *all* nature that there would be indeed nothing that does not exhibit some intentionality or other. We can then say with Whitehead that every actual entity intends every other—not to speak of higher order organisms and minds. I do not want to go in that direction. I suspect—let this much be said at present—that such limitless generalizations tend to obliterate those limits within which a concept such as intentionality could have any significance. The grand metaphysics which then looms on the horizon can be courted only at the cost of paying a fairly heavy conceptual price.

For the present, I wish to raise the following questions in connection with the Sellars-Dretske type of theory. First, a naturalistic theory of intentionality requires that we have an account of representation or representing content which by itself is free from the notion of intentionality. There are obviously only three ways such an account can be given: *either* in terms of resemblance, *or* in terms of causality, or in terms—as with Dretske—of the idea of information. None of these, however, will do. 'Resemblance' will not do, for if A resembles B, B also resembles A, which implies that if a content C represents an object O by virtue of resemblance, O also will be representing C. The resemblance account also cannot explain how the representing content 'this man' will represent only this man and no other, for the content also resembles all other men, at least many others. The causal theory claims to be able to account for the last sort of cases; also, being an asymmetrical relation, the causal relation does not, if C is caused by O, make O a representation of C as well. However, there are other difficulties that beset the causal account of representation. If a representation C must, to be a representation of O, be caused by O, under what conditions can it be a misrepresentation of O? How is false belief possible, in that case?[9] Furthermore, since there are a large number of causes that together produce the putative C, it is not clear why, within the limits of the causal theory, one should be allowed to say that C represents O, and not any of the other causes. Dretske's information theory reduces the content to the information carried, and the information is a function of a nomic relation between events at the two ends. The thermometer carries information as much about the rise of mercury as about the increase in temperature. In that case, there is no reason why C will be a representation of O, and not O of C. However, as Frege said, there is no route from the object to the sense. Any theory of representation which places the object and the content on the same level will fail to account for intentionality, for misrepresentation as well as for the representing function of the content.

Sellars's is a resemblance theory. If the objectivity a R b is being represented by a rat, then in the rat's representing system there must be, in this theory, a symbol a* which stands for a, b* which stands for b, and a relation R*, a counterpart relation to R. However, as in all talk of resemblance, resemblance cannot simply be read off. As Husserl pointed out in his *Logical Investigations*,[10] the *Bildbewusstsein* is a special intentional, interpretive consciousness. A picture is not simply, in itself, a picture of a given thing, it has to be *taken to be so*. In Sellars's view:

$$a \text{ (is) before } b$$

and

$$\begin{matrix} a \\ b \end{matrix}$$

have the *same* syntactical form, namely 'a' and 'b' in a counterpart relation. We may ask, when would 'a' and 'b' *not* be in a counterpart relation? Consider

$$a$$

$$b$$

or

$$\begin{matrix} b \\ a \end{matrix}$$

One can always detect a relation in these two cases which can be regarded as the counterpart of 'before'. We can *construe*, that is, any content as a picture of any object—given suitable rules of interpretation. How, then, is misrepresentation possible?

Dretske's argument—apart from the already mentioned difficulties—suffers from a serious deficiency. He takes a *nomic* relation between F and G to be intentional on the ground that one may *know* something to be F without knowing that it is G. In a thermometer, the rise of mercury is *nomically* connected with the rise of temperature: this leads to the conclusion that the thermometer is an intentional state, and yet a thermometer does *not* know that it is F, without knowing that it is G. In fact, one may even question why an intentional state should be so defined. We know, of course, that in the intentional context substitution by identity does not go through, but we *did not expect* substitution by nomic correlation to go through in any case.

Whereas Sellars and Dretske want to embed intentionality in biological or physical intentional states, Fodor, as it well known, regards the mental act, the propositional attitude, to be related to a mental representation, which belongs to a 'mental lexicon' with its own syntax and semantics. But how do these mental representations refer? What relates them to the world? What is the *meaning* of a mental representation? Are all mental representations linguistic, i.e. discursive, or are there imagistic ones? How does the mental lexicon relate to the many different languages speakers may be using? If the mental representations themselves have to be *interpreted*, in order for us to be able to assign to them a structure and a content, then the mental act is not merely related to a representation but must also contain an 'interpretation function'.[11] One may, for example, ask,[12] in what *sense* is it the case that the internal states of a digital computer are representational. Is it not the programmer who provides the *essential* link between the states of the machine and states in the world? Furthermore, one cannot assign one unique structure to a thing, apart from the interpretation by a human subject. Are not the structural equivalences (between the representation and world) our own making? Finally, can a representation be a representation not merely *of*, but also *for* and *to* a system, unless the system has a subjective point of view?[13]

II

These reflections lead us from cognitive psychology to the phenomenologically descriptive, psychological understanding of intentionality by John Searle. Searle begins by taking intentionality as directedness,[14] but proceeds to further determine this directedness as one of 'representing': 'intentional states "represent" objects and states of affairs in the same sense of 'represent' that speech acts represent objects and states of affairs'.[15] Every intentional state is analysable into a 'representative content' and a psychological mode in which one has that content. Searle emphasizes that his use of 'representation' is different both from its use in traditional philosophy and from its use in cognitive psychology.[16] First of all, there is nothing of ontological significance in his use. The representative content, we are told, when it is propositional, determines a set of conditions of satisfaction of the intentional state: it determines under what conditions a belief would be true, or a desire satisfied. It is not clear what his view is regarding contents which are not propositional. Nor is it clear if he identifies contents with conditions of satisfaction, or regards the content as a representation *of* the conditions of satisfaction. Even if the process-product ambiguity—as between the requirement and the thing required—is kept in mind, one would want to know if an intentional act represents to itself its own conditions of satisfaction, or if its representing content consists of those conditions. In the former case, besides representing the object or state of affairs, the act must also represent the conditions that would satisfy its intention. It is the latter which Searle most likely means. His use of 'content' is not also that of cognitive psychology or AI theories, for he rightly finds the idea of a formal syntactic structure of mental representations unclear. The contents for him are essentially semantic and not syntactical.[17]

All this is very nicely in consonance with classical phenomenological psychology. Every intentional act, according to the latter, has an act-quality (which is Searle's psychological mode) and an act-matter (which is Searle's content).[18] The act-matter determines both the reference and the mode of reference. However, there are two features of Searle's theory to which I want to draw attention: one allies him with naturalism, the other with a sort of Heideggerean holism—both poise him, so it may seem, against Husserlian phenomenology. In the first place, while affirming, with a great deal of emphasis, that 'there really are such things as intrinsic mental phenomena'[19] which are as real as any other biological phenomena, he yet holds that intentional mental states are both *caused* by the operations of the brain and *realized* in the structure of the brain.[20] The causal laws by which the brain can produce intentionality will, Searle hopes, be quite different from the 'strict' laws in current science; they will be as different from those we now employ '(as) the principles of quantum mechanics are from the principles of Newtonian mechanics.' From all this it follows that, for Searle, intentionality is a natural phenomenon. This allies him with Sellars and Dretske.

In the second place, Searle holds not merely that intentional states are in general parts of *networks* of intentional states, but also that they always figure against a background of non-representational, pre-intentional, mental capacities (which primarily include knowing-hows). That intentional states belong to a *network* of intentionalities is a part of Husserl's maturer thesis about intentional implications. But that intentionality rests upon a background of non-representational, non-cognitive skills and abilities characterizing one's being-in-the-world, is possibly Heideggerean in origin. Let me recall that Dreyfus has drawn attention to this alliance between Searle's 'holism' and Heideggerean 'being-in-the-world' (as also, less convincingly, between the cognitive psychologist's methodological solipsism and the Husserlian's egology).[21]

III

This brings me to the third level of understanding intentionality which, as contrasted with the first, i.e. the naturalistic, may be called the existential-phenomenological. In order to be able to bring out its distinctive features, let me briefly refer to a tension in Searle's theory of intentionality. On the one hand, intentionality is taken by him to be naturalistically *caused*, while at the same time the very idea of causation is being intentionalized.[22] Naturalizing intentionality and intentionalizing causality go together in his thinking. But the result is neither naturalism nor intentionalism. We rather seem to be driven towards recognizing a third category hovering before us. I will spell it out in a moment. The other aspect of the tension is the way intentionality is grounded in what he calls the non-representational background of *lifeworld*. If we unify these two aspects—without letting them be in tension—we begin to get a glimpse of the second picture of intentionality as an existential phenomenon.

Let me briefly return to the question of causality. Searle includes causation within the representative content of the experiences of objects (especially of perception and of action). It belongs, for example, to the *content* of perception that it is being caused by the object out there, to the *content* of action that I am performing it. This is intentional causation. If we stress this aspect of the sense of perception and action as intentional acts, then we have at hand the beautiful idea of the *intermingling* of *intentionality* and *causality*, for which I find no clearer and better expression than the following passage from Bernhard Waldenfels:

What we have from the beginning, according to Waldenfels, is 'a givenness of the efficacious and an efficacy of the given'. To suffer from a bodily injury, he writes,

... signifies neither that I do something (I hit something), nor that something happens in the world (something hits something else), but rather that *something happens to me* (I hit myself upon something). What happens to me, I can neither objectify, without remainder, to a factual effect, nor can I ascribe to myself as a free action.[23]

The consequence of this intermingling is: intentionality is neither raised above the causal order, nor caused by it (in the naturalistic sense), but rather inseparable from causality at every point of its life. An opaque weight of corporeality attaches to its being inextricably. Its being and the sense of its being are ambiguous: it neither is pure interiority nor is reducible to pure exteriority. It is being-in-the-world— not, to be sure, as a thing is in the world, but as both constituted by, and constituting, its world. As constituted, it is not fully transparent to itself; as constituting, it is not purely opaque either. It is both at once and therefore ambiguous if judged in terms of that Cartesian-sounding opposition.

Turning now to the notion of the Background, if intentionality is rooted in nature, it is also made possible by a background of non-representational skills and practices. Not only are all mental states *not* representational but what is more: the intentionality of many representational states (such as intending to board a train) presupposes physical skills, knowing *how* to do various things which are not representational states. The two very different kinds of grounding can be explicated thus: A belief as an experience, as an *event*, is caused by the natural order, but the *content* of the belief presupposes the Background. But this only shows that the separation between the two sorts of grounding is artificial. The nature which causes my intentionality as an *event* and the non-representational lifeworld from which it derives its *content* must form a unity: that unity between nature and culture is the world that is meant to be captured by the concept of being-in-the-world.

What this picture, then, grounds intentionality on, is not the non-intentional causal order, but a non-representational but intentional-cum-causal being-in-the-world. Let us call the latter the 'existential intentionality'. Existential intentionality is not representative, nor is it merely cognitive. It is cognitive–affective–volitional in one. Its subject is not the bare point of a pure ego, but a concrete, corporeal, historical and mundane entity whose unity is prior to the Cartesian distinction between the inner and the outer. Merleau-Ponty calls it the body-subject; and this original intentionality is 'operative intentionality' which as much flows from the subject to the world (as the subject's project) as from the world to the subject (as the world's beckoning).

IV

Before moving on to the fourth, i.e. the *transcendental* understanding of intentionality, I need to say why the phenomenological-existential concept of intentionality needs to be surpassed by the transcendental. I have already said why a purely naturalistic account is unsatisfactory. Nevertheless, a few more remarks about the relation between intentionality and causality may be in order. The idea of 'representation' is important in the naturalistic theories, because it is just this pictorial, or imagistic, idea of representation that lends itself, relatively easily, to a physicalistic interpretation. Push the idea of content as *meaning*—rather than as picture image—to the forefront in our theory, and physicalism finds itself incapable of accommodating it. The particular occurrent act-token (or even the act-type) could be meaningfully identified with a physical event, but the same cannot be said of the *noesis-noema* structure. Conceptually, it makes *no sense* even to say that this correlation to an *irreal* entity has its counterpart in a correlation of the physical event and another such pictorial or imagistic structure. *The noema is not a representation*, not a substitute for the object, not 'in the mind' to be acted upon or to be mentally processed.[24]

There are indeed many other reasons why intentionality as noesis–noema structure cannot be inserted into the causal order, all of which I need not rehearse on this occasion.[25] But let us now see what happens to that 'giveness of the efficacious and efficacy of the given' that Waldenfels does, and Searle would, recognize as the intrusion of the causal order into the intentional. The merit of this last thesis lies in its phenomenological, as opposed to the naturalistic-scientific, nature: what it insists upon is that at least certain experiences themselves—perceptual and actional, at any rate—display a causal component in their structure. They have correctly identified a phenomenon, but immediately proceeded to mis-interpret it.

The phenomenon they have identified is the phenomenon of passivity, of being-affected-by-the-given that undoubtedly characterizes a whole class of intentional experiences, the most striking being the case of perception. Perception of an external physical object in particular is *also* an experience of being-affected-by. But there is nothing in this phenomenon that carries the report of a real causality, of the story even in rudiments that physics and physiology tell us. What characterizes the *experiences* under consideration is rather *felt* causality. It is quite a different case when that causality itself is thematized, i.e. made the object of the experience. In this latter case, a real causality is the *object* of experience just as a real external object is the object of normal, outer perception. Waldenfels's example of a sharp instrument hitting my body and causing injury is of this type (falls into this case). In that case, the object is real causality. It would be wrong to interpret the experience as though the *object* of the experience, *qua* its object, is *also* experienced as its cause. While the object, i.e. *real* causal event, is experienced as external and real, the experience itself is *felt to be caused,* the later being a case of what I call felt causality.

Searle proceeds to elaborate precisely this distinction, without recognizing that it would take away the naturalistic interpretation he wishes to confer on his finding. The Humeans, he writes, 'sought causation in the wrong place. They sought causation as the *object* of our experiences, whereas in its most primitive form it is part of the *content of* experiences of perceiving and acting.' The experience of causation is part of 'the conditions of satisfaction that are internal to the experience'. Now if 'the conditions of satisfaction' or internal representation is Searle's reconstruction of the Husserlian noema, then the causation he is talking about belongs *not to nature* but to the noematic sense of the experiences concerned. Searle calls it 'intentional causation'. The 'intentional causation', according to him, is a 'logical' or 'internal' relation, just because one component of 'the conditions of satisfaction' of the intentional experience requires that it be the cause or effect of another component. The noema legislates, predelineates, how it is to be satisfied. All this shows clearly that what Searle has in mind is far from being outer, *real* and natural causality.

If intentional causality is thus appropriated into the *content* of the act, and natural causality ruled out as *inappropriate* (as belonging to a different level of discourse), what happens to that Background, that non-representational life-world in which the intentional content is after all grounded, to the Dasein's being-in-the-world? It is true that the intentional content of a cognitive intentional state is determined in part by the intentional contents of some other cognitive states (beliefs, etc.) but in part also by non-cognitive practices, skills, expectations and abilities (also by sedimented interpretations constituting one's tradition), which one takes for granted in everyday life. Thus, for me to be able to intend to walk from one place to another presupposes not only *beliefs* such as that the ground under me will not cave in, that material objects are impenetrable, etc. but also *skills* to execute proper bodily movements necessary for walking. Such skills are not intentional, they do not have representational contents, they are not cases of knowing-that, but rather cases of knowing-how.

There are several things wrong in thus *limiting* the role of intentionality. First, as McIntyre has pointed out,[26]

. . . even if I do not know how to walk and so do not have the skills requisite for satisfying my intention to walk across the room, I can form that intention if I *believe that* I have the requisite skill and that belief would belong to *my* network.

The point of this argument is that even if *as a matter of fact* there is such a Background for our intentional states, the Background *qua* Background is not necessary. It can be appropriated into the network. Such appropriation may be a never-ending process, but *in principle* there is no reason why it is not conceivable that an intentional being performs his intentional acts with a full reflective consciousness of all those presuppositions, including his ability to form those movements. That, in fact, is the implication of the possibility of transcendental reduction.[27] The skills and abilities under consideration have to be the skills and abilities of the person who is the subject of intentional acts, nor is it necessary that he does have a body. What is needed is that he is able to ascribe to himself abilities such as to move himself around—which is nothing but possessing the (practical) 'I can' sort of kinaesthetic consciousness. What I am saying is compatible with—and perhaps is even implied in—the point Aquila makes in the same connection: what Searle shows is that a set of non-intentional capacities, etc. must be recognized as constituting the matter (in the Kantian sense) *of* a psychological state that has the 'form' of intentionality, and so need not be construed as external to the intentional act.[28]

These criticisms make, I believe, a provisionally strong case for the 'transcendental' interpretation of intentionality. They are intended to show that a strong *internalist* theory of intentionality is a viable one, that intentionality is not derivable from any of the other non-intentional concepts such as causality. The network of intentional acts form one self-enclosed mental life through whose internal *contents* and their concatenations the world derives its various constituting senses. Carried to its utmost possibilities, it yields the result that the world owes its sense to intentional acts. Intentionality, then, is not mere directedness to world, but interpretive of the world. It not only has its own content, it confers meaning on its object, so that its object is presented as having that meaning for it. As constitutive of the sense or senses of the world, intentionality *is* transcendental. As must be apparent, such a conception is a generalization of the Kantian thesis that understanding makes nature possible.

There are three objections against the plausibility of such a thesis, which I wish to briefly comment upon. One is that the theory makes what is out there dependent upon what is in the mind, and thus reverses the original realistic intuition underlying the thesis of intentionality. Second, it leaves no room for a direct, *de re* intentionality. Third, by grounding the sense of the world in the mind, it, like all transcendental philosophies, leaves no room for the variety of discourses that are possible about the world, so that the foundationalism entails a monolithic, non-relativistic picture of the world. The first and the second objections go together; the third is based on a very different philosophical intuition.

First, then, the realistic intuition. There is no doubt such a realistic intuition did in fact underlie the thesis of Brentano. Subsequent development of that idea has shown that while something important in that intuition needs to be preserved, that realism won't do. There are three aspects of the *situation* of intentional reference: there is the being-about that characterizes it at the level of pre-reflective naïvity. Then there is the grasping-of-a-sense in reflective thought. But, ineluctably underlying these, is the 'cunning of intentionality': the *interpretive* function, the *Sinngebung*, which conceals itself under the surface phenomenon of 'grasping'. On various occasions, I have used the metaphor of complementarity—between the particle and wave theories of light—to describe the relation between 'grasping' and '*Sinngebung*'. This also illuminates the complementarity between phenomenology and hermeneutics.

Direct *de re* intentionality—not in terms of a causal theory whose fundamental flaws have been pointed out earlier in this essay, but in terms of a *sui generis* cognitive relationship as forcefully suggested by Barry Smith,[29] such as in veridical acts of perception—needs to be construed, within a transcendental framework, differently from a purely ontological relation. If, in principle, mental acts may have properties *not* transparent to their subjects, we are left *also* with the possibility that the naïvete with which the perceiver construes his act in terms of a naturalistic ontology may only be the surface phenomenon of a deep interpretive constitutive structure. There is no doubt something importantly wrong in construing all acts on the pattern of non-veridical acts or even of veridical acts which are *descriptive:* in both cases, the intentionality of an act is explicable in terms of its being *as-if* directed towards some object or other, and so in the long run—in terms of the concept of *noema*. But it is equally misleading to have a sort of intentionality whose understanding makes us fall back upon 'what may be recognized from the outside, by suitably qualified observers.'[30] For transcendental phenomenology, the truth must lie in between these extremes of a surface description by the subject of his acts and a third-person observer's account. For this, we need a theory of perceptual meaning—not assimilable into a theory of conceptual, or propositional, *noema*; a theory of intuitive acts in which the object is presented with the *sense* of being self-given; and a theory of perceptual interpretation. I will not develop such a theory here, but shall only note that we do not have in veridical perceptual acts a group of acts which force upon us the necessity for a naïvely realistic ontology.

In fact, a transcendental theory of intentionality finds Putnam's 'Skolemization of absolutely everything'[31] a most congenial move to the effect that it is absolutely impossible to fix a determinate reference for *any* term at all, except by *our* interpretations (not by any mysterious mental powers). As Putnam puts it, 'the world doesn't pick models or interpret languages'.[32] *We* do. We constitute our worlds *and ourselves*. It it easy to show that, in that case, the third objection stated earlier expresses an anxiety which is uncalled for. A transcendental theory of constituting intentionality would encompass ontological relativism and is not a plea for a monolithic picture of the world.[33]

V

I have distinguished between four levels of understanding of intentionality: the descriptive-psychological, the naturalistic-causal, the existential and the transcendental-constitutive. In doing this, I have traversed a path that represents a progressive deepening of our comprehension of intentionality. However, it is not a simple linear progression such that the succeeding one leaves behind the preceeding ones. The naturalistic-causal understanding thinks it can do justice to the descriptive-psychological. It claims to supersede the latter by appropriating it into a causal context. What I have questioned is the tenability of these two claims taken together. The existential understanding seeks to preserve the truth of both foregoing theses— but claims to supersede both by freeing the Brentano thesis from its mentalism and the causal theory from its physicalism. The transcendental constitutive interpretation preserves the truth of this last 'overcoming' of Cartesian dualism, for the constitutive intentionality is neither mental nor physical—both these being constituted, and so mundane, orders. The path is 'dialectical' in the sense in which— as in Hegel's *Phenomenology*—the succeeding 'shape' both negates and preserves the truth of the preceeding.

Another way of describing this 'dialectical' path is as follows. One begins, as with Brentano, with a descriptive thesis. This Brentano thesis is then given a 'naturalistic-causal', or 'information-theoretic' and/or 'biological' grounding. The inability of such a 'grounding' to preserve the phenomenon of intentionality leads to a more purified, denaturalized, mentalistic thesis. But one also realizes that the mental contents must be grounded in the natural and cultural orders, which provides the transition from the mentalistic to an existential understanding of intentionality. We face here a typical dialectical situation. The mentalistic thesis has a *representationalistic* idea of intentional content (at worst, an image theory, capable of being appropriated into a physicalistic version.) The existentialist thesis rejects the idea of 'representation' in favour of a *non-representational* idea of *Dasein's* being-in-the-world. This opposition between a mentalistic representation theory and an existential non-representational theory is to be overcome in the theory of intentionality as a transcendental-constitutive function according to which (a) the intentional content is not an internal representation but a publicly sharable meaning, and (b) the world in which *Dasein* finds itself is the result of prior constitutive accomplishments of an intentionally implicated community of egos.

I should like to add that with this progressive deepening of our understanding of the nature and function of intentionality, the relevant philosophical problem also continues to get transformed. Thus, the problem to which the original Brentano thesis was a response was: how are mental phenomena to be distinguished from the physical phenomena? (which incidentally is very different from the contemporary question: how is the mental different from the physical?) This Brentano question gets transformed, in Husserl, into the question: *how* does a mental, or rather any intentional, act refer to whatever is its intentional object? Or, making both the act and its object specific particulars, one may want to ask: how does *that* object become the object of *this* mental act? The answer roughly is, as in much of cognitive psychology, 'through a representational content of the act, a mental representation of that object'. But this way of asking the question appears to be circular, for *that* object must then be identifiable *as* that object or as satisfying any other description, *before* one could ask the question, how does it become the object of this act. In other words, one cannot start with an object which is available only through some intentional act or other. The proper question, then, would seem to be: how does an intentional act refer to whatever happens to be its object. In asking it this way, one is starting with the conscious experience under consideration, but then one finds that having *such and such* object as its intentional object is *internal* to that experience. One then comes to recognize the structure act-*noema* as the irreducible point to begin with. The lesson is something that Frege clearly saw: there is no route from object to sense. We have unavoidably to traverse the path from sense to object—as also from sense to the sense-giving, i.e. the interpretive and constitutive function of intentionality.

NOTES

1. Cf. the correspondence between Sellars and Chisholm on intentionality, reprinted in A. Marras (ed.), *Intentionality, Mind and Language* (Urbana, IL: University of Illinois Press, 1972).
2. W. Sellars, *Mental Events* (pre-print), para 56.
3. Ibid., para 57.
4. Ibid., paras 46–9.
5. F. Dretske, 'The Intentionality of Cognitive states', in *Mid-West Studies in Philosophy*, (eds), Peter French and Theodor E. Uehling, vol. V, 1980, pp. 281–94, esp. p. 285.
6. Ibid., p. 289.
7. Ibid., p. 290.
8. Ibid., p. 291.
9. For these criticisms, see Jerry Fodor, 'Semantics: Wisconsin Style' (pre-print).

10. Husserl, *Logical Investigations* Inv. V, Appendix to § 11 and § 20 (Findlay tr. vol. II, pp. 556–93).

11. Cf. Z. Pylyshyn, 'Imagery and Artificial Intelligence', in *Readings in Philosophy of Psychology*, (ed.) N. Black, Vol. 2 (London: Methuen, 1981), pp. 170–94.

12. Cf. J. Heil, 'Does cognitive Psychology Rest on a Mistake?', *Mind XC*, 321–42, especially p. 331.

13. Cf. R. Cummins, *The Nature of Psychological Explanation* (Cambridege, MA: MIT Press, 1984), p. 177.

14. J. Searle, *Intentionality: An Essay in the Philosophy of Mind* (Cambridge: Cambridge university Press, 1983), p. 3.

15. Ibid., p. 4.

16. Ibid., p. 11.

17. Cf. R. Aquila's review of Searle, *Intentionality* in *Philosophy and Phenomenological Research*, XLVI, 1985.

18. Cf. E. Husserl, *Logical Investigations*, Inv. V.

19. Searle, *Intentionality*, p. 262.

20. Ibid., p. 265.

21. Cf. Editor's Introduction to Hubert L. Dreyfus (ed.), *Husserl, Intentionality and Cognitive Science* (Cambridge, MA: MIT Press, 1982).

22. J. Searle, *Intentionality*, esp. ch. 4.

23. B. Waldenfels, 'Intentionalität und Kausalität', in *Der Spielraum des Verhaltens* (Frankfurt am Main: Suhrkamp Verlag, 1980), pp. 98–125, esp. p. 109. (English translation mine).

24. Cf. E. Marbach, 'On Using Intentionality in Empirical Phenomenology: the Problem of 'Mental Images', *Dialectica*, 38 (1984), pp. 209–29, esp. p. 223.

25. See my 'Intentionality, Causality and Holism', *Synthese*, 61 (1984), pp. 17–34.

26. R. McIntyre, 'Searle on Intentionality', *Inquiry*, 27 (1984), pp. 468–83, esp. p. 479.

27. I am not surprised that Searle himself does not think the thesis about the background to be incompatible with Husserl's transcendental reduction. Cf. McIntyre, ibid., pp. 482–3, n12.

28. R. Aquila, Critical review of Searle, *Intentionality*, in *Philosophy and Phenomenological Research*, XLVI (1985), p. 163.

29. Barry Smith, 'Acta Cum Fundamentis in Re', *Dialectica*, 38 (1984), pp. 157–78.

30. Ibid., p. 163.

31. Hilary Putnam, *Realism and Reason* (Cambridge: Cambridge University Press, 1984), p. 15.

32. Ibid., p. 24.
33. I have shown how transcendental phenomenology is compatible with relativism in a lecture entitled 'Phänomenologie und Relativismus' given at the meeting of the German Phenomenological Society, in Trier, Spring, 1985. A version of that lecture is scheduled to appear in the proceedings of that meeting.

chapter

nine

Intentions of Intentionality:
20 Theses*

1. Something is intentional if it is directed towards some object or other.
2. To an intentional act belongs inextricably an intentional object.
3. There is a many-one correlation between acts and their contents.

II

4. Every intentional act has a sense or meaning through which its object is intended.
5. Every intentional act is meaning-giving or interpretive.
6. Intentionality is either cognitive or practical or affective, as also are their meanings.
7. An intentional act, if it is not an original beginning, functions within a culture.
8. A culture is but a system of sedimented meanings.
9. Every meaning must be, in the long run, originally a gift of intentionality.
10. Intentional acts originate from a subject who refers to herself as 'I' (and in this sense from an *ego*).
11. An ego is not only the source of her intentional acts, but as she performs intentional acts, these acts, founded upon earlier acts, modify the life of the ego.

*First presented at the Bryn Mawr College, Philadelphia in 1996.

12. To be distinguished from I-intentionalities are We-intentionalities, or collective intentionalities.
13. To be distinguished from acts which are being performed by an ego or a collectivity, are those which operate anonymously.

III

14. Intentionality constitutes the world.
15. The world constitutes consciousness.
16. The truly transcendental principle is: consciousness-of-the-world.
17. Objects as presented to consciousness are results of interpreting the given data.
18. Perceptual objects are *passively* constituted.
19. Theoretical, mathematical and logical objects are *actively* constituted.
20. The empirical *is* the transcendental.

chapter

ten

Kant and Husserl[†][*]

usserl wrote to Cassirer on 3 April 1925: 'My own development originally was opposed to Kant [*Meine eigene Entwicklung [die] ursprünglich Kant-feindlich war*], but gradually I came to recognize the value as well as the limits of Kant'.[1] Since when did this change take place? As early as 1908, Husserl wrote to the neo-Kantian Cohn (dated 15 October 1908): 'For several years (and since the appearance of my *Logical Investigations*, with heightened energy) I have been working on a Critique of Reason, to be built up actually from its foundation.'[2]

This idea that Husserl intended to write a Critique of Reason (he does not call it Critique of Pure Reason) provides me with the guiding clue to undertake this enquiry into the relation between Kant and Husserl. I will divide this article into three parts. In the first, I will try to offer a brief sketch of the *Critique* as Husserl would have written it. In the second, I will likewise present a sketch of the *Phenomenology of Pure Consciousness* which Kant may be regarded as having given us. In the third part I will single out some central points of difference between the two philosophers—differences which erupt within a common horizon. This shall also show us a path for the future of transcendental philosophy.

[†]This paper was presented at the Kant Congress held in Memphis, Tennessee in March, 1995.

[*]*Husserl Studies* 13: 19–30 (1996). Netherlands: Kluwer Academic Publishers.

THE CRITIQUE OF REASON THAT HUSSERL DID NOT QUITE WRITE

That *some* problem of Reason weighed heavily on Husserl's mind is evident from his constant reference to 'reason' and 'rationality'. For my present limited purpose at this point, it would be enough to note that for Husserl, the problem of reason is the problem of adequately *grounding* one's truth-claims on evidence. It is very different from the Kantian problem of determining what reason can know *a priori* about the world.

Husserl's continuing concern, however, with a Kantian-like critique is borne out not only by the reference to a transcendental aesthetic in *Formal and Transcendental Logic* but by the large number of pieces, in the *Nachlass*, devoted to the theme of Transcendental Aesthetic. (His use of 'Transcendental Logic' by contrast is more well known from the major published work bearing that title). A manuscript from November 1925 is entitled '*Aus Transcendentale Äesthetik*' (A VII 26).[3] Manuscripts right into the mid-thirties are said by the author to contribute to Transcendental Aesthetic. Some manuscripts continue to hint at what would constitute a Transcendental Analytic. We do not, however, find any suggestion of a Transcendental Dialectic corresponding to Kant's . My present exposition will largely draw upon the formulations in these manuscripts, but I will also, when necessary, make use of the published works of Husserl.

First, it is important to note that Husserl does not deal with 'geometry' in his Transcendental Aesthetic as Kant does. While he does consider the spatiality and temporality of perception, the space and the time of his Transcendental Aesthetic are not yet the space of Euclidean geometry and the time of Newtonian physics. Kant's theory of perception is continuous with physics; Husserl's relates to something prior to and discontinuous with physics. Husserl's Transcendental Aesthetics is concerned with the constitution of pre-scientific perceptual world, with what he, in the *Crisis*, calls the *Lebenswelt*. In the above-mentioned fragment from 1925, he calls his a 'deepening and extension of Kant's Transcendental Aesthetic through phenomenology'. Now how does it proceed?

Every perception lets itself be continued in endless series of perceptions. Every perception can be continued, interrupted and closed. Different perceptions of the same object are unified through recollection. Two perceptions of the same object are possible only at different times. A perception has an open horizon—what is given is a 'pre-belief in hypothetical possibilities' (*Vorglauben hypothetischen Möglichkeiten*). The open horizon is continuously filled with new perceptions. We must distinguish between an open perception, still becoming, and a perception's coming to an end (like a melody coming to an end). The perception is either an originary beginning with regard to its object (no past-horizon of the object) or an open beginning, or an ending perception (either ending with an open-horizon *or* ending because of the end of the object so that there is no future-horizon.)

We have also to distinguish between (a) continuous synthesis of perceptions of the same object, (b) a discrete synthesis, for example, the synthesis of a perception with a recollection, and (c) the total systematic form of possible syntheses in general.

From this Husserl derives the idea of a universal system of experience. The entire concrete experience is inductive. Besides specific inductions, the very *style* of universal experience is inductive and provides 'a framework for infinities of inductive presumptions' (*ein Rahmen Für Unendlichkeiten von induktiven Präsumptionen*), (A VI 21, from 1931). Vary this *style* and we reach the idea of possible experience in general, and also structural (for example, spatio-temporal) necessities belonging to this idea.

Thus Husserl can say (A VII 14) that a possible world has a double eidos: one, more universal, mathematical Idea, and another, special and sensuous. The former belongs to the Transcendental Analytic, the latter to the Aesthetic. Note that the idea of a possible experience is introduced by Kant *only* in the Transcendental Analytic. For Husserl, even Transcendental Aesthetic, dealing with sensuous experience, has room for the idea of a possible experience. Here there are inductively anticipated interconnections, forward and backward reaching presumptions (*vorgreifende Antizipation, rückgreifende Präsumption*) (A VII 14) which are *not yet a priori* rules of the understanding, but which are grounded in the typicalities characterizing the experience even at this level. Synthesis of sensuous perception is not intellectual synthesis.

Transcendental Aesthetics, in Husserl's view, has the following strata:

1. The correlation between things and the concrete perceiving ego with his kinaesthetic and somatic experiences;

2. The structure of the world as pure perceptual world;
3. The structure of a unified experience;
4. The motivation for a transition to ideal considerations.

Of these, as is clear, 3 belongs to Transcendental Analytic, according to Kant. Husserl adds a note (A VII 14, p. 94): 'here we have a phenomenological parallel of the Kantian analogies.' This makes it clear that large parts of Kant's Transcendental Analytic really come under Husserl's Transcendental Aesthetic. These are: the doctrines of synopsis, reproduction and recognition, of imaginative synthesis as preceding reflective conceptualization, and the analogies in so far as they are understood as modes of interconnection amongst perceptions without presupposing the doctrine of the *a priori* dignity of these modes.

Transcendental Aesthetic ends, where—as Husserl writes in a fragment from the 1920s—the mathematics of continuity, of limits, begins, and nature is geometricized and mathematized. Transcendental Analytic, in Husserl's view, should deal with the constitution of pure logic and mathematics, and the way empirical sensuous nature is brought under them. If Transcendental Aesthetics is the doctrine of the essential structure of all possible perceptual worlds, Transcendental Analytic is the doctrine of the essential laws of the constitution of something in general (i.e. of formal ontology) and of a mathematical manifold (A VII 14). The difference from the Kantian Transcendental Logic (especially Analytic) is quite clear: it rests on their differing conceptions of formal logic and mathematics.

Kant's idea of formal logic was Aristotelian, a logic of predicative judgements which also 'corresponds' to the transcendental logic of categorial synthesis which constitutes objects of cognition. Husserl's formal logic is, in the long run, a formal ontology whose domain is the empty region of 'object in general'. Logic, as a purely axiomatic and deductive science of meanings, is not Kantian; for Kant, logic, even general logic, is still concerned with *judgements* though in abstraction from all contents, and judgement is still an act of thinking and so is of cognitive significance. Kant does not raise the question of the *constitution* of formal logic; he simply uses formal logic for access to transcendental logic. Also decisive is the difference between the views of both regarding the relation between logic and mathematics. Kant's theory of mathematics allows for arithmetic of natural numbers, ordinary algebra and Euclidean geometry, but not for real and imaginary numbers, abstract algebras, non-Euclidean geometries and axiomatic systems of pure mathematic. Husserl's is more in consonance with the modern mathematician's mathematics, but Husserl needs a theory for applied mathematics. I shall return to this problem later.

WHAT IF KANT HAD WRITTEN A PHENOMENOLOGY OF PURE CONSCIOUSNESS?

I shall deal with Kant's theory of pure consciousness under several headings. First, what does he mean by 'pure' consciousness? Second, I will briefly answer the question, if consciousness, in Kant's view, is intentional. Third, we need to be clear about what the function of consciousness is, according to Kant. And finally, we need to look at Kant's conception of the unity of consciousness. Of course, in all these respects, we shall have the phenomenological theory of consciousness in mind.

Basic to Kant's phenomenology is a distinction between empirical and pure consciousness. Empirical consciousness is a consciousness in which sensation is a component and in Kant's account 'from empirical consciousness to pure consciousness a graduated transition is possible, the real (i.e. sensation) in the former completely vanishing and a merely formal *a priori* consciousness of the manifold of space and time remaining.'⁴ Empirical consciousness is changing and subjectively different: it appears in various degrees down to the purely unconscious (*CPR*, B 415). Kant seems to hold the last thesis also of pure consciousness; it may be indistinct, but must be always present when there is knowledge of objects (ibid., A 104, A 117). The pure consciousness as belonging to an 'I', as unified in one single self-consciousness, is transcendental consciousness (ibid., A 117), and is the ultimate condition of the possibility of knowledge of objects. It would be perfectly in order to say that for Kant, consciousness as such is intrinsically transcendental, it is only as containing sensations as components that it seems to be empirical. This is in fact what he writes in the essay '*Beantwortung der Frage: Ist es eine Erfahrung daß wir denken?*' (1788–91): 'The consciousness of presenting an experience or of thinking in general is a transcendental consciousness, not an experience' (*Das Bewußtsein also, eine Erfahrung anzustellen oder auch überhaupt zu denken, ist ein transzendentales Bewußtsein, nicht Erfahrung*).⁵ In another essay of that period, he writes that the consciousness that I think is transcendental, and precedes all empirical consciousness which occurs in 'inner sense'. 'Inner sense' is psychological consciousness, the pure apperception is logical.[6] The Kantian pure transcendental consciousness is intellectual; it is even called a 'form' (*CPR*, A 346=B 404), it is not itself 'a representation distinguishing a particular object', but 'a form of representation in general'.

Is this intellectual, formal, pure consciousness also intentional? On this matter, it is indeed difficult to state precisely Kant's view. In a sense, it is intentional, but that sense is not the straightforward Brentano thesis, but may indeed be closer to Husserl's in many respects.

Sensation, for Kant, is not, as such, a content of (pure) consciousness and also is not intentional. Intuition is the most basic intentional item in the Kantian inventory of 'representations'. Empirical intuition has an 'undetermined object' (which Kant calls 'appearance' in A 20=B 34). It is by virtue of the pure intuition of space—the form of intuition—that sensations are referred to something outside me (A 23=B 38). Even if an intuition *as such* is not thought or conceptualized, the intentionality of intuition must precede that of consciousness. When empirical intuition is conceptualized, it becomes at the same time intuition of a determinate object, and a judgement and so cognition of the object—only then do we have intentional consciousness. The intentionality of consciousness is consciousness's own achievement, a product of the synthetic functions of thinking—although it may be regarded as having been *anticipated* by the 'unconscious' activity of imagination.

The 'I think' or self-consciousness of the identical subject does not merely accompany all representations, but is what unifies those representations into the unity of an object—such that the unity of self-consciousness and the consciousness of unity are correlative achievements. The transcendental ego does not merely contain all representation, nor does it merely accompany them, neither is it the source (as with Husserl) of intentional acts. Though 'descriptively empty', the unity of self-consciousness precisely is the condition of the possibility of 'making' out of a manifold of representations a unity of object.[7] Thus even *a* perception as such does not succeed in presenting an object; only as entering into a synthesis with other possible perceptions is there an experience of an object.[8]

For my present purpose it is also important to recall that for Kant, the unity of the object contains the representation of the object = X 'which I think through the predicates' (A 105). Thus the judgement 'this table is brown' amounts to 'the X which is first thought by the predicate "this table", is then thought through the predicate "brown".'

As Cramer makes it clear, the X does not mean the 'this-there' which is designated by the demonstrative, nor does it mean 'the table', nor also 'the this-there which is a table'. The X is the *object* which is referred to through the predicates 'this table' and 'brown'.[9] The object looks like being the Husserlian *noema* with its X component and the predicate components. But is it?

From the above it is clear that when Kant's followers such as Reinhold sought to transform Kant's transcendental philosophy into a theory of elements or representations, they missed the whole point of Kant's concept of consciousness—which neither is a representation nor contains representations, but is a function or activity of unifying itself while unifying representations into the unity of an object. If Husserlian phenomenology, in many respects, stays close to Reinhold, to that extent also it remains at a distance from Kant. The representations, as subjective determinations, belong to the inner sense, to empirical apperception, but *not* to the transcendental unity of apperception. Strictly speaking, there are no *contents* of consciousness; consciousness is always a function, an act of bringing together, and through this bringing together, it brings itself together to an unity.

A Kantian phenomenology of pure consciousness, then, would consist of a description of the fundamental modes of synthesis, of acts of synthesis, whereby the unity of the object as well as the unity of the ego are both constituted. It is no wonder that Husserl and the phenomenologists found the A-deduction, especially the so-called subjective deduction with the doctrine of the three-fold synthesis and with a major role assigned to imagination to be philosophically more important than the B-deduction with its claim to give a *logical proof* of the objective validity of the categories.

A COMPARISON OF THE TWO PHENOMENOLOGIES

(1) The Kantian phenomenology suffers from the lack of an adequate theory of consciousness. By restricting consciousness to the intellectual function of synthesis, and by excluding from the domain of consciousness strictly so-called sensuous, hyletic representations, it either makes all syntheses active and intellectual, or leaves passive synthesis to imagination (which is still not a function of consciousness even if it is a blind faculty of the soul). Husserl has a more comprehensive theory of consciousness, for which consciousness includes the sensuous and the noetic, its synthesis are both passive

and active, perception, imagination and thinking all beings modes of consciousness. Consciousness is not merely thinking (as in Kant), but includes all *Erlebnisse*. Thus there is a certain 'naivety with regard to consciousness' ('*bewußtseinstheoretische Naivität*') in Husserl, such that even transcendental consciousness is said to be parallel to empirical consciousness. It is the same consciousness which as belonging to the world is empirical, and as constituting the world is transcendental. Because of the intellectual nature of the Kantian consciousness, the 'Transcendental Aesthetic' of the *Critique of Pure Reason* is, as Ricoeur rightly pointed out, the least phenomenological.[10] The spatiality and the temporality which the Transcendental Aesthetic grounds in the nature of the human sensibility are the space of Euclidean geometry and the time—in spite of its 'inwardness' (*Innerlichkeit*)—of physics. The enormous, qualitative diversity of space and time as they characterize pre-scientific life-worlds has not been, and cannot be, made the theme of Kantian reflection.

(2) What stands in the way of the Kantian phenomenology coming to its own is, according to Ricoeur, the *justificatory* motivation of his thinking: how are mathematics and physics possible? But it should be emphasized that Husserl's phenomenology is not entirely free from a justificatory intention. Husserl sought to justify mathematics by returning to the originary evidence on which mathematical cognition is based. The result is a theory of constitution of mathematical objects. Kant's theory of mathematics—of natural arithmetic and Euclidean geometry—contains, on the one hand, a theory of the *constitution* of numbers and geometrical figures: numbers are constituted by counting and geometrical figures by construction, and both are founded in the intuition of time and of space. On the other hand, the theory of constitution also shows how mathematical cognition is possible and what is more, how mathematics applies to the perceptual world. If the Husserlian theory is different, it is because Husserl had a more formalistic concept of mathematics, but he too asks how mathematical *objects* are constituted and how they apply to the perceived world. For the latter question, he had to come up with a more complex answer than Kant. Since he begins with the life-world, he had to have a theory of how the life-world could be 'idealized' in order to be amenable to mathematization.

(3) For genuine phenomenology, a theory of justification of cognition has then to be a theory of constitution of the appropriate objectivities, and the latter, as we have learnt from Husserl, has to be a description of the evidences, beginning with the most basic, as they

build up step by step the givenness of the objectivities under consideration. Naturally, the category of intuition is fundamentally limited in Kantian thinking: limited to sensory intuition of contents and *a priori*—not intellectual, to be sure—intuition of forms of perception. There is, in Kantian thinking, neither the Husserlian eidetic intuition of essences (which can only be *concepts*, i.e. modes of comprehension of intuitions) nor categorical intuition (of syntactically formed objectivities) *nor* reflective intuition of one's own inner mental life. Correspondingly, the Kantian category of 'object' is very restricted in scope, when compared to Husserl's for whom there are objects of different strata: basic real particulars, essences, states of affairs, eidetic singularities, persons, and of course intentional acts and their contents which can be objectified.

(4) As regards *persons*, Husserl is led to the problem of the constitution of the other ego. Husserl needs the idea of intersubjectivity for recovering the strong senses of objectivity, and he needs this strong sense of objectivity for he has no use for the idea of Being as contrasted with that of objectivity. Kant has the contrast between phenomena and things in themselves, and he thinks he can have a theory of constitution of phenomena without bringing in other egos. Consequently, the Kantian transcendental 'I' wavers between *my* ego (in so far as it is *I*) and the universal function of thinking. If it is the latter, then the problem of intersubjectivity becomes only the problem of knowing other minds, and loses an ontological significance over and above this simple epistemological question. But when—as it seems to me the only occasion—Kant reverts to this problem, he wonders if it does not seem strange 'that the condition under which alone I think, and which is therefore merely a property of myself as subject, should likewise be valid for everything that thinks', and comes up with two suggestions in response. First, 'we must assign to things, necessarily and *a priori*, all the properties that constitute the conditions under which alone *we* think of them' (A 347=B 405) (emphasis mine). This answer leaves unanswered the question whether *we*—I and the others—think under the same, i.e. a common set of conditions, and how are we to ascertain that the others do—which precisely was the worry. This anxiety can be removed only if we can say that the other thinking beings think exactly as I do. To show this, Kant goes on to assert (A 347=B 405): 'objects of this kind [meaning thinking beings] are nothing more than the *transference* of the consciousness to other things, which in this way alone can be represented as thinking beings.' Note this concept of 'transference' which Husserl uses

in the 5th Cartesian Meditation to elaborate his concept of 'analogizing apperception'.

(5) I want to restrict my observations to the common horizon of Kant and Husserl, and so do not wish to introduce Husserlian themes which totally transcend Kantian phenomenology or *vice versa*— themes such as *historicity* of constitution of sense. So even if we for the present leave out the theme of history, we cannot pass by the theme of temporality which is so profoundly Kantian. It would be a natural way of looking at Husserl's original thoughts about internal time consciousness to regard it as a deepening of the Kantian intention. It was Kant who first in modern times located the origin of time in the inner sense, in the ordering of the contents of the mind (*Gemüt*). It may appear as if for Kant the time-order of our representations is the same as the time-order of events occurring in outer nature, but does not he also insist that while the order of our perceptions is sometimes reversible, the order of *events* in nature is always irreversible? I can, if I so wish, perceive the floor of a room first and then the ceiling, or I can, if I so wish, perceive the ceiling first and then the floor. However, the perceptions considered as occurrences in nature, are in an irreversible order. The first perception of the floor will not return in order to occupy a different temporal position; what I can do is to have a numerically distinct perception of the floor after perceiving the ceiling. The same *representations* are not then assigned a different temporal ordering. There is only one time-order—be it of inner or of outer events. This is where Husserlian phenomenology parts company. Bracketing the mundane time of the world (including both the inner and the outer), it discovers a new dimension of experience of time which is unknown to Kant—but which Kant could have discovered had he asked the question: does the self-constitution of the unity of the self-consciousness occur in time? The intellectual and formal transcendental ego is raised by him above time. Had he recognized that the *acts* of synthesis themselves (as constituting objectivities, and so not themselves as objects) were also temporal, and had he made use of his own recognition (in the A-deduction's doctrine of three-fold synthesis) that the pre-objective representations themselves were temporal, he would have recognized a level of temporality that is the *pre-objective* foundation of objective time. Here we need not add anything to Kant's thinking from outside, we need only make explicit all those elements which are already implicitly there.

(6) Finally, regarding 'intentionality' and 'truth', let me introduce this concluding observation by recalling an issue in Kant interpretation which has attracted some attention in recent times. In a famous but

intriguing text (A 58=B 83), Kant, after saying that the nominal explanation (*Namenserklärung*) of 'truth' as correspondence is here taken for granted, goes on to maintain that no general and sufficient criterion of truth is forthcoming, for any such criterion has to take the content of cognition into account and this content varies from cognition to cognition. Formal logic, he tells us, gives us only the negative criterion of truth, but nothing about the positive, general and sufficient criterion of truth. There are several intriguing questions about this text, which I cannot take up now. If Kant had held that not merely formal logic, but even he, in his transcendental logic, cannot come up with a general and sufficient criterion of truth then one wonders why he characterizes transcendental analytic to be a logic of truth. One answer, suggested by Prauss,[11] is that what Kant gives a theory of, in transcendental logic, is 'objective validity' which means 'truth value difference' (*Wahrheitsdifferenz*), i.e. the property of being either true or false—but not of truth as such. Hans Wagner has argued, as against Prauss's interpretation, that to the negative criterion of formal logic, Kant adds the transcendental-logical criterion, i.e. conformity to the fundamental principles (*Grundesetze*), but that also is not adequate to separate truth from falsity, which eventually calls for actual intuition.[12] I have argued, in an unpublished paper, that the idea of 'possible experience' provides the transcendental-logical criterion of truth. 'Possible experience' may be so construed as to contain within it *the actual* sensory perception as its core to which one then applies the *Analogies*, and then one arrives at the idea of an open-ended system of perceptions. A cognition is true if it belongs to 'possible experience', false if not. Without developing the theory here, and without defending this exegesis of Kant, I want to further maintain that this 'coherentist reconstruction of the notion of correspondence' brings us to the close vicinity of the Husserlian criterion of truth as confirmedness of a claim by the ongoing unfolding of its internal and external horizons. Husserl's notion of 'possible experience', then, would not be in terms of the Kantian Analogies as much as in terms of 'anticipations' constituting the horizons of the present experience—extending up to the horizon of all horizons, namely the World. The antinomies would then be traceable to treating the world as a thing, not as the ultimate horizon. Both the Kantian 'possible experience' and the Husserlian 'World' would be constituted by 'rule-governed' anticipations of the course of experience.

It is within such rule-governed anticipation that intentionality referring to a determinate object is possible. Here is the crucial Kantian text:

We have representations in us, and can become conscious of them. But however far this consciousness may extend, and however careful and accurate it may be, they still remain mere representations . . . . How, then, does it come about that we posit an object for these representations, and so, in addition to their subjective reality, as modifications, ascribe to them a kind of objective reality that I do not quite understand ['*ich weiß nicht, was für eine*'—here I depart from Norman K. Smith's translation 'some mysterious kind of . . .']. (A 197=B 242)

Kant's answer is:

. . . objective meaning cannot consist in the relation to another representation (of that which we desire to entitle object), for in that case the question again arises, how this latter representation goes out beyond itself . . . If we enquire what new character *relation to an object* confers upon our representations, what dignity they thereby acquire, we find that it results only in subjecting the representations to a rule, and so in necessitating us to connect them in some one specific manner. (A 197=B 242).

For Husserl, this rule is constitutive of the *noema;* truth requires that the implications of the *noema* are not contradicted by the unfolding of the course of our experiences. To further explore the vicinity which is now visible, we need to ask: what kind of theory of meaning did Kant have. We have already seen earlier that the X which Husserl locates in the texture of the *noema* appears as the X-transcendental object in the Kantian concept of object. The Husserlian 'Object' ('*Gegenstand*') is ambiguous as between the *Sinn* component of the *noema* and the real object out there, just as the Kantian 'objective validity' (*objektive Gültigkeit*) is ambiguous as between truth-value difference (*Wahrheitsdifferenz*) and truth (*Wahrheit*) (as opposed to falsity (*Falschheit*)).

Taking cues from both Kant and Husserl, we are then in a better position to understand transcendental idealism. 'Existence', like 'non-existence' is a *thetic* predicate of the noematic *Sinn*, a predicate that is 'merely the positing of a thing'—not a real predicate, i.e. a concept which can be added on to the concept of a thing.

NOTES

1. Edmund Husserl, *Briefwechsel* (Husserliana Dokumente III), ed. Karl Schuhmann in collaboration with Elisabeth Schuhmann (Dordrecht: Kluwer, 1994), vol. V, p. 4.
2. Ibid., vol. V, p. 14.

3. As here, references to Husserl's unpublished manuscripts will be made in the body of the text using the standard Husserl Archive designations.

4. Immanuel Kant, *Critique of Pure Reason*, tr. N.K. Smith, B 207. Subsequent references to this work will be made in the body of the text using the abbreviation *CPR*.

5. E. Cassierer (ed.), *Immanuel Kants Werke* (Berlin: Verlag Bruno Cassierer, 1922), vol. 4, pp. 520–3.

6. Ibid., vol. 8 (Anthropologie, 1.T.§7), p. 27.

7. K. Cramer, 'Einheit des Bewußtseins and Bewußtsein der Einheit', in Hans-Dieter Klein, *Systeme in Denken der Gegenwart* (Bonn: Bouvier, 1993), pp. 138–9.

8. Ibid., p. 130f.

9. Ibid., pp. 128–9.

10. Paul Ricoeur, *Husserl. An Analysis of His Phenomenology*, tr. Edward G. Ballard and Lester E. Embree (Evanston: Northwestern University Press, 1967), p. 181.

11. G. Prauss, 'Zum Wahrheitsproblem bei Kant', in G. Prauss (ed.), *Kant. Zur Deutung seiner Theorie von Erkennen und Handeln* (Köln: Kiepenheuer & Witsch, 1973), pp. 73–88.

12. H. Wagner, 'Zu Kants Auffassung bezüglich des Verhältnisses zwischen Formal- und Transzendentallogik,', *Kant-Studien*, 68, (1977), pp. 71–6.

part

two

chapter

eleven

The System and the Phenomena: The Kant-Interpretations of Nicolai Hartmann and P.F. Strawson*

In his *The Bounds of Sense, An Essay on Kant's Critique of Pure Reason* (London, 1966), P.F. Strawson undertakes the task of disentangling those doctrines of the *Critique* which depend on Kant's system—the transcendental idealism—from other analytical and descriptive theses contained in the same book but independent of that system. The obviously underlying attitude towards Kant's great work is that it has 'two faces'—one of which is not longer acceptable or even promising[1] and the other 'the blander, the more acceptable'[2] consisting of doctrines that remain 'fruitful and interesting'.[3] Strawson recognizes that in Kant's mind these two sets of theses were interdependent, or rather the analytic, descriptive theses were regarded as being dependent upon the thesis of transcendental idealism. Strawson's intention, however, is to show that Kant was mistaken in this, that the analytical, descriptive theses may be made to stand on their own and that transcendental idealism cannot be used to support them just because it is in itself an incoherent thesis and also because Kant has not been able to establish it by any convincing argument. Using the distinction made by Strawson in his *Individuals* (London, 1959), one may say that what he attempts to do is to separate the descriptive from the revisionary parts of the *Critique*.

*Jan Brokman and Jan Knopf (eds), *Konkrete Reflexion*. Festschrift für Hemann Wein Zum 60. Geburtstag. The Hague: M.Nijhoff, 1975.

Nearly half a century before Strawson's book on Kant, Nicolai Hartmann delivered a lecture before the Kantgesellschaft in Berlin in the year 1922 entitled 'Diesseits von Idealismus und Realismus. Ein Beitrag zur Scheidung des Geschichtlichen und Übergeschichtlichen in der Kantischen Philosophie.'[4] Transcendental idealism, Hartmann tells us, is only one standpoint amongst others, it has its point of strength and weakness. It belongs to history, and is not for us today, except for historians of philosophy. But the thought of every great philosopher, and so also that of Kant, contains elements which are supra-historical, which are beyond standpoints. Not all theses of Kant required the support of transcendental idealism; many of them are in fact indifferent to it and contribute nothing to it. There are others which even contradict it, directly or indirectly. The task of the time, in its relation to Kant, is to disentangle these two sets of elements. Hartmann's lecture is meant to be a prolegomena to such a work:

Was ich hier vorlegen möchte, ist das Program zu einem Kantbuche, das ich selbst nicht schreiben werde, das aber geschrieben werden muss, und das ich als eine Aufgabe unserer Zeit ansehe.[5]

Could Strawson's *The Bounds of Sense* be regarded as a major fulfillment of the task?

The purpose of this essay is to institute a brief comparison between these two attempts to disentangle two different strands—one descriptive, the other speculative, one supra-historical, the other historical, one neutral as against standpoints and the other determined by standpoints—of Kantian thought. The comparison, it is hoped, would contribute not merely (a) to a clear appreciation of the material issues in Kant interpretation involved (for we shall be dealing with two philosophers who come out of entirely different philosophical traditions, one from the Marburg Neo-Kantianism and phenomenology, and the other from the tradition of Oxford linguistic analysis), but also (b) to throw some light on issues far beyond the interests of a Kantian scholar, which tend to coverage on one central methodological question: how far may philosophical description be free from, and neutral as against, 'systems' and 'standpoints'.

II

According to Nicolai Hartmann, what is merely historical in Kantian thought consists in those elements which are determined by the metaphysical standpoint of transcendental idealism. They are 'historical' in the sense that in the history of philosophy transcendental idealism is one system amongst others with as much and as little claim to finality as the other systems. The supra-historical elements, on the other hand, are those (a) which are grounded in genuine philosophical *problems* and not in systems, and (b) which are descriptions of irrefutable phenomena. Thus, there are two kinds of 'supra-historical' elements in any great thinker: the *aporetik* and the phenomenological. These are not superseded in the course of history, but remain permanent acquisitions.[6]

The elements in Kant's philosophy which are, for Nicolai Hartmann, *not* supra-historical are the following:

1. The thesis that all objects are rooted in and conditioned by subjective functions.

2. The thesis that the *a priori* is formal and subjective and must be a function of synthesis, that—as a consequence—there are no material, contentual, objective *a priorities*.

3. The thesis that space and time are *nothing but* forms of intuition and do not characterize things in themselves. (The thesis is based, according to Nicolai Hartmann, on a failure to distinguish between the concept of 'being-in-itself' and the concept of the 'Unknowable' or the 'Irrational.' Since there may be irrational appearances [*Erscheinungen*] as much as knowable being-in-itself, the Kantian thesis that whatever is perceived in space and time cannot be thing-in-itself is not justified, unless one accepts the prior thesis that space and time, being *a priori*, must be subjective functions.)

4. The thesis that the fundamental principles (*Grundsätze*) are judgements, and not directly ontological principles of things themselves. This thesis, according to Nicolai Hartmann, leads to the absurd consequence that perception (of things) presupposes judgements.

5. The thesis that the possibility of synthetic *a priori* judgements is, in the long run, grounded in the transcendental subject or consciousness in general which, according to Nicolai Hartmann, is nothing but 'das ins Groβe, Allgemeine, Überempirische projizierte menschliche Subjekt.'[7] What, however, is needed for explaining the possibility of synthetic *a priori* judgements is not such a transcendental subject which is the unity of empirical subject and empirical object, but *a partial identity* of the principles of thought and principles of being.

6. The thesis of the distinction between 'appearance' and 'thing-it-itself' which in its peculiarly Kantian form certainly depends upon transcendental idealism.

7. The thesis of the primacy of practical reason which is invoked to save human freedom, but is really not necessary for that purpose.

Contrasted with these are the 'neutral', supra-historical elements which are independent of transcendental idealism and which would survive even if one rejects the Kantian system. These, according to Nicolai Hartmann, are the following:

1. There is first what Nicolai Hartmann calls 'the classical phenomenology of judgements' in the Introduction to the *Critique*, which includes the three-fold division of judgements into: the analytic-*a priori*, the synthetic-*a posteriori* and the synthetic *a priori*. This phenomenology constitutes what may be called the *questio facti* which then have to be subjected to the *questio juris* with regard to their possibility.

2. This is followed, in the Transcendental Aesthetics, by the phenomenology of space and time which brings out their priority to empirical data, their non-discursive and intuitive character, their singularity and uniqueness (there is but one space and one time), the givenness of their infinity and the way they are conditions of the possibility of empirical perception. These descriptive findings have to be kept apart from the system-dependent thesis of the ideality of space and time. Nicolai Hartmann proceeds to point out that an analogous phenomenology of the categories is missing in the *Critique*, and we have instead a dubious derivation of the categories from the table of judgements.[8]

3. Kant's rejection of empirical idealism and avowal of empirical realism is taken as a proof that Kant knew how to respect the weight of phenomena, more specifically, of the 'Phänomen der Realität'.[9] But after extending recognition to this phenomenon of reality, Kant wishes to reconcile it with the demand of the system and he can do this by holding that the same object which is real from the point of view of empirical consciousness is also ideal from the point of view of transcendental subjectivity. Such a move is required by the 'standpoint', not by the phenomena or the problems at hand.

4. A further element of phenomenological importance in Kantian philosophy is, according to Nicolai Hartmann, the doctrine of the two sources of knowledge. In Hartmann's words:

Dem Phänomen dieser Dualität kann man auf alle Fälle nicht entgehen, ohne das Grundproblem der realen Gegenstandserkenntnis zu verfehlen.[10]

Complementing this thesis of duality of the sources of knowledge is the famous Kantian thesis that concepts without intuitions are empty while intuitions with concepts are blind. For Nicolai Hartmann, this is but a recognition of the undeniable fact that truth is not a matter of logical structure alone but the agreement of our ideas with the things themselves.[11]

5. While one who is interested in the system, i.e. transcendental idealism, would look upon the doctrine of the Transcendental Unity of Apperception as containing the central point of the Analytic, one whose interest is in the problems would look elsewhere for the same. Nicolai Hartmann himself finds it in the section entitled, 'The Highest Principle of all Synthetic Judgements' (A 154–158; B 193–197). He rejects Kant's derivation of the principle as unhelpful and misleading, but considers the last of Kant's several formulations of the principle, namely that 'the conditions of the possibility of *experience* in general are likewise conditions of the *possibility of the objects of experience*, and that for this reason they have objective validity in a synthetic *a priori* judgement', as capable of being made self-evident as soon as one looks at it from the point of view of the problem of objectively valid synthetic *a priori* judgements. What the principle asserts, to account for the possibility of such judgements, is that there must be an identity of principles between the knowing mind and the known object, between the *Erkenntnisprinzipien* and the *Seinsprinzipien*—not a total identity between subject and object, which would be more than what *a priori* knowledge needs, but a *partial* identity of their *principles*. Such a formulation of the principle is 'von Kants eigenen *Systemvoraus setzungen unabhängig*'[12] and indifferent to both realism and idealism. Whereas idealism would reduce the principles of objectivity to the principles of subjectivity, realism would take the opposite course. It may be true that Kant himself chose the first move, but the content of the principles is totally 'indifferent' as against these possible metaphysical moves.

6. This partial identity between the principles of subjectivity and the principles of objectivity leaves room for an 'irrational remainder' in the object, and Nicolai Hartmann could therefore say that the concept of thing-in-itself is '*das beredeteste Zeugnis fur das Übergewicht der aporetischen Denkweise in Kant.*'[13] The object is knowable only to the extent in which its principles are identical with the principles of knowledge; beyond this limit, the object is unknowable. The positive and acceptable content then of the much maligned Kantian concept of Ding-an-sich lies in what Kant himself calls the 'transcendental object' which is nothing other than '*das verlängerte "empirische Objekt"*':[14] it is that 'part' of the object which lies outside the reaches of possible experience, and therefore also of the categories.

7. And finally to the Kantian reconciliation of freedom of will with the universal reign of the law of causality in the domain of nature: here again one has to disentangle the standpoint-dependent from what is independent of any standpoint. Nicolai Hartmann begins by distinguishing between two components of the Kantian doctrine of freedom: the idea of autonomy of the moral will and solution of the causal antinomy.[15] Regarding the first, that the autonomy of the moral law shall be grounded in the autonomy of practical reason is another manifestation of the Kantian transcendental idealism; but that the moral law itself is autonomous over and against the laws of nature is an insight which no moral philosophy can deny. The doctrine of the autonomy of the moral law has then to be kept separate from the doctrine of the freedom of the moral will as self-legislative. This latter doctrine, while depending upon transcendental idealism, has also provided the strongest inner motive for idealism. If moral law is autonomous, if the autonomy of the moral law is a radically different sort of autonomy than that of the natural laws, and furthermore if the former sort of autonomy, by its very essential nature, directs itself towards a will that is free—then the freedom of will may be derived from the autonomy of the moral law and the central thought of the second *Critique* may be salvaged from the idealistic metaphysics into which it has been inserted. Likewise, Kant's solution of the 'third antinomy' aims at showing how freedom is compatible with universal determinism: freed from the system, this solution, according to Nicolai Hartmann, rests on the insight that two totally heterogenous forms of determination coexist in the same world, a thesis which has no intrinsic connection with the concept of nature as mere appearance.

To sum up: what Nicolai Hartmann rejects is the Kantian doctrine of subject in general (*Subjekt überhaupt*), the 'prescription' of laws through reason, the synthetic construction of objects by the understanding, the transcendental ideality of space, time and the categories, and the concept of the moral will as self-legislative. What he recognizes as elements of undeniable and permanent phenomenological value are the phenomenology of judgements, the phenomenology of space and time, the notion of *a priori* freed from formalism, subjectivism and intellectualism, the duality of the sources of knowledge, the empirical realism, the concept of the transcendental object, the doctrine of the *a priority* and autonomy of the moral law and the coexistence of freedom and causal determination in the same world.

III

Let us now turn to Strawson's project of disentangling what he calls the 'two faces' of the *Critique*. Amongst those elements of the *Critique* which Strawson wants to set aside as dispensable, the following may be noted:

1. There is first the overwhelmingly psychological idiom used by Kant in ascribing all necessities to the nature of human faculties.[16]

2. There is next what Strawson calls 'the associated picture of receiving and ordering apparatus of the mind'.[17]

3. Central to all this is, of course, the doctrine of transcendental idealism which, Strawson argues, Kant has never substantially proved but which he often uses to support these which could stand on their own.[18]

4. It has been commonplace amongst critics of Kant, in recent times, to point out—and Strawson joins this group—that many of Kant's theses depend upon the state of scientific knowledge of his time, more specifically on Euclidean geometry, Newtonian physics and Aristotelian logic. If the theory of space depends upon first, the doctrine of the categories depends on the other two; to the extent they are so dependent, these doctrines need to be relegated to history of thought, but to the extent they, or certain components of them, may be salvaged from such dependence, they may form parts of those Kantian theses which are still acceptable and useful.

5. The doctrine of synthesis as a story in transcendental psychology is rejected by Strawson on the ground that we can claim no empirical knowledge of its truth. It is 'one of those aberrations into which Kant's explanatory model inevitably led him.'[19] The transcendental deduction as 'a description of the transcendental workings of the subjective faculties whereby experience is produced' is set aside in favour of the deduction as 'an argument about the implications of the concept of experience in general'.[20] The doctrine of the transcendental unity of apperception, in so far as this doctrine is connected with the doctrine of synthesis and the doctrine of the subjective constitution of the world, is set aside as belonging neither to empirical psychology nor to analytical philosophy of mind, but to 'the imaginary subject of transcendental psychology'.[21]

6. The transcendental interpretation of the *a priori*, the thesis that the *a priori* must be 'within' us, is 'ignored' by Strawson[22] and sought to be replaced by what he calls a more 'austere interpretation' of the concept.

7. The connection between belief in supersensible reality and the idea of moral freedom has not been established by Kant,[23] and Strawson sees no logical connection between them. In fact, even if freedom is a property of supersensible beings, unless such beings are in some sense shown to be identical with us humans, that freedom would be irrelevant for our moral situation, and yet—according to Strawson—Kant has not shown how the two are related.[24]

However, Strawson's book is also a remarkable attempt to extract from the *Critique* a set of theses which can supposedly stand on their own independently of transcendental idealism and its connected doctrines, and to reformulate and interpret them accordingly. The most important of them may be stated as follows:

1. The Kantian dualism between concepts and intuitions is regarded by Strawson as a 'fundamental duality, inescapable in any philosophical thinking about experience';[25] but, at the same time, the Kantian thesis has to be freed from the psychological idiom of faculties.[26] What remains after such purification is the distinction between general concepts and particular instances; and any concept of experience must have room for experience of particulars as well as for recognizing and classifying them as such and such.

2. The Kantian dualism between the *a priori* and the empirical is likewise accepted, but only after the transcendental and subjective interpretations of the concept of *a priori* have been replaced by 'a relatively austere interpretation'.[27] By '*a priori*' structures are now meant those which are indispensable for any intelligible conception of experience, and the empirical are 'those less general ideas corresponding to features of our experience which we can abstract from without imperiling the entire structure of the conception of experience itself.'[28]

3. Freed from the subjective and the 'epistemological slant',[29] the major part of the Kantian philosophy of space and time survives. That they are forms of intuition means now nothing other than that space and time are the forms of particularity; that they are *a priori* means that any concept of experience that we can render intelligible to ourselves would be the concept of experience of particulars in space and time, however otherwise these particulars and their relationships may differ. That there is one space and one time means that a single spatio-temporal framework is needed for such an experience. There is nothing in these theses as such to suggest the transcendental ideality of space and time.

4. Though Strawson sees the way Kant's metaphysical deduction of the categories depends upon the Aristotelian logic's table of

judgements which can hardly be regarded as beyond reproach, he does nevertheless make a heroic effort to save what can be saved from the Kantian argument. If the issue concerns the minimum that the logician must have to recognize in the way of logical forms, Strawson is led to the formally atomic proposition in which a one or more place predicate is applied to one or more specific objects of reference. The distinction then between particular objects and universal characters seems basic to any logic, and may be used to derive what concepts or categories must be true of any object of experience at all. At least this is advanced as the bare outline of an argument which could very well replace Kant's metaphysical deduction, without completely upsetting his doctrines in the deduction and the Principles.

5. As with metaphysical deduction, so also in the case of transcendental deduction: while rejecting the Kantian doctrine of synthesis, Strawson yet wants to salvage from it an argument about the implications of the concept of experience in general. The most important of these implications are: first, that a temporal series of experiences must belong to one consciousness; second, in order so to belong to a single consciousness, the members of the series must exhibit a certain rule-governed connectedness such that they constitute experiences of a single objective world; third, the concept of an experience of an objective world requires the distinction between the objective order of how things are and the subjective order of how experiences of those things are.

6. Though rejecting transcendental idealism with its associated doctrines of synthesis, Strawson nevertheless attempts a very positive assessment of the Kantian doctrine of the transcendental unity of apperception. The Kantian thesis that 'The "I think" must necessarily be able to accompany all my representations' (B 131) is now seen as the contention that 'experience must be such as to provide room for the thought of experience itself.'[30] And the possibility of this self-reflexiveness is entailed by the possibility of distinguishing between the subjective order of experiences and the objective order of the things that are experienced. Thus, the reflexivity thesis and the condition of objectivity are shown to be interconnected. Transcendental self-consciousness in the sense of this necessary self-reflexiveness of experience provides the condition for the possibility of ascription of empirical states of consciousness to oneself, i.e. of empirical self-consciousness, and may well be regarded as being 'transcendental' in this, not altogether un-Kantian, sense.

7. Finally, the Kantian limitation of knowledge is admitted, but not in the form in which Kant, under the influence of his system, formulated it. Thus writes Strawson: 'We can even and should, find room in philosophy for a concept which performs at least some of the negative functions of the Kantian concept of the noumenal.'[31] It is surely dogmatic to hold that reality is completely comprehensible by our conceptual scheme, as much dogmatic as the Kantian thesis that our conceptual scheme has no point of contact with reality at all. We need not go into the incoherencies Strawson points out in Kant's own version of the unknown and unknowable thing-in-itself—these incoherencies have been pointed out by critics ever since Kant propounded his doctrine. What Strawson will concede is that the nature of reality is not exhausted by the kinds of knowledge we have of it; and yet he insists: 'we do not have to deny that we know things of some kind about some kinds of things there really are'.[32] There may well be kinds of reality we know nothing about.

To sum up then: Kant's metaphysics of experience contains at least the following theses which are 'acceptable' by themselves and need no support from his transcendental idealism. Experience is of a world consisting of spatio-temporal particulars characterized by general features. The particulars belong to, and are individuated in, one comprehensible spatio-temporal framework. In order that experience may be of such a world, the temporal succession of the experiences must be distinguishable from the objective succession of things that are experienced. Furthermore, the experiences must belong to one consciousness, and they must have a necessary possibility of self-reflexiveness. Finally, certain principles of permanence and causality must govern the objective world. These constitute the core of Kant's description of the most general features of any objective experience. But there is no *a priori* guarantee that this *a priori* conceptual structure must fully exhaust the nature of reality.

IV

Striking similarities and differences between the Kant-interpretations of Nicolai Hartmann and Strawson should already have been obvious.

1. Whereas Nicolai Hartmann speaks of the 'supra-historical' and 'phenomenological' elements in Kant's philosophy, Strawson wants to isolate the 'conceptual' and 'analytical' arguments in Kant. What both wish to reject are the system-dependent elements, especially

those dependent on transcendental idealism. Nicolai Hartmann calls them 'historische' and 'standpunktliche' elements; Strawson calls them 'speculative' and also elements of a 'transcendental story', etc. Although Nicolai Hartmann wants to purge Kantian thought of what he calls historical elements in it, he does not make an attempt to show in what way those elements he discards are dependent on the historical intellectual situation in which Kant thought; all that he shows is dependence on transcendental idealism. But transcendental idealism, like any other system, is not a merely historical phenomenon, it is also a *recurrent* phenomenon. On the contrary, many of those Kantian theses which Nicolai Hartmann singles out as being 'phenomenological'—like what he calls the phenomenology of judgements would seem to be dependent, at least in the way Kant formulates the distinctions between 'analytic' and 'synthetic', on the state of logic in his time. Little does he show his awareness of the way Kantian philosophy depends on its triple historical foundations: Aristotelian logic, Euclidean geometry and Newtonian physics. By saying this, I do not wish to suggest that those elements of Kantian thought—like the philosophy of geometry, the table of categories, the Analogies—which depend on these historical foundations have to be expurgated; there are other means of taking care of this overall objection to Kant. To Strawson should be given the credit of at least having made a painstaking effort to 'save' something of Kant's philosophy of geometry, metaphysical deduction and the Analogies. One may even be more heroic, and contend that the three 'historical' disciplines, though supplemented by modern developments in logic, geometry and physics, nevertheless constitute undeniable cores of those and are still as valid as before of a limited segment, a central core, of human thought and experience—so that the Kantian theses, dependent on them, are not simply to be rejected but ought to be put in their proper perspectives.

2. Neither of the two want to reject metaphysics altogether. Both find in Kant a certain sort of metaphysics which is different from speculative, transcendent metaphysics. However, the sorts of metaphysics they ascribe to Kant are different. The descriptive elements which Nicolai Hartmann has singled out are not for him metaphysical, they are rather called phenomenological. Nevertheless, in his view:

Der Gegensatz, Kritik—Metaphysik' ist gar nicht Kantisch. Wie hätte Kant sonst die Kritik der reinen Vernunft als ein Prolegomenon künftiger

Metaphysik meinen können! Es gibt Probleme, die ihrem Wesen nach metaphysisch sind. Kant bezeichnet sie als die unlösaren und doch zugleich unabweisbaren.[33]

There is, according to Nicolai Hartmann, a 'natural metaphysics of problems' which Kant does not seek to demolish. But there is another sort of metaphysics which consists in giving to these problems solutions by force: this is the 'dogmatic' metaphysics which the *Critique* certainly attacks.[34]

While there is no doubt that, in Kant's own view, metaphysical problems have an inevitability about them, that they spring from the very nature of human reason—it is not at once clear how Nicolai Hartmann can make room for *this sort of* inevitability of metaphysical problems after he has got rid of the Kantian transcendental idealism and all its other implications, including the belief in a supersensible reality and the thesis that sensible nature is phenomenal. The concept of thing-in-itself which Hartmann is willing to admit, which is but the concept of '*des verlängerte "empirische Objekt"*' does not allow of a distinction between problems about objects that are soluble and problems that are, in principle, insoluble.

Strawson, however, in continuation of the tradition laid down by Paton, looks upon the Aesthetic and the Analytic as together constituting a 'Metaphysics of experience'. Using a concept familiarized by him in his earlier book *Individuals*, we may say that what he finds in Kant is a descriptive metaphysics whose purpose is 'to show what the limiting features must be of any notion of experience which we can make intelligible to ourselves.'[35] In the words of *Individuals*, such a metaphysics describes 'the actual structure of our thought about the world'.[36] This structure, or at least a core of it, has no history: 'there are categories and concepts which, in their most fundamental character, change not at all.' In this sense, the structures discovered by descriptive metaphysics may well claim to be '*überzeitlich*' and '*standpunktfrei*'.

But it is not clear whether these are structure of the world we experience, or of our experience of the world, or of our concept of any possible experience of any possible world. Strawson himself speaks of them as 'structures of experience', also as 'structures of ideas in terms of which alone we can make intelligible to ourselves the idea of experience of the world',[37] 'the conceptual structure',[38] and 'the intuitions'. For Nicolai Hartmann, this shows that knowledge, and hence truth, is not merely a case of logical coherence of ideas, but needs empirical confirmation in intuition. For Strawson, any experience of an objective world must be of particulars as characterized by general features. Just as language has both 'referring' and 'descriptive' components, so our experience consists in 'awareness in experience of particulars' (which Kant calls 'intuition') and 'capacities for recognition and classification' (which Kant calls 'understanding'). Intuition provides the 'occasions for the exercise and development of these capacities'.[42] It is striking that while admonishing Kant's psychological idiom, Strawson yet speaks of 'capacities'. How exactly this talk of 'capacities' is to be interpreted save by way of their possible reduction to their actual exercise on appropriate occasions, if we are to be consistent with that rejection of the psychological idiom, is not clear.

5. Transcendental idealism is rejected by both Nicolai Hartmann and Strawson, but Strawson shows a more sustained effort to *understand* the thesis of transcendental idealism. For the purposes of this essay, it is not necessary to go into the various senses of transcendental idealism which he distinguishes and to ask, if there is not any other sense in which the Kantian thesis may be understood. He is certainly at his best in his efforts to salvage the Kantian doctrine of the transcendental Unity of Apperception. Nicolai Hartmann brushes it aside in a rather cavalier fashion:

Es ist das ins Große, Allgemeine, überempirische projizierte menschliche Subjekt.[43]

Transcendental Apperception is only an analogical extension of the phenomenon of empirical self-consciousness. What is still more: with this notion of transcendental self-consciousness, transcendental idealism falls.

... in den Atavismus der von ihm so heftig bekämpften dogmatischen Systeme, in denen die Fiktion des intellectus infinitus, archetypus oder divinus dieselbe überbauende Rolle gespielt hat.[44]

One of the most fruitful achievements of Strawson's Kant book is to have offered an interpretation of this key Kantian concept which takes it outside of the system of transcendental idealism, and yet retains the two essential functions Kant ascribes to it: its function as the condition of the possibility of empirical self-consciousness, and its function as the condition of the possibility of objective experience. Besides it also takes into account what may be regarded as a 'phenomenon', namely the necessary possibility of self-reflexivity of experience.

Both reject the usual version of the Kantian thing itself, the unknown and the unknowable, supersensible 'noumenon', and yet both want to retain something of the Kantian limitation to human knowledge, and in this there would seem to be a close agreement in principle. By collapsing the two Kantian concepts of 'thing in itself' and 'transcendental object', Nicolai Hartmann understands, as we have seen, the noumenon as but 'the extended empirical object' by which may be meant those aspects of the object (of experience) which fall outside the reaches of human knowability. But why should any object or any aspect of it fall, in principle, outside the reaches of human knowledge if the fault, the limiting factors, do not lie in the structure of the human mind? Since Hartmann does not want to reject, unlike Strawson, the psychological idiom of faculties altogether, he could say that the limiting factors lie in the structure of the human cognitive faculties, i.e., in both sensibility and understanding. But neither space and time, nor the categories are, for him, merely subjective forms of the human mind, they are also forms of thing themselves. The fact then that we perceive whatever we do in space and time and conceive of all objects that we think of under one or more of the categories does not as such entail any limitation of the range of human knowledge, for these forms are also forms of being. For Nicolai Hartmann, then, the limitation lies in the fact that the principles of human knowledge and the principles of being do not coincide at all points. Space, time and the categories represent those points of coincidence; beyond them, there is the unknown and the unknowable which is still to be understood as an 'extension' of what is known and knowable. Strawson concedes that 'the conception of reality is not bounded by the types of sensible experience we actually enjoy',[45] and allows to the noumenal the modest, negative meaning of 'those aspects of reality, if any, of which we have not, as things are, any conception.'[46] But at the same time, he also emphasizes that the formal concepts like 'individual', 'identity', 'relation' and 'property' would surely continue to have 'new types of employment or exemplification' to altogether new types of things or new aspects of the familiar world. Strawson's then is a weaker version than Nicolai Hartmann's.

V

In the above section, I have drawn attention to certain central issues that arise in connection with disentangling some of the Kantian theses from the general context of Kant's transcendental idealism. These issues revolve round the question: to what extent, even if we reject transcendental idealism, can we altogether dispense with his psychological idiom and yet ascribe the salvaged theses to Kant? Is it not rather the case that the reference to the subjective pole is a necessary aspect of the structure of experience being described, so that Kant may not be simply expressing the supposedly objective structures in an arbitrarily chosen psychological language, although the particular type of psychological idiom he chooses, for example the language of faculties, may have been historically conditioned. The picture of consciousness *producing*, through its spontaneous acts of synthesis, the world of experience may be a misleading metaphor, but the picture of the world from which reference to consciousness has been eliminated or at most in which consciousness has been assigned a place as one of the items amongst others, is an equally misleading theoretical construction. Experience shows a necessary pole of subjectivity as much as a necessary pole of objectivity, and the subjective pole shows besides a necessary possibility of self-reflexiveness.

In this concluding section, I want to raise several interconnected methodological questions. We have followed the attempts of two philosophers, coming from two entirely different philosophical traditions, to dissect the Kantian philosophy into two sets of theses: one set would consist in a number of theses that are independent of Kant's overall systems, that are grounded in descriptive phenomena which no philosophy of experience can afford to overlook, that in effect are likely to survive the fluctuating destiny of systems through history; the other set consists in theses that are system-dependent, that operate with speculative and imaginative models and that may well be abandoned at no great risk. The questions that I wish to raise are: is this sort of dissection possible in the case of any great philosopher? Is it not possible to say that every philosophical *system* undoubtedly contains a phenomenological core, in other words, that it is based on some descriptively valid foundation? If this question be answered in the affirmative, one may go on to ask, further, whether the speculative flight or system construction does not proceed from the descriptive base in accordance with a certain informal logic? To put the last question in a different manner, does the speculative philosopher make use of the descriptive-phenomenological core in a wildly arbitrary manner, constructing 'imaginative stories', possibly to satisfy repressed unconscious desires, or are there certain common patterns that are discernible in all such movements of thought and/or imagination? It seems to me that all these questions have to be answered in the affirmative.[47] It is true, to anticipate a possible objection, that a pure interpretation-free description is an ideal, for all that philosophers wish to be accepted as system-free, uninterpreted data are not truly so. In Strawson's case, this is particularly so in the way he accepts the Principle of Significance (which is but a Kantian version of the positivistic principle of verifiability), which is far from being descriptively grounded. A descriptive philosophy cannot operate with a general criterion of significance. However, as Strawson himself remarks in the Introduction to the *Individuals*, 'the task of descriptive metaphysics . . . has constantly to be done over again.'[48] In Nicolai Hartmann's case, likewise, the warnings against idealism and the emphasis on the phenomenon of reality, on Realitätsgegebenheit, is unexceptionable, but is he not also operating—not unlike the idealist—with a theoretical prejudice in favour of realism? What I am trying to draw attention to is that like idealism realism is also a theory, and that like realism idealism also contains a descriptive phenomenological core. A truly descriptive philosophy which would be 'diesseits von Realismus und Idealismus' would be 'neutral' as against both and seek to capture the phenomena on which they both are founded. This would lead to the last of the questions formulated above, and here, along with various patterns of the movement of speculative thought, it would be particularly instructive to look for the decisive roles of 'models and metaphors'.

NOTES

1. P.F. Strawson, *The Bounds of Sense, An Essay on Kant's 'Critique of Pure Reason'* (London: Methuen, 1966) (henceforth referred to as *BS*), p. 16.

2. *BS*, p. 19.

3. *BS*, p. 16.

4. Originally published in *Kant-Studien*, 29, 1924; now reprinted in Nicolai Hartmann, *Kleinere Schriften* (Bd. II, Berlin: Walter de Gruyter, 1947). All references to this essay are to the paginations in this latter volume.

5. *Kleine Schriften* II (henceforth referred to as *KS*), p. 279.

6. Cf. Nicolai Hartmann, 'Der philosophische Gedanke und seine Geschichte', *Abhandlungen der Preussischen Akademie der Wissenschaften*, 1936, Phil.-Hist. Klasse, Nr. 5. Now reprinted in *KS*.

7. *KS*, p. 286.

8. *KS*, p. 293.
9. *KS*, p. 294.
10. *KS*, p. 297.
11. *KS*, p. 299.
12. *KS*, p. 303.
13. *KS*, p. 307.
14. *KS*, p. 289.
15. *KS*, p. 312.
16. *BS*, p. 19.
17. *BS*, p. 22.
18. *BS*, p. 91.
19. *BS*, p. 32.
20. *BS*, p. 88.
21. *BS*, p. 97.
22. *BS*, p. 49.
23. *BS*, p. 241.
24. *BS*, pp. 247, 249.
25. *BS*, 20.
26. *BS*, p. 30.
27. *BS*, p. 49.
28. *BS*, pp. 49–50.
29. *BS*, p. 60.
30. *BS*, p. 107.
31. *BS*, p. 42.
32. *BS*, p. 262.
33. *KS*, p. 283.
34. *KS*, p. 284.
35. *BS*, p. 24.
36. P.F. Strawson, *Individuals. An Essay in Descriptive Metaphysics* (Anchor Books edition, 1963), p. xiv.
37. *BS*, p. 15.
38. *BS*, p. 18.
39. *BS*, p. 44.
40. *KS*, p. 285.
41. *BS*, p. 68.
42. *BS*, p. 48.
43. *KS*, p. 286.
44. *KS*, p. 288.
45. *BS*, p. 269.

46. *BS*, p. 269.
47. I have worked out some of these patterns in my 'Philosophical Description', in Kalidas Bhattacharyya (ed.), *Philosophical Papers*, First Series (Santiniketan, India, 1969). This essay is reprinted in this volume as chapter 20.
48. *Individuals*, p. xiv.

chapter

twelve

Phenomenology and History*

I n this essay, I will be concerned with only one question, namely
whether history can be a phenomenon for phenomenology? I
think this fundamental question, and the apories connected with
it have simply been bypassed by phenomenologists who, *qua*
phenomenologists, have taken history seriously. In order to bring out
these apories, I would need to further clarify the question by specifying
the senses in which the crucial terms in the question have to be taken.

First, by 'phenomenology' I mean 'transcendental phenomenology', i.e. a phenomenology which is not simply ontic in Heidegger's
sense which describes the structures of the world, but which rather
describes the structures and contents either of the constituting consciousness or of the *Dasein:* in the former case, we have transcendental phenomenology; in the latter case, fundamental ontology. Both,
for me, are transcendental.

By 'phenomenon', I mean not ontic structures, states of affairs,
events or processes which can be observed and described, but such
structures and contents as belong either to the transcendentally
purified consciousness, i.e. consciousness purified of ontic naivities
and self-understandings in terms of received opinions and beliefs,
or to the *Dasein's* being-in-the-world understood purely ontologically

*Originally presented as a lecture at the meeting of the *Internationale Institut de
Philosophie*, Helsinki, 1995.

and not in terms of an anthropological, psychological or sociological theory of man.

What do I mean by 'history'? In this case, I need to recollect a number of distinctions which are an inheritance of standard phenomenological wisdom. To begin with, an obvious distinction needs to be made between 'time' and 'history'. Being temporal is a necessary but not sufficient condition for being historical. Events and processes of nature are temporal, but we do not want to say that they are historical. One may begin by saying that only what pertains to human existence in general, to the human world, society and culture, has history. Nature may be said to have history—as my Gottingen teacher Carl F.V. Weizsäcker says—in so far as it is nature for man, for example in so far as it is the subject matter of natural science which is historical in the straightforward sense of being a human accomplishment. It is then appropriate to say that culture is historical, and that nature is also historical in so far as it enters into culture, or as Marx said, has been humanized.

Another very familiar distinction is between history as a science (as what is done by the historians) and history as the subject matter of this science. Currently there is a tendency to obliterate this distinction. For an illustration of this tendency, let me quote Gadamer:

Wahrend der Gegenstand der Naturwissenschaften sich idealitar wohl bestimmen lässt als das, was in der vollendeten Naturerkenntnis erkannt wäre, is es sinnlos, von einer vollendeten Geshichterkenntnis zu sprechen, und eben deshalb ist auch Rede von einem Gegenstand an sich, dem diese Forschung gilt, im letzten Sinne nicht einlösbar.[1]

I think this view is right in emphasizing the historicity of historical research, but wrong in rejecting the simple idea that history, as a science, has its object domain in the same way that natural science has. One way of recovering this simple idea is to emphasize that there is an everyday experience of history preceding history as a science, analogously as the everyday experience of nature precedes the sciences of nature.[2]

This last distinction prepares us for another one that has played an important role in contemporary phenomenology, namely the distinction between history (in either of the two above-mentioned senses) and historicity (Geschichlichkeit). For my present purpose, it will suffice if we focus upon two usages of this term, one by Heidegger and the other by Husserl. This distinction between history and historicity is closely connected with, but not identical with, the distinction between time and temporality. This latter distinction goes back to Husserl who distinguished between objective time in which events occur and enduring entities endure, and the temporality of inner, phenomenologically 'reduced' consciousness. In the latter, Husserl discovered the 'originary temporal field' consisting of primordial impressions, retention and protention, and whose unity is also called by him the concrete living present which is caught up in a continuity of iterated modifications. Out of this perpetual flux of the living present, reproduction and recollection constitute, through idealization, an objective temporal order existing in itself to whose positions I can return again and again by way of identification. As has been by now well recognized, Husserl came more and more to be convinced that the time-constituting consciousness cannot itself be temporal (for there would otherwise be an infinite regress), and even came to hold that the time-constituting consciousness cannot in itself be grasped attentively, but is grasped only as 'quasi-inserted in time.[3]

II

What precisely was Husserl's concept of history and historicity? Even when, in the texts from the time of the Krisis,[4] Husserl comes to focus upon history, he is not interested in the 'external' history (of historians), in the history of facts, or singular events. A mere factual history is, for him, incomprehensible. His concern is rather with 'inner history', but more specifically with four different, though interrelated themes. Placing the external, factual history within brackets, Husserl focuses upon the history of meanings. This is what he calls 'intentional history' which is concerned with sedimentations of meanings as they must have been constituted successively. It is not a question of when the meaning constitution took place and by whom it was initiated, but of how it came about, of what it consists in, and in what constitutive order. This is the sort of work Husserl does in the Krisis in the chapter on Galileo, a sort of archaeology.

This brings me to the second of Husserl's concerns with regard to history: sedimentations of meanings make a tradition. Much of Husserl's concern with history is to understand how a tradition comes about. What Husserl does in the text on 'Origin of Geometry' is to show that geometry is a tradition and how, depending on what conditions, this tradition could have come about.[5] But geometrical propositions, in Husserl's earlier, more well-known theory, are ideal objects. At first, ideal objects were said to be a-temporal. Later on, this a-temporality was construed as omni-temporality. Now we are told that ideal objects themselves are historical. The idealities arise out of the life-world: '*Ihre bleibende Seinsart: nicht nur eine beweglicher Fortgang von Erwerben zu Erwerben, sondern eine kontinuierliche Synthesis, in der alle Erwerbe fortgelten . . .*'⁶ But in this process the 'original evidence' underlying the ideal object's coming into being is lost in and through the tradition. This naturally raises the question of the identity of an ideal object. Husserl wants to preserve identity, while allowing that each thinker from within his own historical perspective, has a different thought about it. The ideal object nevertheless, carries with it its original sense of being an ideality. There is here a seeming contradiction. While not willing to abandon the earlier thesis of ideal objects, Husserl will nevertheless historicize them. How can he have it both ways? We now have a new conception of history. History, in the strict sense, is history of ideal meanings (not of brute singular facts).

This leads me to Husserl's third theme: the idea of the '*a priori of history*'. The *a priori* of history, he tells us, is that 'all entities are comprehended within historical having-been-ness and change, or in their essential and appropriate being as tradition and being-tradited'. Jacques Derrida comments:

Howsoever large our ignorance of actual history may be, we know *a priori* that every culturally being—present—and along with it every scientifically being-present—in its totality implies the totality of the past.⁷

The historical 'now', from the very beginning, is the irreducible place and movement of this totalization and traditionalization. This historical now is grounded in the living present, not of one transcendental ego but of 'the being with and through one another' of a community of egos, i.e. 'our present', which Husserl tells us, is 'historically, in itself, the first'.⁸ Every possible culture and tradition must conform to this *a priori* condition. Finally, history in the sense of '*die lebendige Bewegung des Miteinander und Ineinander von ursprünglicher Sinnbildung und Sinnsedimentierung*'⁹ (in which all the above three concepts are implicated) is possible because each ego (not merely the empirical ego but also the transcendental ego) is historical.

This brings me to the fourth concept, i.e. the concept of transcendental historicity, or the historicity of the transcendental, constitutive subject. Stripped of all Husserlian technical jargon, what this means is that the life of consciousness of an I, even after phenomenological reduction, is a temporally-flowing, yet standing, 'standing-strömend' 'streaming' in the sense of being a flux, but also standing in the sense that at any moment it is a unity of its own history (for example, 'that history is my history') in which its past is integrated. The I, called transcendental ego, as constituting meanings takes up meanings from the already constituted world and advances it by its own being-to-gether-with the other egos.

Thus, although Husserl's original perspective—his essentialism, his search for necessary truths, his ontology of ideal objects, and his severe critique of historicism—seems to have excluded all possibility of a serious concern with history, the actual development of his thought turned out to be otherwise. The streaming, intentional consciousness is recognized to be historical, the life-world turns out to be the concrete historical world with its traditions and ever-changing meaning structures. The transcendental foundation of all knowledge and experience, the ego and its life of consciousness, becomes a historically developing process.

III

Let me now turn to Heidegger. In his Marburg lectures of 1919–20, Heidegger distinguished between several senses of 'history': history as a science, history as the domain of enquiry, history as the merely past, history as tradition, and history as a unique decisive event. Of these, he regards the first, second, and third as being inauthentic, derivative and not *urprünglich* in relation to concrete existence. The fourth can be either authentic or inauthentic. The fifth is the most *urprünglich*. The two authentic conceptions of history, for Heidegger, are tradition and the unique decisive event in one's life. For the latter, he cites the locution 'this person has had a sad history'. In the authentic sense, tradition is not simply a past accumulation of accomplishments, but is also having this accumulation as a component of one's self-consciousness in the present. In this sense, historical consciousness is not knowledge of history (as recorded in books) nor simply knowledge of the objective past, but rather is the awareness of the way the past, as sedimented structure of meanings, is present as constitutive of ones self-understanding. A people, he tells us, may have history (as *Vergangenheit*, as past), and yet may have no history in the sense that their past does not play a role in their mode of being.[10]

In *Being and Time,* we are presented with a slightly different set of meanings of 'history'. These are: (i) what is past, whether as active now or simply as not-active; (ii) what arises out of the past and runs through the present, a *Wirkungszusammenhang;* (iii) the totality of entities which changes in time, but excluding nature; and (iv) the inherited tradition. Putting these four together, Heidegger characterizes history as the specific happening, giving itself in time, of existing *Dasein* (*'das in der Zeit sich begebende spezifische Geschehen des existierenden Dasein's'*).[11] All the four meanings relate to human existence, and in all four there is a specifically determining role of the past. These two features point towards the nature of historicity. Originally historical is the *Dasein;* secondarily historical are the inner worldly entities, including equipments, which belonged to the *Dasein's* world. What is past is the world. An entity belonging to a past world may still be present, but such an entity possesses a character of being past and historical inasmuch as it belonged to and comes from a world which has been as the world of a *Dasein* which was there. *Dasein* and only *Dasein,* has and can have history, because its being is characterized by historicity.

The historicity of *Dasein* does not mean that a transcendental world-less subject is historical. The historicity of *Dasein* is also, and essentially, the historicity of its world. The mode of being of *Dasein* is being towards death and so future-oriented. History, therefore, cannot begin with the present. What is to be an object of history has to be *chosen* from the perspective of a possibility for *Dasein.* In concrete working out of its temporality, *Dasein* chooses its own fate. But *Dasein* is also essentially being-with-others, not a solipsistic ego. Thus, there is a common fate, or destiny, which *Dasein* can return to as the ground of authentic possibility of the community. Thus *Dasein's* choice of its own possibility is the primary source of historical meaning and coherence. This meaning does not derive from the objective process of historical development, but from *Dasein's,* the community's, the *Volk's*[12] choice of its own destiny drawing upon the resources of its own tradition.

Gadamer has maintained that Heidegger's philosophy of history was basically *'eine radikale Abkehr von Idealismus',*[13] guided by the belief that 'life' is irrational, that experience of history is not conscious-ness of history, that history is not fundamentally the object of a cognitive consciousness.[14] We also have to recognize that in spite of deep differences in their thinking, there is a common philosophical move on the parts of Husserl and Heidegger. History as science, and history as a succession of interconnected temporal human events both presuppose a more fundamental structure called historicity. For Husserl, this structure belongs to the constituting transcendental subjectivity and, for Heidegger, it characterizes the mode of being of *Dasein*. Furthermore, for Husserl, historicity requires intersubjectivity, for Heidegger being-with-others. In Husserl's thinking, historicity begins with the present, and reaches back into the past, i.e. the constituted tradition, and into the future. In Heidegger's thinking, historicity centres around future possibilities from which a community chooses in accordance with its past tradition. For both, phenomenology provides an access to history, and a new kind of thinking about history. Nevertheless, Husserl's thinking is closer to the traditional inasmuch as he ascribes a *telos* to history, which is total self-knowledge on the part of the transcendental ego, whereas Heidegger's thinking dispenses with any such goal for history in general, for authentic history is constituted by the community's choice of its own possibility.

IV

For all such thinking about history, I would like to raise one fundamental question: is history, or even historicity, a *phenomenon*? It can be claimed that unlike temporality, history is not given to us in certain experiences which have 'historical' written all over them. If historicality is not experienced by us as a phenomenon, how then do we think about it in phenomenology? To construct a transcendental argument of the sort (which both Husserl and Heidegger do): 'History is possible because of the historicity of . . .' remotely sounds like Voltaire's parody: 'Opium makes you sleep, because it has soporific power'. The point of this comparison is that we seem to have no idea of historicity save through our idea of history. Or, do we? How different is the argument in the case of 'time': 'Time is possible because of the temporality of . . .'? Do we likewise have an idea of temporality independent of the idea of time? I want to maintain that we have an experience of temporality (as also of time) in a manner in which we experience neither history nor historicity. History is a construct, historicity is a construct to account for that construct.

So let me take up the question: how do we experience history? I shall consider various answers to this question given by phenomenologists. These are: by experiencing historical entities, through the experience of 'being overtaken by', by the experience of fate or destiny which cannot be reversed, by anticipation of an epoch, by experience of an epochal event, through understanding as a project, through a sense of tradition, through autobiographical consciousness, through experience of the past *qua* past through recollection, through forgetting, or through the experience of the past as working on me now.[15]

Let me begin with the idea that autobiography gives us an access to the Erlebniszusammenhang which constitutes history. It is following this idea that Georg Misch undertook the Diltheyan project of a history of autobiography, but this very project shows that history is more than autobiographies. Although an autobiography presents an '*erlebte Vergangenheit*' and '*selbsterlebte Geschichte*', what we have is, at its core, a psychological continuity, but, to be sure, not an entirely uninterrupted continuity. Discontinuities, forgotten intervals, are filled in by stories told by others, and overall there is a self-interpretation which goes beyond mere recollection. While, at best, providing material for the historian, autobiography does not present historical consciousness.

Perhaps, the most forceful occasion for historical consciousness, for history as a phenomenon, is encountering what may be called historical entities, which Heidegger describes as 'all the things that the human being who is historical and exists historically in the strict and proper sense creates and shapes and cultivates: all his culture and works'. Such entities are inner-world entities: the ruin of a temple, a tool from an ancient and lost civilization, an inscription, a text, a painting. Experience of such entities is also experience of history as entailed in their very mode of being. Now, I would like to distinguish between perceiving—between coming across a cultural entity not as a cultural entity, but simply as a thing, experiencing it, if it is a ruin, as a ruin, as a survivor from another culture that may or may not be past—and experiencing it as carrying historical information from a forgotten past. There is thus a possible reference to a past and in that sense a possible experience of history. But note that neither Husserl's history as meaning sedimentation nor Heidegger's history as tradition and/or a unique event, is a desideratum of that all-too-familiar experience of 'so-called' entities. What I am insisting on is that neither Husserl nor Heidegger can point to our familiar experiences of cultural objects as necessarily presenting history in their respective senses as phenomena.

Now it may well be that the temple that is standing over there in ruins marks the end of one historical epoch and the beginning of another, and so satisfies the Heideggerian requirement, but that is something we learn and know from learning history as a science or as a story. What Husserl, and especially Heidegger, is referring to is a pre-theoretical, pre-cognitive experience, and not to what the historians have told us.

It would seem that our taking phenomena or entities as historical, or—in the hermeneutic mode of speaking—our interpreting them as historical all presuppose appropriately specific historical knowledge. This applies as much to ascribing 'epochal significance' or applying the claim to be an absolute epochal cut—to the birth of Christ, which Gadamer does, for example—as to considering any such event as a decisive event and in that sense regarding it as historical in an authentic sense. Events may have been experienced as epochal, but may not turn out to be so. Events may have been experienced as commonplace, but may turn out to have changed the destiny of a people.

Gadamer has, rightly in my view, emphasized the role of discontinuities in history, but the discontinuities he has in mind, the *Epocheneinschnitten*, are those brought about by events such as the birth of Christ or the French Revolution.[16] However, if my present argument is correct, there is both truth and error here. Discontinuities in history are important, but they are not to be construed as simple cuts in a temporally unfolding process. To understand discontinuities in that way would be still to be clinging to the traditional idea of one history, a world-history even if marked by breaks, cuts, transformations along the way. I think what modern historiography, especially that of the post-modernists, has discovered is that this idea of one history is spurious. There are histories in the plural: one, a history of madness, another a history of sexuality, and another a history of prisons. In these histories, new modes of discourse, new thematic concepts are constituted. Each of these histories is again diversified with regard to different regïons in space. Certainly, the history of sexuality in China and that in Europe do not form one homogeneous history of sexuality. In any case, history is history, in Husserlian jargon, of ideal meanings.

The prejudice that experience of history is an experience of violence, like that of a storm which sweeps you off your feet, of something unexpectedly new, so that the world would never be the same, is deeply influenced by western prejudice, which leads to the judgement that where this sense of violent upsurge or breaking-in is lacking there is no historical consciousness. When Gautama, the Buddha, first taught, he said he was only one of the many Buddhas, others had taught the same truth before him. Why is that not also a sense of history, unless you define 'history' or 'sense of history' in the familiar jargon of epochal cuts or unique decisive events? There may be a quite, unobtrusive, peaceful experience of history, experience of repetition, recollection, and ego-lessness.

Thus, where you find what sort of historical experience is a matter of interpretation. No wonder, Heidegger's original fundamental onto-logical understanding of history was replaced by the hermeneutical.

V

A perceived material object *qua* perceived, a mental act of hoping *qua* intentional in its own specific manner of intending, a social institution such as a ritual, can be phenomena inasmuch as each of these can be thematized by reflection *as present*. By reflecting upon the inner flow of my consciousness I can catch hold of my inner temporality i.e. my consciousness as 'now', as retaining its grip on what is just past and as anticipating what is just not-yet. But can I likewise focus on my (our) historicity or on the historicity of a cultural object?

Suppose I am listening to a recital of *sarod* by Ustad Allaudin Khan. By reducing this experience to 'listening', I can lay bare the temporal structure of my listening, but not the historicality of what I am encountering, unless of course I already *know* the history, the historical background of that composition. In listening to it, I can allow myself to live through a great chapter of the Indian musical tradition, but only if I *know* that history, not otherwise. Otherwise, there can only be a vague, formal, temporal reference to the past.

A phenomenology of mathematics, including a theory of the con-stitution, for example, of the real number series, requires knowledge of mathematics. No appeal to the fundamental rationality of existence is of help. The same is true in the case of history.

There is no doubt that it is a merit of phenomenological philosophy that it opens up the possibility of different modes of givenness, including the pre-reflective, everyday experience of things. Also, higher order reflective modes of givenness (of numbers and functions to the mathematicians, or of historical discontinuities to the historians) are to be recognized and subjected to genetic analysis. We may still have a phenomenology of history, but we should beware of smuggling reflective concepts derived from interpretations of history into the allegedly primitive pre-reflective life.

In this regard, Husserl's thinking, as always more cautious, presents only a formal-universal framework of thinking about history, without interpolating into that account, in the name of authenticity, concepts derived from historical–scientific interpretation of theological writings of a specific tradition.

I wish to emphasize at the end, one of the results of Husserl's thinking about history. This result has been brought to the foreground by Derrida in his introduction to Husserl's text on the origin of geometry. There can be no history of a unique thing, of a this–there, *tode-ti*. The this–there comes to be. There is change, production, creation, but not history. History must be history of an essence, of what Husserl calls an ideal object. History is history of an 'X', where this 'X' takes in constants such as 'music', 'warfare', 'painting'. Only ideal entities are historical. Nominalistically conceived real particulars arise and perish. The claim 'all things are historical' is nonsensical. 'All things' is a formal concept, not an ideal object.

VI

It may appear that my contention in the above paragraphs is not compatible with my earlier assertion that there is an everyday experience of history preceding history as a science analogously as the everyday experience of nature precedes the sciences of nature. It is therefore incumbent on me to say in what sense the latter thesis is to be understood so that it would be consistent with my statement that 'history' and 'historicity' are not phenomena in the sense of transcendental phenomenology.

Let me for this purpose quote the following text from Husserl's *Nachlass* (A VII 5):

Jeder Mensch und jedes Wir hat eine gewisse patente Tradition, die Erinnerungssphäre, die generative Erinnerung, die vorwissenschaftliche Geschichtlichkeit. Das innerhalb der verschlossenen dunklen Tradition, die im fertigen Sinne der jeweiligen Umwelt niedergeschlagen ist: latente Geschichtlichkeit. Wird sie enthüllt, so entspringt die eigenliche, die patente Geschichte. Aber die Geschichte im gewöhnlichen Sinne ist nur eine Schichte, ein erster Ansatz.

What Husserl is saying here is that we all have a sphere of memory which he calls 'prescientific historicity'. The tradition to which we belong is, in an obscure manner, indicated in our surrounding world. When this is brought to light, we have explicit history. Our memories of our past, through generational stories inherited by us, through going back to the origins, myths, and mythologies, are parts of the cultural world in which we pre-scientifically grow up; in this sense, our everyday life is permeated by a sense of history. Where philosophers go wrong is when they impute to our mode of being, to *Dasein*, a heavily loaded, philosophically interpreted sense of history which, if true, can only be derived, not from phenomenologically describing the structure of everyday life, but from a lot of relevant historical knowledge appropriately interpreted. This is what I have sought to reject in this lecture. The reference to the past, through memory— stretching back through memories of past generations surviving through stories told and retold—and the hopes of a future promised again in stories received in the tradition, are not being denied. If we abstract from the content of such stories, what characterizes the mode of existence, or the consciousness, of us humans is temporality. History adds content to this temporality. The mere reference to the past is transformed into stories about the past, for example, when we factor in the everyday experience of history.

NOTES

1. Hans-Georg Gadamer, *Wahrheit und Methode* (Tübingen; JCB Mohr, 4th Auflage, 1975), pp. 268f.

2. Karl-Heinz Lembeck. *Gengenstand Geschichte. Geschichtswissenschaftstheorie in Husserls Phänomenologie* (Dordrecht: Kluwer Academic Publishers, 1988), p. 47.

3. Bernet, Kern and Marbach, *Edmund Husserl, Darstellung seines Denkens* (Hamburg: Felix Meiner, 1989), pp. 105–6.

4. E. Husserl, *Die Krisis der Europäischen Wissenschaften und die transzendentale Phänomenologie* (Husserliana VI) (The Hague: M. Nijhoff, 1954).

5. Husserliana VI, Beilage III, pp. 365–86.

6. Ibid., p. 367.

7. Jacques Derrida, *Husserls Weg in die Geschichte am Leitfaden der Geometrie*, German tr. Hentschel und Krop (München: Wilhelm Fink Verlag, 1987), p. 145. (Eng. tr. mine.)

8. Husserliana VI, p. 382.

9. Husserliana VI, p. 380.

10. Martin Heidegger, *Sein und Zeit* (Tübingen: Max Niemeyer, 1953), pp. 384–5.

11. Ibid., p. 379.

12. Ibid., p. 384, where Heidegger uses the word 'Volk.'

13. Hans-Georg Gadamer, *Hegel, Husserl, Heidegger* (Gesammelte Werke, Bd. 3) (Tübingen: JCB Mohr, 1987), p. 217.

14. Ibid., p. 220.

15. Gadamer, *Gesammelte Werke* Bd. 2 (Tübingen: JCB Mohr 1986), p. 145.

16. Ibid., pp. 136–8.

chapter

thirteen

Some Thoughts on Time, History, and Flux*

One must distinguish between:
(1) Everything is in time; and
(2) Everything is (in) a process of change.
It has often been taken as self-evident that (2) follows (1). But (2) follows from (1) only on the further assumption that time is one-dimensional and consists of a series of perishing instants. (I am not even sure if this assumption suffices for deriving (2) from (1). It certainly is necessary). But duration is also a modality of time, and to endure is a mode of being in time, so that something can be in time without being a flux in which nothing abides. It does not therefore necessarily follow from (1) that nothing is ever the same, that identification and re-identification of a thing can only be ontologically misleading—even if pragmatically useful (as the Buddhists held).

Two kinds of philosophical moves are possible at this point: one descriptive, the other revisionary. The revisionary move starts with the premise that everything is in a flux, and argues that any ontology which admits abiding things must be abandoned. The descriptive move starts with the fact that in the world as we experience it we perceive things (and persons) which we recognize as being the same, and so holds that there must be some things which are temporal in

*Krausz and Shusterman (eds), *Interpretation, relativism and the metaphysics of culture: Themes in the Philosophy of J. Margolis*, Amherst, N.Y.: Humanity Books, 1999.

the sense of abiding and enduring, even if not everlasting. Unless an independent argument which does not beg the issue is advanced for its premise, I would prefer the descriptive over the revisionary move.

But on what ground is the premise 'everything is in a flux' to be justified? Not on the basis of (ordinary) experience, for we do not perceive, relate, act upon bits of flux, but rather things which can be again and which we recognize and identify as being the same. The only arguments known to me are the one advanced by the Buddhists, and the one making use of elementary particle physics. It can be shown, I believe, that none of these two can prove that things—all things— are in a flux. They both would be under obligation to show why and how things that abide could consist of elementary particles which do not.

II

If (2) does not follow from (1), it is also questionable if (1) is true in any non-trivial sense. To begin with, (1) should be distinguished from

(1*) All experience is temporal.

An experience may be temporal while the object of that experience may not be. But what is it to be temporal, or to be in time? Clearly, something is in time or temporal (these two again need to be distinguished, though for the present I would do without undertaking that work) if predicates such as 'came into being at time t_n,' 'goes out of existence at time t_n,' can be meaningfully predicated of it. Of an experience—a perception, a memory, an imagination, a thinking, for example—one can always meaningfully ask 'When did it occur, at what point of time, and when did it cease to exist?' But there are objects precisely of those experiences—a proposition, a theorem, a number, an arithmetical truth, a theory—of which such questions cannot be meaningfully asked. A locution such as 'The Pythagorean theorem began in the year___, month___, and day___, at such and such hour and such and such minute' is not false but meaningless. The question 'When did the number 0 begin to exist?' makes no sense. Some objects then are not in time, not in the sense that to say they are in time is false, but in the sense that ascribing temporal predicates of them does not makes sense.

I should add here, without stopping to take up these matters in this essay, that there are various kinds of objects in so far as their relation to time is concerned. These are:
• those, like the ones mentioned in the preceding paragraph, in whose case questions of beginning and end just do not make sense;

- those to whom a beginning is to ascribed, but no end (ask, when did Shakespeare write Macbeth? but not, When will Shakespeare's Macbeth cease to exist?);
- those to whom a beginning cannot be assigned, but an end can be (compare the question 'When did you begin to be ignorant of Quantum Mechanics?' with 'When did you cease to be ignorant of Quantum Mechanics?.)

But, in case of each such object, its experience is temporal. We then have to face up to a most serious question: how do experiences which are intrinsically temporal, present objects which are not temporal (in the aforementioned sense)?

III

There is no one unique conception of 'Time', to which, according to some philosophers, all experiences and all objects belong. One must, at the least, distinguish between:
(a) the cosmological time to which supposedly all Nature belongs;
(b) the physical time, meaning by it the time of physics;
(c) the historical time, in which history of mankind takes place; and
(d) the inner, phenomenologically lived time in which the internal stream of consciousness flows.

But, if we do not presume to know what the real time is, or even what the real time is under any of (a) (b) and (c), we are faced with various possibilities under each of these headings. Under (a), for example, we may have the Greek conception of circular time, or the Newtonian infinite linear time. Likewise, under (b), we have the Newtonian time (which is also the time of Newtonian physics), or the conceptions of time implied by space-time geometry of Relativity theory, the second Law of Thermodynamics and the Indeterminacy principles of Quantum Mechanics. For some, the very distinction between (a) and (b) would have to be given up. Consider now (c): unless one has one Universal History of Mankind, there need be no talk about one historical time. If there are many histories, there would have to be a plurality of times (as Foucault was led to suggest), and between these times one could affirm temporal relations only by violating categorial laws preventing mixing up temporal predicates from different domains. What I am suggesting is, that the concept of time of a domain is co-constituted with that domain, and we do not have available—as Kant, Bergson or the physicists would have us believe—one (concept of) time in terms of which we could non-trivially assert that everything is temporal. One would have to ask, 'temporal' *in which* sense? Thus, monistic and absolutistic claims on behalf of either (a) or (b) or (c) would fail; (a) is incurably cultural, (b) is theoretical, (c) differentiates itself in terms of a plurality of histories.

Only (d) promises to present a monistic framework, not for all things but for all experiences. All experiences regarded as immanent within the mental life of an experiencing self, are in this immanent, lived time with its retention–protention–now structure. For the present, it is not important that Husserl's exact description of this structure be true. As a matter of fact, he modified his version several times. What is important is that there is such an immanent temporality to be distinguished from both the world-time, the time of physics and historical time. But this immanent time does not comprehend physical objects, historical events or ideal entities such as numbers; it comprehends our experiences of all transcendent objects, also of all immanent objects such as acts, sensory data, thinking, imagining, remembering, etc. regarded not as events occurring in nature but as belonging to a stream of experience constituting the mental life of a transcendental ego.

We still do not have a satisfactory formulation of the thesis 'All things are in time'.

IV

From both (1) and (2), we must sharply distinguish (3) 'All things are historical'.

If (1) does not entail (2), and if neither (1) nor (2) seems to be true (for what cannot be formulated as a thesis cannot be taken to be true, and this holds good of (1), nor does (1)—even together with (2)—entail (3). What could one mean by saying that all things are historical?

Being in time or being temporal is a necessary but not sufficient condition of being historical. What else must be added to temporality in order to make historicaly possible? One answer, widely accepted in contemporary philosphy, would run something like this: the possibility of history, or of being in history, lies in the historicity of being. Unless one accepts the thesis pressed by Karl Löwith amongst others that mundane history is a reflection of *Heilsgeschichte*, there is no clear meaning to be assigned to the locution 'historicity of being' other than the straightforward 'being of history'. In that case, the answer is trivial, for it amounts to saying that the possibility of history lies in the being of history. A more substantive and plausible answer is: history is possible, because of the historicity of human existence, of what Heidegger calls *Dasein*. From this point of view, only what pertains to human existence, in general human world, society and culture, has history, and nature can be said to have history only in so far as it is nature for man, for example in so far as it is the subject matter of natural science which is historical in the straightforward sense of being a human project and a human accomplishment. It is then appropriate to say that culture is historical, nature is also historical in so far as it enters into culture, or has been, as Marx said, humanized. So (3) needs to be modified into (3*) All things of human significance are historical.

Only under the assumption that 'All things' and 'All things of human significance' are co-extensive, even if extensionally, would (3) still be true, but that assumption needs justification in a nontrivial manner. But neither (3) nor (3*) entails (2): to be historical is not *eo ipso* to be in a process of change. The idea of history involves both change and endurance, besides the idea of human significance. Obviously, I am now speaking not of history as a science (as what is done by historians, let us call it H_2), but of the subject matter of the historian's scientific concern (let us call it H_1).

Although the idea of historicality (*Geschichtlichkeit*) goes back to Hegel, in its present usage it is derived from Heidegger and Jaspers. For Heidegger the historicity of *Dasein* does not mean being in a social world, but rather the very ontological mode of being, not an ontic feature. Ontologically, *Dasein* is always ahead of itself, and exists in the sense of *ek-sistenz*, to be stretched outside of itself; it is being-towards-death, consequently finite, which makes possible its temporality and historicity in one. In his Marburg lectures of 1919–20, Heidegger distinguished between several senses of 'history': history as science (what I have earlier called H_2), history as a domain of enquiry (H_1), history as the merely past, history as tradition, history as a unique decisive event. Of these, he regards the first, second and third as being inauthentic, derivative and not *ursprünglich* in relation to concrete existence. The fourth can be either authentic or inauthentic. The fifth is the most *ursprünglich* for concrete human existence.

Without agreeing with Heidegger's analysis, let me, however, single out the two *authentic* conceptions of history: the tradition and the unique event in one's life. (For the latter, Heidegger cites the locution 'This person had a sad history'.) Tradition, in the authentic sense, is not simply a past accumulation of accomplishments (that would be close to the first and the second senses of 'history') but having this accumulation as a component of one's self-consciousness in the present. In this sense, historical consciousness is not knowledge of history (of the books) nor simply knowledge of the objective past, but is rather an awareness of the way the past, as sedimented structure of meanings, is present as constitutive of ones self-understanding. Historical consciousness requires consciousness of the past as constituting the present and as heading towards the future. This would not be possible if all were in a flux (unless we give a different meaning to 'flux' than the word would normally be taken to mean). Consciousness must have the ability to gather together what is past and what is present. It must be able to retrieve and reactivate the traces of what is past. The past must have, in Whitehead's words, 'objective immortality' which historical consciousness can capture in an act of subjective appropriation.

It can, as a matter of fact, be claimed that without some thematic identity, one cannot speak of 'history of . . . .' We need not decide right now whether this identity is pre-given or 'constructed'. Even if the identity is constituted, it is constituted along with its history. 'History of X' as an item is constituted along with the constitution of X. There is not history which is not a history of . . . . It is in the light of this remark that we will be able to reflect on the meaningfulness of the locution 'All things are historical'. 'All things' is a formal concept, and cannot fill in the empty place in 'history of . . . .' There is no history of all things. Nor can there be a history of one unique thing, of a this-there, *tode ti*. The this-there comes to be. There is change, production, creation, but not history. History must be history of an essence. Nominalism has no place for a concept of history.

V

It is well known that the theme of history comes to the centre of Husserl's thinking in the late work *Crisis* (although the theme of time was there ever since 1905). It is to be noted that Husserl uses 'history' in the *Krisis* mostly within quotation marks—which suggests that he was not using it in the standard sense (of either H_1 or H_2), but rather in an unusual sense. Elisabeth Ströker has identified this sense as 'intentional history'. Intentional history is the history of constitution of meaning, and explores its genetic constitution—as Husserl does in the case of Galilean mathematization of nature (and

Foucault does in the case of 'madness'). It is therefore in the nature of things that for Husserl the ideality of meanings and essences is not only not incompatible with their historicity, but historicity precisely requires ideality. Only ideal entities are historical. Nominalistically conceived real, particular events only *perish*.

If H_1 is history of meanings, and H_2, as science, requires ideal meanings as well as facticity (the historian, *writing* a la Derrida, for example), we can assert the equivalence of (3) and (3*) with

(4) History is history of meanings.

Sedimented meanings constitute a tradition. In this sense, a tradition is both the result of history and makes history possible. History is history within a tradition, even when it takes us beyond the given tradition and opens up new possibilities.

But is anything whatsoever possible? Can history take any direction in the next moment? Logically, yes. Really, no. Real possibility is motivated possibility, motivated by the course of experience up until now. Mere logical possibility is free possibility, for which nothing in the course of experience up until now counts. The idea of motivated possibility is narrower than free, merely logical possibility, but is wider than real possibility construed as what is compatible with the known laws (of nature or of society). In this sense, the future of history is unpredictable but not everything is possible.

VI

What I have argued for, in classical metaphysical terms, is the thesis that change, time and history all involve something invariant, abiding—if not everlasting. This classical thesis seems to be opposed to what seems to be Margolis's fundamental thesis about flux and radical history. Sometimes, the best you can do to pay homage to a philosopher friend is to set up for him an opposition which he can then set out to demolish. I am sure, Margolis would love doing that.

chapter

fourteen

Phenomenology of Religion and Human Purpose*

The title 'Phenomenology of Religion' has been used by many authors in recent times with no complete unanimity however regarding its subject matter, methodology and purpose. Holsten, writing on Phenomenology of Religion in *Religion in Geschichte und Gegenwart*,[1] distinguishes it from both History of Religion and Theology. It is not concerned with the historical development of religion. Unlike theology, it is concerned only with such phenomena as show themselves. The phenomenologial *epoche* forbids us to look behind phenomena. More precisely, phenomenology of religion, according to Holsten, knows only of human acts in relation to God, not of God's acts. However, Holsten recognizes that since the religious phenomena is itself historical, phenomenology of religion cannot remain totally unconcerned with history.

Kristensen also distinguishes between phenomenology of religion and history of religion.[2] History of religion is neither systematic nor comparative. Phenomenology of Religion seeks to 'classify' and to 'group' religious phenomena of the same category (e.g., sacrifice, prayer, sacrament, etc.) appearing in different religions and at different times to get at their inner meaning and ideal connections. Just as this would be going beyond history, it would also be stopping short of philosophy, for Kristensen would not let phenomenology

*W. Horosz (ed.), *Religion and Human Purpose*. The Hague: Nijhoff, 1987.

try to extract the essences of such phenomena. For him 'essence' is a philosophical concept, and so beyond the scope of phenomenology. But Kristensen also allows that phenomenology of religion is the systematic treatment of history of religion.[3]

However, the distinction between phenomenology of religion and history of religion is important and should not be obliterated. It is a misuse of the word 'phenomenology' when it is used to designate the study of history of religions.[4] Eliade rightly sees that the historical conditions of an experience do not tell us what a religious experience ultimately is and what it means.[5] Religious phenomena may be historical, but they reveal a behaviour which, Eliade rightly remarks, goes far beyond the historical involvement of man.[6] In other words, phenomenology of religion cannot remain confined to a mere empirical study of religious phenomena, it has also to seek for their meaning, structure, significance or essence. What Kristensen regarded as a philosophical but not a phenomenological concern is precisely the concern of a phenomenological philosophy. It searches not for a metaphysical essence but for the morphological essence which shows itself in the phenomena.

But what sort of phenomena are religious phenomena? In one sense, religious phenomena are the whole spectrum of religious ideas, activities, institutions, customs, symbols, and myths; one cannot even exclude religious art and literature from the purview of such a study. But at the same time it is also true that phenomenology operates with a definite conception of 'phenomenon' which does not coincide with the ordinary conception of it.

The basic concept of phenomenology is the concept of intentionality. Introduced in modern times by Brentano with a view to distinguishing between mental and non-mental phenomena, this concept has demonstrated its effectiveness beyond that limited purpose. It in fact defines the whole subject matter of phenomenology, and also defines its methodology. Whatever is intentional comes under the scope of a possible phenomenological investigation precisely in so far as it exhibits intentionality; phenomenological description is not an empirical description of the Humean variety, but is intentional analysis making use of the key methodological notion of noetic–noematic correlation. Keeping this in mind, we may say that what a phenomenological study of religion has to do is not merely give an empirical description of the religious 'data' but to uncover the living intentions behind them, the acts and intentions through which the religious 'data' are constituted precisely in their character of religiosity.

As is well known, the concept of intentionality developed, in the writings of Husserl, through three distinct but interrelated stages: intentionality understood as the simple directedness of consciousness towards an object, intentionality as noetic–noematic correlation, and intentionality as constituting function. One may also need to recall the later Husserlian notions of intentionalities that are not acts, of unconscious intentionalities and finally the notion of operative intentionality. In post-Husserlian phenomenologists, this key notion took on the forms of the concepts of being-in-the-world (Heidegger), of transcendence (Heidegger and Sartre), nihilation (Sartre) and of bodily intentionality (Merleau-Ponty). These notions cannot be relevant for any discussions of phenomenology of religious experience.

Max Scheler, one of the pioneers in the field of phenomenology of religion, divides it into three parts; the first part is to be an essential ontology of the divine being ('*die Wesensontik des Göttlichen*'), the second part is to be a doctrine of the forms of revelation in which the divine reveals itself to man; and the final part is to be a doctrine of religious acts through which man prepares himself for the acceptance of the content of revelation.[7] However, it is highly doubtful if a theory of God's revelation to man can claim to be a phenomenology. Revelation is not a phenomenon, as Van der Leew rightly says. What is a phenomenon is rather man's reply to revelation.[8] The same may be said regarding Scheler's first topic for a phenomenology of religion. Phenomenology can concern itself with the divine only in so far as the divine is the noematic correlate of religious acts. In other words, phenomenology has to study the religious acts, both in their noetic and their noematic aspects. God or the Divine, after the phenomenological *epoche*, appears as the noematic correlate, as the intended object *qua* intended. It is with the religious intention that the phenomenologist is primarily concerned. The question, for example, whether God exists is of no concern to the phenomenologist. What concerns him is, what religious acts constitute, for the religious person, the divine being as an existent reality and as divine. He is concerned with the *meaning* of God's existence, and not with his actual existence which has been placed within the *epoche*.

II

A phenomenology of religious acts has been made possible by the modern discovery that feelings are not merely subjective states but are intentional in as much originary sense as cognitive acts. In other words, intentionality is not a characteristic of the cognitive states alone. Brentano, of course, in a famous passage[9] speaks of love and hatred as being intentional. But while many would concede the seemingly uncontroversial fact that love implies an object loved, yet for most traditional philosophers love is not an originary intentionality inasmuch as it presupposes the intentionality of cognitive acts. An object that is loved is necessarily an object that is represented. As Brentano put it, every mental phenomenon is either itself a representation, or presupposes a representation. This Brentano doctrine, if taken seriously, leads to an intellectualism for which the primary intentionality is cognitive. Feelings may add a noematic quality. By being an object of love, the object may acquire a new noematic property of being loved, but its basic disclosure is to an act of representation. Now, one of the major philosophical insights we derive from the writings of Heidegger and Merleau-Ponty is that this intellectualist thesis is false. Feelings are originary modes of disclosure, they do not merely add colour to what has already been disclosed. This makes possible a further noetic and noematic study of religious acts which are basically non-cognitive in character. With the modern insight into the intentional structure of feelings, we need not any longer outright reject Schleiermacher's famous characterization of religious experience. The 'feeling of absolute dependence' is meant to be an intentional experience, and not a mere subjective state.

The first and indispensable prerequisite for a satisfactory phenomenology of religious acts is that we bring into operation the phenomenological *epoche*, by which is meant that we neutralize our belief in the reality of the objects of religious acts (analogously with the neutralization of the belief in the reality of the world in a phenomenology of perception, and with the same meaning and methodological significance of 'neutralization'). We, instead of naïvely living in those acts, reflect upon them without disturbing their naïvity, and yet we try to catch hold of their living intention directed towards their respective objects precisely as they are intended without taking it for granted that those objects are ontologically real or otherwise. For, as said before, the aim of a phenomenology of religion is not to arrive at a decision regarding the ontological status of the objects of religious acts, but to explicate their sense of those acts themselves.

The possibility and also relevance of such an *epoche* is brought out by the following logical features of intentional discourse. It has been brought out by Chisholm and others that intentional discourse is characterized by such features as truth-value indifference, existence-independence and referential opacity.[10] In other words, if a sentence whose main verb is an intentional verb (e.g. 'S believes that p') with a propositional clause as its object ('p') then from the truth of this sentence nothing follows regarding the truth or falsity of the propositional clause. Further, if the main intentional verb has a name or a definite description for its accusative, then from the truth of the sentence nothing follows regarding the existence or non-existence of the entity referred to by the name or the description. Again, in intentional contexts substitution of extensionally equivalent expressions does not preserve truth-value. These logical features of intentional discourse reinforce the point of view that the mere fact that there is a certain intentional act directed towards an object does not entail either the existence or the non-existence of such an object. Intentionality is not a relation relating a mind to an object in a certain specific manner, for if it were a relation the subsistence of this relation would have implied—as with all relations—the reality of both the terms involved; whereas in the present case only the reality of the mental act is entailed; not the reality of the object of that act. This should warn us against making a too hasty transition from phenomenology to ontology, from a phenomenology of religious acts to an ontology of divine being or beings.

III

In the light of the above general remarks regarding intentionality, we may examine some of the claims made by Scheler about religious acts. First, Scheler regards relatedness to God as an essential feature of all religious acts. Acts directed towards any other sort of content— humanity, the nation, or ones own self—are not religious unless they all in the long run are directed towards God.[11] Now this seems to me to be a very narrow conception of religious experience, for there are obviously important religions which do not admit of God. Within the tradition of these religious communities—for example of Buddhism and some Hindu sects—religious experiences are recognized which however are directed towards God (as understood in the Christian-Judaic tradition) but towards the Self (Ātman) or the Nothingness (Sunyatā). To say that for these religions, the Self or the Nothingness itself serves as the God is to turn the thesis of Scheler into triviality, for in that case whatever a religious act may intend ultimately would become God for that act. We have then to look for a more generic characteristic of religious acts than the property of having God for their last intention.[12]

Religious acts, Scheler next tells us, belong essentially to human consciousness not because it is human (in the inductive-empirical sense) but because it is a finite consciousness.[13] The first secure truth of all religious phenomenology, according to Scheler,[14] is that man, irrespective of the stage of his religious development, always and from the very beginning looks up at an ontological and axiological realm which is basically different from the empirical world. To look for the development of man into the religious point of view is absurd. Religion develops autogenetically and not heterogenetically. Now here again one should take care not to go astray from the path of phenomenology. It is one thing to plead for the uniqueness of religious acts, for their irreducibility to any other kinds of acts and to regard causal—psychological, sociological or otherwise—explanations as being irrelevant for a proper understanding of this uniqueness of religious acts *qua* religious. It is quite another thing to say that they follow necessarily from the finiteness of human subjectivity. How can one say that man in all ages and climes was and has been religious save through an empirical-inductive generalization? Surely the absence of the religious point of view in a human community is not inconceivable, and if we apply Husserl's method of free imaginative variation we may be entitled to refuse to give our assent to Scheler's proposition that the religious acts belong essentially to the human nature in so far as it is a finite consciousness. We may at best insightfully agree to the proposition that a finite consciousness must be characterized by transcendence and intentionality, but it does not seem evident that this transcendence should necessarily be a religious one. In fact, a phenomenology of religious acts need not take upon itself the larger task of ascertaining the essence of man; its humble task is to ascertain the essential features of religious acts themselves.

Religious acts cannot be mere desires or needs, just because they relate to objects of an altogether different type than the empirical objects towards which our desires and needs are ordinarily directed. They are thus not only altogether different from other sorts of acts of human consciousness, they are also not formed out of combinations of other intentional act types: ethical, aesthetic or logical. If by this attempt to separate the religious acts from the other types of intentional acts, Scheler intends to highlight their specific point of difference from the others he is surely justified. Religious experience is neither morality touched with emotion, nor the finite reason aware of its own infinite potentialities. The moralist and the rationalist are both apt to miss the uniqueness of the religious act. However, it is not true that religious acts are given in isolation from the rest of man's conscious life. In fact, they are inextricably blended with, and they in fact lend colour and tone to, the entire conscious life of the religious man. Eliade recognizes that there are no purely religious phenomena and that it is by an *epoche* that we come to apprehend the purely religious moment.[15] In this sense, a phenomenology of religious acts should end up with the recognition that it can only be a phenomenology of the religious moment in the total life of a religious man. The religious acts do not exist side by side with the other acts, as do our intellectual acts, without touching them. They have the tendency to overpower them, suffuse them with their own aura and to transform the entire life. In this sense, every religious act has *global* intention, which Scheler owing to his emphasis on the other-worldiness of the religious object fails to recognize.

There are three other secure marks of religious acts, according to Scheler.[16] First, in their intentions they transcend the world, not merely the actual world which includes all things and persons even the religious person himself, but also any possible world.[17] The second feature follows from the first: the intentions of religious acts are fulfilled only through the divine understood as a world-transcending reality. Lastly, the religious acts, as distinguished from all other cognitive acts, even those of metaphysical thinking *demand* a reply, a reciprocal response from the object towards which the acts are directed. Revelation, in the broadest sense, is nothing but the mode of givenness of a divine being, such a mode being strictly correlative to the religious acts.[18] One therefore understands Scheler's contention that a doctrine of revelation and of its various forms ought to constitute a major part of a phenomenology of religion.

Again we note Scheler's over-emphasis on the other-wordliness of the religious attitude, which in fact renders his characterizations too narrow. For one thing, not all experiences which intend a transcendence of the world are *eo ipso* religious. Heidegger, as is well known, emphasizes certain ontological moods, like care and anxiety, where there is no specifiable object towards which they are directed but in which the world of entities becomes meaningless, insignificant, and in so far transcended. Such acts are not however for Heidegger religious. Further, not all religious acts transcend the world in their intention, they may discover a new significance in the world—and such a discovery would be precisely what fulfills their intention. Again, it is only in the context of theistic religions that one can speak of the demand for a revelation of the divine being in response to the religious acts of man. Outside that context, the notion of revelation becomes insignificant. The notion of discovery or disclosure becomes more important.

IV

Where Scheler's phenomenology fails, it is conditioned by his inability to take the multifarious forms of religious phenomena into consideration. It is precisely in this respect that the phenomenologies of Rudolf Otto, Van der Leew, and Mercia Eliade deserve our consideration, for all three are aware of and take into consideration the vast domain of the religious phenomena that lies outside the Judaic-Christian tradition. Otto makes the notion of the holy his central notion, Eliade operates with the notion of the sacred, while Van der Leew accords central place to the notion of power.

Otto bases his phenomenology on Kantian-Friesian philosophy.[19] Accordingly, he searches for the *a priori* structure of religious experience. But Otto's *a priori* is not Kantian, but Friesian. The *a priori* for Fries is not a function of transcendental subjectivity as it is with Kant, but a psychological function, an inborn *Anlage*. Otto regards the complex category of holiness as an *a priori* element in this sense. He refers it back to the *Seelengrund*,[20] the bottom or ground of the soul. Otto gives a sort of proof that we have in the Holy an *a priori* category. He says that this proof can be had through introspection and 'a critical examination of reason such as Kant instituted'.[21] But the examination he undertakes is simply to show that the numinous experience involves beliefs and feelings which are qualitatively different from anything that natural sense–perception is capable of giving us. While this latter proposition may be conceded, this is far from entailing the truth of the thesis that the idea of the holy owes its origin to 'a hidden substantive source'. Phenomenology is under obligation to recognize the uniqueness of intentional acts where such uniqueness impresses upon us as a phenomenon, but this uniqueness need not lead us to find out a special faculty in the human soul as its source. Let us therefore pass over this part of Otto's doctrine, and turn to his analysis of the idea of the holy as the peculiar category of value that is experienced in religious acts. Religion in fact for Otto is *Werterleben*, experience of value; and the peculiar value that is experienced in it is the Holy. The idea of the Holy is indeed a complex idea consisting in both rational and non-rational components, and what interests Otto are the non-rational components of the *mysterium tremendum*, the *mysterium facsinosum* and the numinous value. The object of religious act is felt as absolutely overpowering (giving rise within us to the 'feeling of our creaturehood'), as awesome and majestic, as the wholly other but also as uniquely fascinating. Otto claims that even the 'void' of the eastern mystics, the sunyatā of the Buddhist, the identity of the Ātman and the *Brahman* which the mystics of the Upanishads strived to realize—all these conform to his characterization of the Holy as the wholly other and the *mysterium tremendum*.

We may now make a few remarks regarding Otto's phenomenology of religious experience. In so far as Otto separates the idea of the Holy from that of God, he is on a more secure ground than Scheler.[22] But at the same time, in making this idea as an *a priori* category he also reduces it to a level of generality which raises itself above the diversity of religious acts and phenomena. In fact, what Otto gives us is a theory of the object of the religious act, and not a phenomenology of those acts themselves.[23] His is therefore not an act-phenomenology. But he, at the same time, seeks to provide religious experience with an ontological guarantee by making the acts themselves *a priori*, instead of showing, as does Scheler, that the acts being *sui generis*, demand *a real object that is *sui generis*. Both attempts to provide an ontological guarantee for religious experience fall outside the scope of a phenomenology of religion, for such a phenomenology can only explicate the *sense* of the truth-claim of religious acts and *not substantiate* that claim.

Van der Leew operates with a more self-conscious phenomenological methodology. He is aware of the limitations, in fact self-imposed limitations, under which a phenomenologist has to work. For example, he knows that phenomenology is not metaphysics and that existence is unattainable to the phenomenologist.[24] He also knows that 'Before revelation Phenomenology comes to a halt'.[25] Also: 'For Christian faith, the figure of the mediator is no 'phenomenon'; the phenomenologist cannot perceive where and how it enters history'.[26] However, though revelation is not a phenomenon, man's reply to revelation, his assertion about what has been revealed, is a phenomenon.[27] Again, 'Of heaven and hell however phenomenology knows nothing at all; it is at home on earth, although it is at the same time sustained by love of the beyond'.[28] Further, in recognizing that the phenomenon is neither pure subject nor pure object but the subject as related to the object and the object as related to the subject,[29] he is aware that the phenomenon, for the phenomenologist is defined by the notion of intentionality with its implied notion of noetic-noematic correlation. The range of the phenomena which he studies is also wide enough to help him avoid hasty generalizations.

Just as the central category for Otto is the idea of the Holy, for Van der Leew the central concept is that of Power. For the religious consciousness, things or persons have either power or not. Those that are powerful are sacred, those that are not are profane.[30] Phenomenology has to describe man's response to this Power. The sense of being in relation to a Power generates in human consciousness both fear and attraction. Man is also seized with dread and yet he loves it.[31] In directing itself to Power, human life is touched by Power and becomes sacred life.[32] Though much is *given* as sacred, life is yet regarded as something always to be filled with Power. Hence the importance of rites. Dread indicates the tension that exists between man and the Power. A man seized by dread may either live continuing to ignore the Power, or he may try to seize Power through *tapas;* or, he may rely on habit established through the rites and customs and feel secure; or he may fall back on faith in a possible reconciliation.[33] Thus religion is not mere acceptance of life as given. In one of its major strands, religion seeks power in life, seeks to elevate life, to enhance its value. It is 'the extension of life to its uttermost limit'.[34]

On the basis of this conception of religious life, Van der Leew works out in detail a phenomenology of the various forms of religious acts. Thus service with its active, rhythmic swing of the body dramatizes the active participation of man in the Power and becomes a sort of 'sacred game'. The celebrations of festivals repeat what are regarded as the sacred moments of time—thereby implying the distinction between profane time and sacred time. While secular time and secular life are linear, sacred life and sacred time are cyclic. Every cult and rite is repetition. They do not symbolize events in linear time, they symbolize a cyclic order in which man seeks to participate. Like sacred time, sacred space has to be recognized as distinguished from profane space. Holy space is characterized by the existence of Power. Its effects are as it were visible there. Thus in all its dimensions, human life is touched, seized and transformed by Power. This, for Van der Leew, is the most essential feature of religion. This general feature makes room for various strategic moves that man may make in adjusting his relationship to Power. Man in fact takes up the challenge, but his responses are many and varied. Hence the diversity of religious phenomena.

Long complains that Van der Leew's phenomenology is too much under the influence of the objective and eidetic bias of the early

Husserl.[35] This much is true that Van der Leew does not bring out the deep existential meaning of the religious phenomena. Reading his monumental volumes, one does not learn that religious acts arise out of existential needs of man and that they cannot properly be understood unless they are seen in that perspective. For these insights we have to turn to Eliade. It may also be said that Van der Leew overemphasizes the notion of Power. All religious experiences do not conform to this pattern, especially the Hindu search for the Ātman and the Buddhist striving after *nirvāna*. These latter religious hankerings have their origin in existential situations like pain and suffering and not in man's attempt to adjust himself to Power. There may be a sense of tapas according to which man seeks to acquire power to be equal to the gods. But this is not the primary, or even the main, motivation of the Hindu and Buddhistic religious life. Van der Leew interprets the Hindu ideal of seeking harmony with the universe as an attempt to unify human and cosmic powers.[36] But I have grave doubts if this interpretation can be sustained. What are sought to be harmonized are the individual consciousness and the spirit that is supposed to pervade the universe, the Ātman and the Brahman. And the notion of consciousness or spirit in the Hindu philosophies does not coincide with that of Power. However, to be fair, it must be said that one of the welcome features of Van der Leew's phenomenology is that he has brought out the active, self-directing thrust of man in relating himself to the world and the Power. In fact, what a study of religious phenomena clearly brings to light is that man is not a passive instrument or medium for the working out of divine purpose, but that human intentionality, in its multifarious forms, constitutes and recreates the forms and patterns of life and behaviour which suit his existential needs.

The great merit of Eliade's studies on religious phenomena lies in their contribution towards relating the complex variety of religious phenomena to man's existential situation. Eliade is primarily concerned with the myths inasmuch as it is in the myths that the original intentions of religious consciousness are preserved and can be read off. Myths are not primitive tales nor are they pre-scientific and pre-rational attempts to explain the origin of the universe. But what is intended in the myths? According to Eliade, the myths preserve the sacred history, the primordial history.[37] But sacred history is not history in our ordinary sense, it is not a linear succession of events. It is rather a cycle of significant archetypal patterns which the myths preserve and which the cults want us to repeat. Myth is the language of the sacred, and through myths man lives again in a timeless world. The distinction between the sacred and the profane is central to Eliade's thought. But the distinction does not mean a complete separation between the two worlds. For religious consciousness what is most important is 'the eruption of the sacred' in the profane world. The sacred space, for example, creates a centre through which not only communication with the transworldly is possible but also an orientation for the profane world first becomes possible. Similarly, sacred time, as relived in rites and services, gives a new significance and perspective to profane time which otherwise would be an endless series of moments. In general, the profane world receives organization, meaning and significance from the sacred, so that the world becomes apprehensible as a world first by being limited by and then by being diffused by the sacred. The myths show man's nostalgia for the sacred world. Eliade rightly insists that the existential situation is not as such a historical situation. There has been a modern emphasis on man's historicity which, for a true religious consciousness, errs by over-emphasis.[38] Religious consciousness rather tries to transcend historical existence, existence in profane history, towards an existence in sacred time. When therefore Eliade traces back the myths to man's existential situation he should not be understood as referring to man's historical existence. There is rather an essentialist strain in his thinking. The existential situations which the myths express are eternally there, and therefore their relevance for man is never superseded. The sacred is an element in the structure of consciousness, not a stage in the history of consciousness.[39]

Eliade's concept of the Sacred has certain decided merits. It is wider in its application than Otto's notion of the Holy or Van der Leew's notion of the Power. Eliade's Sacred is not merely a structure of man's awakened, developed consciousness but also characterizes his subconscious. Symbolisms like the sky-symbolism, the symbolism of the 'unclean' and 'purification', the symbolism of origin belong to man's subconscious; myths are the language of the sacred. It is therefore an important philosophical task to relate the mythical element of the subconscious with the Freudean analysis of it. This task is undertaken by Paul Ricoeur.

The notions of sacred space and sacred time, as worked out by Eliade, are phenomenologically valid. But Eliade seems sometimes to be speaking the language of two worlds, so that for him religious consciousness would seem to be concerned with the sacred as distinguished from the profane. It is true, he also speaks of 'the eruption of the sacred' in the profane world, but the distinction and the consequent *via negativa*, seem to stand out prominently in his thought. This needs correction in two directions. First, it needs to be shown that the sacred world *qua* sacred is constituted by the peculiar intentionalities of religious consciousness—'constituted' in that peculiar sense of 'constitution' in which Husserl used that word. It needs also to be pointed out that the goal of religious life is not the distinction itself but its annulment. For the truly religious soul, the profane is also the sacred. As the Buddhist philosopher Nagarjuna said, *samsara* and *nirvāna* are one and the same.

The creativity and constitutive function of religious conscious-ness is amply recognized by Eliade when he says, as a final remark to his *The Quest, History and Meaning in Religion*, that spiritual creation is irreducible to a pre-existent system of values and that in mythological and religious universe every creation recreates its own structures.[40] To be noted is that he says 'recreates'. The phenomenologist cannot but be impressed by the recurrence of some fundamental patterns. But eidetic phenomenology must yield place to constitutive phenome-nology. Patterns of religious expressions (myths, symbolism, rites, cults, etc.) must show the way to patterns of religious intentionalities in which they are constituted.

V

Ricoeur[41] distinguishes between three dimensions of religious sym-bolism: the cosmic, the oneiric and the poetic. Man first reads the sacred on the world, on some elements or aspects of the world—the heavens, the sun, the moon, waters and vegetation. There is then a gradual movement away from the cosmic symbol towards the psy-chic which is best expressed in dreams. The cosmic and the psychic are two aspects of the same reality. 'I express myself in expressing the world; I explore my own sacrality in deciphering that of the world.'[42] As a philosopher, Ricoeur proceeds with the principle: 'Symbols give rise to thought'.[43] First there are the symbols as contingent cultural facts. Then, from amongst the world of symbols the philosopher chooses his own orientation: in Ricoeur's case it is the Judaic-Christian tradi-tion which determines his point of view. It is good that he explicitly says this. Finally, he is led into the 'depths' of the intentionalities imbedded in the symbols. 'To understand (for phenomenology) is to display the multiple and inexhaustible intentions of each symbol, to discover intentional analogies between myths and rites, to run through the level of expression and representation that are unified by the symbol'.[44]

Every symbol, for Ricoeur, is finally a manifestation of the bond between man and the sacred. It is also an index of man's situation at the heart of being. The symbols like those of deviation, wandering, captivity and myths like those of chaos, blinding, mixture, fall—all these speak of the situation of man's existence in the being of the world.[45] Perhaps to this it should be added that man's situation in the heart of being is not as such religious unless a religious intention intervenes to relate man's existential situation to the sacred.

It was said before that one of the tasks with which a phenomenology of religious symbolism is confronted is that of reconciling its findings with the Freudean psycho-analysis. For, as Ricoeur has pointed out, every symbol has these two aspects in one: the cosmic and the psychic. The attitudes of phenomenology and psycho-analysis also differ.[46] Phenomenology does not seek to explain, but describes. Psycho-analysis tries to understand the religious symbolism by its function, not by its intention. Phenomenology entertains the question of the truth of symbols in so far as the intention calls for fulfillment. For psycho-analysis the symbolism is an illusion and nothing more than it. Phenomenology of religion looks upon the symbols as expressing man's relation to the Sacred, for Freud they express the 'return of the repressed'. Can these different systems be unified? Ricoeur considers each to be legitimate within its own order. In fact, he allows for two different ways of understanding consciousness: either by going back to the pre-conscious or the unconscious, or by going forward to its more comprehensive unfolding in the Absolute. The latter is the path of Hegelian phenomenology of spirit, the former is the path of Freudean psycho-analysis. It is a measure of Ricoeur's deep insight into the human situation that he rejects both these extremes. Both 'humiliate consciousness' and 'decenter the origin of meaning'.[47] Consciousness has this two-fold dependence: on the Sacred as much as on the Unconscious. Symbols are symbols of this dependence.

It is this ambivalence in the human situation which the religious symbols best express, this unstable union of passivity and spontaneity, of non-being and being, of evil and good. This is what Ricoeur calls man's 'affective fragility', the 'fault' of man's being, the *dukha* of the human existence (according to Buddhism). Religious symbolism both gives expression to it and points towards its transcendence through its annulment.

VI

The Indian philosphers started philosophizing with reflection on the fact that human existence is characterized by the basic fact of suffering (*dukha*). So did the Samkhya and also the Buddha. By 'suffering' or dukha they did not mean the mere fact that life is characterized by pain and frustration. They had in mind a more fundamental ontological fact that human existence is characterized by passivity and receptivity as also the fact that it is characterized by a perpetual self-transcendence. It is this experience of being subjected to a state of passive receptivity (of pleasure or pain) which generated in them the idea of freedom and complete spontaneity. Ever since the time of the Upanishads, this ideal of freedom and complete spontaneity has remained the goal of Indian spiritual life. What interests us in the present context is the fact that the religious acts have their origin in a certain human situation, they are always existential in their significance. The notion of 'religious intention' has been used earlier in this essay. These intentions have their origin in peculiar existential situations, but they are not merely reflections on those situations. Reflection leaves the situation out of which it arises untouched. But the religious acts, arising out of pre-reflective human situation, tend to modify those situations by conferring on them a new noematic quality. Thus situations like death or frustration, trust and love, situations of the sort which Karl Jaspers called the *Grenzsituationen*, may generate religious intentions which *transform those situations from being merely human experiences into being experiences* of the holy, the sacred or the Power.

While thus a pre-reflective (and even pre-religious) existential situation may be transformed by an overwhelmingly religious intention into a religious *concern*, this concern at the same time posits its own object demanding a total surrender on the part of human subjectivity, an object which is such that, in the pertinent words of Paul Tillich, it 'makes us its object whenever we try to make it our object'.[48] We meet here with one of the most puzzling and yet compelling results of a phenomenology of human consciousness. Human intentionality is not only both receptive and constitutive, it confronts as given precisely that which it has constituted. To be an object for it is to be constituted by its meaning-giving function. The religious intention dominating an existential concern constitutes an Absolute, the correlate of an unconditional concern, which demands utter passivity and self-surrender on the part of the constituting intentionality. This is not to say that God or whatever else may be the object of Tillich's unconditional concern is an imaginary projection. To be constituted is not the same as to be projected by one's imagination. The religious object is the noematic correlate of the religious intention, and the sense of the reality or givenness of this object is the sense of such intention being fulfilled. Phenomenology cannot go beyond this point and recommend that there are or are not appropriate modes of fulfillment of the religious intention. What is pertinent in the above remarks is the contention that an existential situation, and an existential concern, is not *eo ipso* a religious situation, or a religious concern. Attempts to show that existentialism has to end up in an existential theology if it wants to be consistent are doomed to failure. Neither Heidegger nor Sartre have the least temptation towards a religious philosophy. This fact does not prove anything, but suggests that the transition from existential thought to religious thought is not straight and logically compelling, not even existentially compelling. But there is a way, the doors are not closed. The Buddha took this road. Many others did the same. The leap requires the coming into play of a religious intention of some sort, which generally arises out of a therapeutic motive. Thus Tillich concedes that whereas modern existentialism does not provide any way of overcoming the ontological threat[49] and whereas psycho-therapy cannot remove the ontological anxiety,[50] religion provides the answer: 'Divine love is the final answer to the question implied in human existence, including finitude, disruption and estrangement'.[51] This is alright so far as it goes (we may have to substitute 'divine love' by 'fulfillment of the religious intention'). But the answer presupposes the question, and the question presupposes a definite orientation towards the existential situation. It is at this last point that the transforming creativity and spontaneity of the religious intention comes into play taking the decisive step.

By way of conclusion it may be said, that a phenomenology of religion does *not* show that man is in his essence a religious being, it does not show that human consciousness, situated as it is, is bound to transcend towards the Absolute of religious consciousness—while it *does* show that the religious phenomena are constituted by a form of intentionality that is *sui generis* but which makes use of other constituted domains, especially of nature, art and the human situation, to constitute the peculiarly religious noematic quality which is grafted on to them. The combination of active spontaneity and receptivity which characterizes religious experience is nothing strange, for it characterizes the intentionality of human consciousness at all levels.

But at all levels, intentionality is constitutive. The peculiarly novel component of the religious intention is the therapeutic motive, the motive of overcoming the human limitations, of getting beyond 'dukha', of achieving freedom. The noematic correlate of this intention is precisely the supreme object of religious concern. In this sense, and it is only in this sense that human purposiveness underlies religious phenomena. But the basic category is not so much the concept of purpose as that of intentionality. We come face to face with a strange and novel form of human intentionality operating in all the diverse forms of religious phenomena, and this intentionality does not merely disclose, it is not merely *of* an object; it, like all intentionality, also constitutes that which it is of.

NOTES

1. W. Holsten, 'Phänomenologie der Religion', in *Die Religion in Geschichte und Gegenwart*, Dritte Auflage, Band V (Tübingen: J.C. Mohr, 1961), pp. 322–4.

2. W.B. Kristensen, *The Meaning of Religion, Lectures in the Phenomenology of Religion*, Eng. Tr. by John B. Carman (The Hague: Martinus Nijhoff, 1960).

3. Ibid., pp. 1–3.

4. J.D. Bettis (ed.), *Phenomenology of Religion* (New York & Evanston: Harper Books, 1969), pp. 2–3.

5. M. Eliade, *The Quest, History and Meaning in Religion* (University of Chicago Press, 1969), pp. 52–3.

6. M. Eliade, *Images and Symbols*, Eng. Tr. by Philip Mairet (New York: Sheed & Ward, 1952), pp. 32–3.

7. M. Scheler, *Vom Ewigen im Menschen, Gesammelte Werke*, Bd. 5 (Bern & München: Francke Verlag, 1954), p. 157.

8. Van der Leew, *Religion in Essence and Manifestation*, Eng. Tr. by J.E. Turner (New York, & Evanston: Harper & Row, 1963).

9. F. Brentano, 'The Distinction between Mental and Physical Phenomena', in R.M. Chisholm (ed.), *Realism and the Background of Phenomenology* (New York: The Free Press, 1960).

10. Cf. R.M. Chisholm, 'Intentionality', in P. Edwards (ed.), *The Encyclopedia of Philosophy* (New York, 1967).

11. M. Scheler, *Vom Ewigen* . . . p. 240.

12. See also J. Hessen, *Religionsphilosophie*, Bd. I (Basel: Ernst Reinhardt Verlag, 1955), p. 268.

13. M. Scheler, *Vom Ewigen* . . . . pp. 242–3.

14. Ibid., p. 170.

15. M. Eliade, *Patterns in Comparative Religion*, Eng. Tr. by Rosemary Sheed (London & New York: Sheed & Ward, 1958).

16. Ibid., p. 244 f.

17. Thus Scheler writes: 'Transzendenz im allgemeinen ist eine Eigentümlichkeit, die jeder Bewusstseinsintention zukommt . . . Aber erst wo das also Transzendierte die Welt als Ganzes ist (mit Einschluss der eigenen Person), haben wir Recht, von einen religiosen Akt zu reden'. (*Vom Ewigen . . .*, p. 245).

18. Ibid., p. 249.

19. R. Otto, *Kantische-Fries'sche Religionsphilosophie* (Tübingen, 1909).

20. R. Otto, *The Idea of the Holy*, Eng. Tr. by John W. Harvey, Fifth Impression (Oxford University Press, 1928), p. 116.

21. Ibid., p. 117.

22. Cf. J.E. Smith, 'The Experience of the Holy and the Idea of God', in Edie (ed.), *Phenomenology in America* (Chicago: Quadrangle Books, 1967). Smith argues that there is no necessary logical connection between the experience of the Holy and the Judaic-Christian conception of God. The former belongs to the structure of life and the world and is not dependent on any definite religious belief.

23. Cf. J. Hessen, *Religionsphilosophie*, pp. 288–9.

24. Van der Leew, *Religion in Essence and Manifestation*, II, p. 675.

25. Ibid., p. 565.

26. Ibid., pp. 666–7.

27. Ibid., p. 679.

28. Ibid., p. 688.

29. Ibid., p. 671.

30. Ibid., p. 47.

31. Ibid., p. 49.

32. Ibid., p. 191.

33. Ibid., pp. 468–9.

34. Ibid., p. 679.

35. Cf. C.H. Long, 'Archaism and Hermeneutics', in J.M. Kitagawa (ed.), *The History of Religions; Essays on the Problem of Understanding* (Chicago: University of Chicago Press, 1967), p. 70f.

36. Van der Leew, I, p. 36.

37. M. Eliade, *The Quest*, p. 72f.

38. M. Eliade, 'It has been too lightly assumed that the authenticity of an existence depends solely upon the consciousness of its own historicity'. In fact, for Eliade, the more consciousness is awakened, the more it transcends its own historicity (*Images and Symbols*, p. 33).

39. M. Eliade, *The Quest*, Preface.
40. Ibid., p. 173.
41. P. Ricoeur, *The symbolism of Evil*, Eng. Tr. by Emerson Buchanan (New York, Evanston & London: Harper & Row, 1967).
42. Ibid., p. 13.
43. Ibid., p. 19.
44. Ibid., p. 353.
45. Ibid., p. 356.
46. I have derived the following material on Ricoeur's views on Freud from Stewart, J.D., 'Paul Ricoeur's Phenomenology of Evil', *International Philosophical Quarterly*, vol. IX, no. 4 December 1969, 572–89.
47. Quoted by Stewart in his article cited in footnote 46.
48. P. Tillich, *Systematic Theology*, vol. I (Univeristy of Chicago Press, 1951), p. 12.
49. Ibid., p. 189.
50. Ibid., p. 191ff.
51. Ibid., p. 286.

chapter

fifteen

What is Special About Phenomenology of Religion*
(Remarks on Works on Phenomenology of Religion by Steven Laycock and Anna-Teresa Tymieniecka)

The question 'What is special about phenomenology of religion?' may mean, depending upon where one places the emphasis, either 'What is special about *phenomenology* of religion, compared to other ways of philosophically dealing with religion (such as rational theology)?' or What is special about the phenomenology of *religion qua* phenomenology, that is to say, as compared to, for example, phenomenology of perception?'

I intend to touch upon both senses of the question—the former in so far as I am interested in religion, which I believe is an important and central concern of philosophy, and the latter in so far as I am interested in phenomenology, in its strength and weakness as a method.

In dealing with both these questions, I will be commenting on two books on phenomenology of religion: Steven Laycock's *Foundations for a Phenomenological Theology* and Anna-Teresa Tymieniecka's *The Three Movements of the Soul*. The two books are as different from each other in their central project, styles of execution, and methods as is conceivable within an overall framework of phenomenology. Whether this last term entails a significant commonality needs to be asked; and if it does, then it is worthwhile to make an effort to precisely bring out that commonality.

Let me begin with a few remarks on the two questions. One way

*A.T. Tynieniecka (ed.) *Analecta Husserliana* XLIII, 253–64. Netherlands: Klnwer Academic Publications.

of bringing out the difference of phenomenology from the standard philosophies of religion is to ask: What sorts of questions that figure in the central core of the standard philosophy of religion do not figure in phenomenology of religion? Or, if there are important questions that translate from the one to the other, how do they—their sense and import—get transformed thereby? I think it may be fair to say that two kinds of questions are ruled out in a phenomenology: questions that ask for a rational argument for a thesis (such as proof that God, answering the Judeo-Christian description, exists), and questions that have a hypothetical 'If–Then' form (such as, If God is omniscient, omnipotent, and good, how can there be evil?). Much standard philosophy of religion is concerned with questions such as these, and phenomenology, with its appeal to the evidence of originary experience, has no need even of taking these concerns seriously. However, phenomenology's abjuring of such issues belonging to rational theology need not be construed as entailing that phenomenology is indifferent to the particular religions in their particularities. It would seek for each, not an argument, but an experience as the original source of meaning and validity.

But this last remark leads me to the second of the two questions asked at the beginning: how is phenomenology of *religion* distinguished from phenomenology of, say, perception, or of mathematics, or of logical thinking? It does appear, at the very outset, that there is a problem which seriously affects the fortunes of phenomenology of religion but which leaves phenomenology as applied to the other areas of experience untouched. This is the problem of radical alternation—of either–or—and not of conjunction, summation, or equalization. One is either a Hindu or a Buddhist or a Christian. The perceived world is not so divided: one perceives the same world under descriptions which are commensurable. That is why a phenomenology of perception, of perceptual experience (not of the perceived world, to be sure) can come up with eidetic descriptive features (such as perspectivity, temporality, historicity, and the like) which are indifferent as to *what* one perceives and as *what.* Can we say the same of phenomenology of religious experience? Faced with the radical alternation that divides religious life, should it immediately ascend to an eidetic level and focus on religious experience as such (with a capital 'R' possibly)? And what guarantee is there that eidetic reduction has not too hastily persuaded us to take what is a dispensable feature of Religion for an essential feature (even though it be essential for one religion in particular)?

But are not the fields of logic and mathematics (or also of art) split by similar radical alternations? You are either a classical mathematician or an intuitionist. Much of what makes sense for the former (such as Cantor's transfinite sets) does not make sense for the latter. You either accept a logic of two truth-values, or a logic of many such. Consider also the deep divide between classical physics and quantum physics. If you are doing phenomenology of these disciplines, how do you proceed? Skipping over differences, and proceeding by a hasty eidetic reduction to the logical as such, the mathematical as such, to art as such? No. Here eidetic reduction must give way to a transcendental-constitutive phenomenology which lays bare the many different processes of meaning-giving underlying the many different object domains before capping the enquiry with an eidetic reduction. So do I think at present, and the case is not very different in the case of religion, although in the case of religion the plurality is bewildering, for you cannot consider the world-religions only, you need also to take into account the so-called pre-literate religions.

My concern with phenomenology of religion is partly due to this: here is a good testing ground for phenomenology as a method, with its twin methodological stances, eidetic reduction and transcendental-phenomenological constitution analysis. A good phenomenology should be able to keep them in a proper balance. But more of this later.

However, we encounter questioning from another direction—in effect, a calling into question the very possibility of extending the transcendental-phenomenological constitution analysis to the domain of religious experience. Tymieniecka joins a host of thinkers, more notably Levinas, in this fundamental questioning. I will focus on this questioning in a little while. For the present, let me look at the two books which provide the occasion for these remarks.

The word 'phenomenology' is often used in a broad, liberal, open-ended sense in which the only constraint on its application is laid down by the imperative of validating one's theoretical–cognitive claims, and of clarifying one's meanings, by the evidence of originary experience. In a narrower, historically-grounded sense, one means by 'phenomenology' Husserl's work, and whatever carries that work forward in conformity with its guiding intention. Tymieniecka's work, if I understand her right, is closer to, even if it does not coincide with, the first sense of 'phenomenology', and Laycock's is closer to the second sense. I hope Dr Laycock will understand that having been concerned with understanding and interpreting Husserl's works for exactly four decades, his conceptualization of the basic demands of religious experience comes closer to my way of looking at things, and that criticism of his project, then, will serve to highlight the significance of Dr Tymieniecka's project. But then again, I will return from her work to his in order to bring out just where my questioning of her work precisely lies. In thus contrasting two such different projects, each carried out with exemplary care as to details, we may begin to see where the path to a satisfactory phenomenology shall take us.

Strangely enough, Laycock's basic question is: What would it be like to see the world as God sees it? (Recall Nagel's question, what is it like to be a bat?) Is this very questioning not phenomenologically illegitimate? Is this not the sort of hypothetical 'If–then' question I ruled out at the outset? 'If there is God, how does he see the world?' In addition, does not the question bypass the *access* through human intentionality and seek to go directly over to the divine intentionality intending the world—when all that we are legitimately permitted to ask is, how is the sense 'divine intentionality intending the world' constituted in the appropriate sort of human intentionality?

As a matter of fact, Laycock's move is not as phenomenologically illegitimate as I have just made it out to be. What he is doing is starting with an eidetic reduction to the eidos 'mind'. Finite minds are characterized by intentionality, teleological directedness, perspectival character, and intersubjectivity. Such features must apply to divine mind, if there is a divine being. Consequently, for Laycock, divine consciousness is teleogically directed towards *its* object pole—and what should be its object save the world as a whole? Ruled out is divine omniscience—on purely eidetic grounds—as being incompatible with the necessarily egological character of God, for the eidetic structure of intentionality requires as much an ego-pole as an object-pole. Again, not unlike finite human intentionality, divine intentionality also requires a hyletic datum, this being provided by the universal intersubjective community. Consequently, God perceives the world through, and only through, our eyes. Laycock gives us the idea of a finite, developing God whom absolute presence of the world eludes, but who, he nevertheless tells us, is 'implicit' within each act of finite consciousness in the form of a *de jure we* (in so far as asserting a proposition is claiming that *any one* will assent). Through a synthesis of perspectives, this *de jure*, implicit we moves towards being actualized, which is nothing other than the constitution of an ever higher humanity, of what Husserl calls *Gottes-Welt*. In this sense,

God's empty intending of the world-pole is concretized through our 'compassionate' practice of mutual understanding. God's future is thus in our hands. How nicely does Laycock succeed in fitting together elements from Husserlian thought to give shape to a concept of God?

But can he avoid the question of access? Is such a God given to us in religious experience? He may bracket the question of the real existence of such a (or any other) God, but he cannot bypass the question, is God so described also presented to human intentionality? To this question, Laycock has an answer. Phenomenology, he tell us, can only be concerned with the God-phenomenon. Thus far, he is right, but then he goes on to add: the God-phenomenon is God *as experienced by me in my reflective act*. Since nothing is revealed to me through reflection which is not itself either a consciousness or a moment or structure of consciousness, the God-phenomenon is possible only if it is a divine consciousness partially congruent with mine. We can reflectively imagine what it would be like to see as God sees. If divine mind is in no way revealed through reflection upon my lived experience, there will be for me no God-phenomenon.

I think Laycock's one move here is both crucial and highly questionable. If God is to be a phenomenon, one may wish to argue, it can be so only to the pre-reflective consciousness. If numbers are phenomena, they are so to the intentionality of the mathematician, not to our—the philosopher's—reflection. We as phenomenologists need to be able to catch hold of that pre-reflective intentionality in order to focus upon what was to it its intended object. If this is the case, Laycock still has on his hands the problem of access. He cannot bypass the question of religious experience and simply base all on the eidetic congruence between finite consciousness and divine consciousness. What prevents one from saying that the eidos he depends upon is not the eidos 'mind in general' but, rather, the eidos 'finite mind in general'?

Whereas Laycock gives us a picture without, providing an access (note that he provides a conceptual access, not an experiential access), Tymieniecka provides us with that access, a genetic phenomenology of religious experience, but with no picture of that to which it is an access. She knows her phenomenology well, and so rejects the role of intentionality altogether in such matters. Let me therefore focus on this last issue, so crucial for the very conception of a phenomenology of religion.

I can only begin by formulating the issue my own way. One of the questions I have been asking myself for some time is: Is there any specifically religious intentionality? I mean an intentional act of a type such that its object is only a religious object. One speaks of love, faith, worship, prayer, for example, as religious acts. So they are. But they are not presumably specifically religious acts, for they take on objects which are not religious. Otto, Scheler, and Stavenhagen, amongst others, tried to identify some. This is not the place to go into the question of why I am not satisfied with their answers.

Failing to identify such specifically religious acts, one may choose either of two alternatives. Either deny that religious experience is at all a mode of intentionality and assert that true religiosity requires transcending the intentional (Levinas takes this route), or hold that religious experience, not an intentional experience *sui generis*, is rather an interpretation of the totality of all our intentional experiences (cognitive, affective, and volitional)—in which the totality of relationships to the world and others is given in some deep and profound sort of sense. Tymieniecka has something in common with both these views, but she forges her own unique path. Is the path phenomenological?

She starts with the idea that man is involved in an ongoing process of self-interpretation in existence and traces out a route from the 'pre-experiential evidences' of this process up to the 'ultimate fulfillment' of the soul. The secret intention which guides this process is to transcend and be free from all objectifying sense.

Note that if the specific hallmark of religiosity is sacredness, for Tymieniecka nothing that is 'outside' the human soul (nature, soil, vegetation) is sacred. Only the human soul is capable of acquiring sacredness, and of thereby investing the world with that significance. She asks a sort of transcendental question: How is the human being— a natural being of the world—capable of sacredness and also of conceiving the sacred as emerging from an other-worldly sphere? The emphasis is on 'other-worldly'—if I understand her aright.

In dealing with this question, Tymieniecka claims to have reversed the direction of classical phenomenology. Classical phenomenology focused on consciousness, she focuses on life. Consciousness is only a moment in the process of life's self-individualization. Classical phenomenology privileges intellect, cognition—in fine, objectivating intentionalities; she privileges the creative, emotional life. Classical phenomenology, we are told, starts with transcendental consciousness; she starts with life at its pre-empirical 'stirrings, strivings, pulsations', with 'brute vital forces'. While doing this, Tymieniecka also wants to remain a phenomenologist, and that—as far as I can see—on two scores. First, she resolves to be faithful to the primacy of the *intuition* of religious experience over all other approaches to the religious phenomenon. By 'religious experience' she means—what one cannot just set aside—mystical experience. Second, not unlike Heidegger in his course on phenomenology of religion, Tyumieniecka insists that religious experience has to be examined in the context of man's situation in the life-world, his inward development, and his quest for the destiny of his soul. However, in doing the last-mentioned, she undertakes what looks like her version of Husserl's genetic phenomenology: spiritual experience is traced back to its genesis in that life-process from which all else originates.

There are two distinctive features of all this which bear examination. First, there is the concept of *life* which Tymieniecka expounds with a great deal of vigour, and second, the account of the spiritual act that she gives. The first, to my mind, moves towards a metaphysics of life; the second shows genuine phenomenological restraints.

Looking back briefly to classical phenomenology, it is interesting to note here how in the course of time (and partly under the influence of Dilthey) Husserl's expressions 'intentional act', 'consciousness', and their derivatives slowly gave way—beginning in the twenties— to the language of 'life' ('intentional life', 'life of consciousness'). This was not a mere change of locution. The change of locution reflects Husserl's perception of the interconnectedness of acts, of their horizontal structure, and of their teleological directedness. But when Tymieniecka speaks of 'stirrings of life', of brute vital powers, she is talking about a domain that lies at the borderline of biology and psychology. To come to terms with the issue of the phenomenological accessibility of the stratum of life in what I take to be Tymieniecka's sense, we can best begin by asking to what extent the Freudian discourse is amenable to appropriation and then extend that query to Tymieniecka's seemingly expansive claim. Note that there is nothing as such wrong in this expansive claim about a subterranean life. The question is whether such a concept can be phenomenologically validated—a question that also arose in connection with some similar ideas of Max Scheler.

Let us now take up Tymieniecka's conception of 'spiritual act'. Her description of the specific traits of spiritual acts largely, but not entirely, coincides with that of Scheler. She lists the following: immanent perception of such an act is accompanied by the conviction of a presence; a spiritual act penetrates the entire depth of consciousness;

a spiritual act wants or demands to be continued and makes claim
to a validity superior to that of objectifying acts; it has an affective
quality of peace and serenity; it does not 'aim at an object', it has no
noetic-noematic structure; it eventually aims at transcending all
objectivity; it is not a cognitive act, it has no distinctive contours
and structures; it always appears to be unpredictable, sporadic, and
ephemeral; it appears devoid of a horizon of possible acts—'out of
context', so to speak; it involves a tonality, a harmonic and polyphonic
unity lived at many different conscious levels. The spiritual act contains a message about which Tymieniecka has many important things
to say. The message itself has several levels of meaning. In this act all
human faculties participate. As and when a spiritual act emerges, it
shows the limits of objectification, of intentionality, of the transcendental-constitutive system. The constitutive act aims at rest and
stability (of the constituted objectivity), the spiritual act is characterized by a restless dynamism to transcend the objective world. The
spiritual act is not a positional act, it is rather proclamatory. It pro-
claims a truth, makes an appeal, and it also seeks to communicate.

Two general features stand out in Tymieniecka's account of the
spiritual act (besides its non-objectifying and non-intentional
character): its telos towards world-transcendence, and its demand
for communication with the other. We are given marvellous accounts
of the stages by which the spiritual soul passes beyond the natural
finitude of man, and yet the 'message' of the spiritual experience,
though personal and situational, requires communication with
others. In her inimitable language: 'The Unknowable One is . . . our
Star in the attempt to surpass finiteness', while 'other human beings
are the soul's only and last hope (p. 86)'. Added to these two features,
is the continuing theme of the genesis of the spiritual life in elementary
nature, in pre-predicative life. As a matter of fact, we are told the
story of how the human condition arises out of this vital substratum
and how it struggle to transcend its mundaneity, a story of which
only the broad landmarks can be given, in terms of the traces left
behind by the emerging spirituality.

Commenting upon Laycock's work, I have said that he gives us a
picture of divine life but does not tell us how we can have an access
to it. Tymieniecka gives an account of the genesis and the path of
spiritual life, but no clear conception of the goal emerges. This may
well be a merit of her work: her concern is with the nature of spiritual
experience and how it is related to the totality of human life; it does
not seek to validate any specific theory of religious reality (God, or

anything else). In this respect, it is a phenomenological work. My concerns, after all its undoubted merits are recognized, are: How precisely does one understand the non-intentionality of the spiritual act? One reason why the spiritual act is taken to be non-intentional is the anxiety that if it were intentional, then its telos, i.e. God, would be an *object*, and so would be open to 'constitution' by the transcendental ego. In other words, the ontological primacy of God as the creator of all things and as Being which is *causa sui* would have to be given up. God would become constituted, rather than being the ultimate ground of all constitution. Thus, from the religious point of view, transcendental phenomenology would seem to be an inversion of the true order of things. To protect, then, the primacy of God, one must either limit transcendental phenomenology to the domain of objects, or do away with the transcendental project altogether in favour of an ontological thesis such as Heidegger's which leaves human existence open to transcendence but does not constitute it.

Religious thinking moves along either of three different paths: either it posits its 'object' (which is a non-object) as the first cause and *causa sui;* or it posits it as a person, a transcendent subjectivity; or it thinks of its goal as an impersonal spirit which is the ground of all things. Transcendental phenomenology puts within brackets that imperious validity which religious life claims for its 'object', reduces that validity to a validity-claim, the putative object to a noematic structure; and it is to this noema, to this sense, that it assigns a constituting subjectivity. To a certain extent, neither the external world (which claims to cause the states of consciousness within an ego) nor the other person (who is encountered as an irreducible other) gives in to this constituting analysis without protest. They too have their claims to transcendence. But it is precisely their sense of transcendence—not those things out there—that transcendental phenomenology seeks to capture in its genesis. If this be so, then the resistance that religious belief and religious experience offer to transcendental phenomenology should be nothing new in principle. It is only that the transcendence-claim of this new 'object' is far more imperious, its putative transcendence far in excess of that which the external world and other persons carry with them. It would not cut deep, then, if one conceded to transcendental subjectivity in all domains save and except the religious. One thus understands Levinas' refusal even to concede that the other person, in his otherness, can be a proper 'object' for transcendental phenomenology. Let us, for the present, leave it undecided whether Husserl's attempt to exhibit the constitution of the ego of the other succeeds or not. But quite apart from the fate of constitutive phenomenology, should one even deny that the other person, in his otherness, becomes the object of a whole class of intentional acts— acts such as love, sympathy, and moral judgement? One still needs to ask whether these acts could be specifically religious in the sense articulated earlier in this commentary.

It is in this connection that we begin to see the relevance of a much larger question which, for phenomenology, seems to have been decided in advance, namely whether there is a dimension of consciousness that is non-intentional, and if there is such a dimension, what is its relevance for religion, on the one hand, and for transcendental phenomenology, on the other?

To be fair to Husserl, it should be noted that the domain of consciousness, even for him, is far wider than the narrow region of intentional acts. First, there is the horizontal intentionality which is a sort of pointing without being an object-directed act. Inner time consciousness is characterized by such horizonal intentionalities (retention and protention amongst others). The account of the constitution of temporality leads Husserl to what he characterizes as the streaming flux which yet remains the standing living present. This dimension of consciousness, again, is not an act. I need not recall here how Husserl extended the account of transcendental constitution beyond the static theory of *Ideas* I. It is in the light of this enriched theory, then, that the question of the role of intentionality within religious experience needs to be re-examined.

A brief remark about 'experience': sometimes it is held that what must constitute the core of religion must be some non-conceptual, non-intentional experience beyond the subject-object distinction. This sort of view is emphasized in many different forms by different thinkers. I do not want on this occasion to go into a detailed treatment of these in their specificities. The remark I want to make should be relevant to all such views in general. No experience, however overwhelming, strong and impressive, tells its own story. The story that emerges is the result of either an interpretation of that experience, or of the role that experience may play in fulfilling a prior empty intention. Without such a conceptual intention coming into relation with the experience, not much can be said about the experience. This is not to say that there is no such religious experience, or no mystic experience. But the cognitive value that we ascribe to any such experience involves an interpretation in terms of some already available conceptual scheme (either Christian or Judaic or Hindu or Buddhist). The pure uninterpreted experience that sweeps you away off your feet, flows into your empty vessel (so the Yogasutras describe it), and simply dazzles you does not *tell* you anything.

chapter

sixteen

Religion and the Sacred*

I begin with the remark that 'is sacred', like 'is beautiful', but unlike
'is red' is not a determining, but rather a modifying predicate
(in Brentano's sense of that distinction). The way I am now using
the distinction between determining and modifying predicates has
to be understood in the following manner.

For one thing, determining predicates and modifying predicates
are not simply different predicates, but are *qua predicates* different.
They are *radically* different predicates. Now, modifying predicates
themselves are of various kinds; of these I choose two for my present
purpose. These are aesthetic predicates such as 'is beautiful' and 'is
sublime', and religious predicates such as 'is sacred', or Rudolf Otto's
'mysterium tremendum'. I want first to press the point that these
predicates express the *how* of a certain mode of working. To say that
a thing is beautiful or that it is sublime is to say that it is working
upon the speaker in an appropriate manner. Let me call it, using an
inelegant locution, 'beautiful-working', 'sublime-working'. A beautiful
thing, i.e. a thing described as beautiful is one which works on the
describer as beautiful, it produces on him an impression-of-beauty.
This is what 'beautiful-working' consists in. Note that the impression-
of-beauty is not a beautiful impression, it is rather an impression of
beauty (or of-elegance, or of-sublimity). When one is speaking of a

*Originally read at a Meeting of the American Society of Aesthetics in 1991.

clear or a fleeting impression, one describes the impression. But an impression of beauty is such that beauty is its immanent, constituent object (not as red resides on the surface of a piece of red paper). The same, I contend, is true of 'is sacred'. If I describe a thing as sacred, the thing is working on me in a certain manner, this working consists in producing in me an impression-of-sacredness.

Let me again go back to aesthetic effects. As Josef König pointed out—and my present ideas go back to him[1]—when Goethe says that art works maintain one in the face of the destructive power of the world, this maintaining is very different from the sense in which an air raid or torando shelter protects you from a bombing or the fury of a tornado. This 'working-as-maintaining', which is not a *real* protecting, is an aesthetic effect. Looking at the Strasbourg cathedral, Goethe said that it raised him to the heavens. This 'working as lifting one up to the heavens' is an aesthetic effect. This does not mean that the cathedral produced in Goethe an effect which raised him up to the heavens.

Contrast with this the feeling good which some news may produce in me. The news is a thing. The feeling good is a thing (a mental state). This is a case of non-aesthetic effect. The pleasant news *eo ipso* pleases someone, in this case, me. A sublime landscape works-as-sublime, not *for* any one. Its being sublime and its working-as-sublime are one and the same.

A non-aesthetic impression may be investigated by either physiology or psychology. An aesthetic effect is not a possible subject matter for investigation by a special science.

Describing a non-aesthetic impression ('It pleases me', or 'That is red') is 'describing' in a radically different sense than that in which describing an aesthetic impression is so. This difference may be expressed thus: One who describes a thing may describe it correctly or incorrectly, describe it well or poorly. One who describes poorly also describes. But a bad poet is not a poet. The aesthetic impression is its own description, it is itself poetic. The description of an art work is like a description of a thing. But an aesthetic impression is not. It speaks, as it were, for itself, bears its own testimony. 'X is beautiful' describes the impression-of-beauty. Aesthetic sensing and aesthetic describing are inseparable moments of one experience of beauty. This is what 'is beautiful' means, and it should not be construed to mean that X only appears to be beautiful. We are not permitted to make that distinction between being-beautiful and appearing-to-be-beautiful. The aesthetic judgement is objective.

If you want other examples, here are some: an impression-of-spatial-depth is what originally presents spatial depth. But if something appears as a man, it may or may not be one. Similarly, an impression-of-vitality is what originally presents vitality. The same is true of impression-of-sublimity. The important question is, by what mechanism can such an impression be produced from without? My contention is, it cannot be. But this last assertion only gives rise to problems of great difficulty, which I cannot attempt to answer on this occasion.

The sentence 'A is blond' is true if and only if A is in fact blond. Here truth is, in some sense, correspondence. The poetic speech, 'That is beautiful' is true by the very occasioning of the utterance, and its truth is the ground of the fact that the fact is as the sentence says it is. The meaning of 'truth' in the two cases is radically different.

I will pursue this strange contrast one step further, and maintain that we have here two senses of 'being': in the one case, being is simple *Vorhandenheit* (as Heidegger understands it); in the other case, it means *acting* in a certain manner, being efficacious, being in the verbal, intensive sense. In the latter sense, to be is to be efficacious, to produce an effect. Such an entity, working in such and such a manner, is *qua* so acting, is a being that is essentially so—beautiful or sublime or sacred, as the case may be. No 'Sein' holds good of all such cases as a generic property, but each one has its own being. In an important sense, this *distributive*, particularized sense of 'being' as being-efficacious-in a-certain-manner, is the only sense of 'being' which does not allow itself to be analysed as 'being the value of a variable' (Quine) or 'being a thetic predicate which is the correlate of an act of believing' (Husserl). Shall we then say, as opposed to the suspicion that being-beautiful or being-sublime is merely subjective being, rather the very opposite holds good, that only in such efficacy does one encounter being as such?

Everything that I have said, following Josef König's most remarkable thoughts, I want to say about the modifying predicate 'is sacred'. To say, on originary evidence, that something is sacred, is to be acted upon by that thing in a certain manner, and this working *is* being-sacred. It is in and through the feeling of sacredness (impression-of-sacredness) that a sacred being is precisely as it is. A sacred being (like a sublime or a beautiful being) is not first a *vorhandenes* entity, which then has a property called sacredness (sublimity or beauty—just as a red thing is first a *vorhandenes* thing which, over and above that, has the property of being red. It is sacred, its very being consists in acting-as-sacred, it is an activity. With this, I have sought to capture both the claims about the sacred—that the sacred must be an original being, and that it is a power, not a thing (*Ding*).

After having presented in barest outlines what I would regard as the nature of the originary concept of the sacred, I would now, again very briefly, indicate how I think the relation of this concept to religion needs is to be best construed.

Here, a paper by Dr. Pratt of New Zealand, which I heard being presented at the Australasian Society of Phenomenology meetings in Melbourne, showed me the way, just when I was groping for it. Pratt distinguished between what he called pre-religion and religion. If I understood him right, the contrast is between an original religiosity exhibited, for example, in the founder prophets and apostles or the experiences underlying the basic texts, and its objectification and institutionalization in texts, dogmas and churches. The importance of this distinction is much lessened if we simply relegate pre-religion to the chronological beginning of every religion. It becomes a more interesting distinction if one recognizes that the pre-religious and the religious co-exist as but two strata of religious life, with the latter founded upon and yet covering up the former, and with the former making the latter possible as its originary source and continuing support. Taking the distinction in this sense, the closest that one need look for illumination of it within phenomenology is Merleau-Ponty's distinction between the pre-objective and the objective. The objective world (correlatively, objective thought) is founded upon pre-objective perception. The task of phenomenology is to grasp the objective world as it emerges out of the pre-objective background of operative intentionalities.

My contention is, that although within the established religions with their objective texts, dogmas, rituals, institutions, laws, communities there is the distinction between the sacred and the profane, the originary source of meaning of the predicate 'sacred' lies in the pre-objective impression/feeling-of-sacredness, through which the *event* of working-as-sacred emerges into the world.

NOTE

1. For the relevant works of Josef König, reference may be made to his *Sein und Denken* (Halle: Max Niemeyer, 1937) and *Vorträge und Aufsätze* (ed.) G. Patzig (Munich: Alber Verlag, 1978).

chapter

seventeen

Phenomenology and Psychology*

I am honored by the invitation extended to me to speak on the relevance of phenomenology for psychology to this august body of psychologists. With a few words of introductory remarks regarding the way the relation between the two disciplines has developed in history, I will address myself to the central theme as I perceive it. The relation between phenomenology and psychology has been nothing short of tortuous. A Freudian might say that the founder of phenomenology, Edmund Husserl, had a sort of love and hate relationship to psychology. One of his first philosophy Professors in Leipzig was Wundt, and what is more important, he and Freud were fellow students of Brentano. He learnt a great deal of psychology—both introspectionist and associationist—and also psycho-physics. If in his 1900 work on Logic[1] he launched a vigorous critique of psychologism, that by no means should be construed as a critique of psychology. Psychologism was a theory which made psychology the foundation of all other sciences—in Husserl's critique, especially of logic. It is this that Husserl critiqued and ruthlessly exposed. The interest in psychology, however, continued. As late as the early twenties he gave courses on 'phenomenological psychology',[2] and in the *Krisis*[3] lectures he made psychology a

*An invited lecture given at the American Psychological Association, New York, 1995.

gateway to the philosophical theory he was developing under the title of 'transcendental phenomenology'. In doing this, he also offered a critique of objectivistic and naturalistic psychologies, which follow the model of the natural sciences, and argued for recognizing the irreducibility of subjectivity.

Following Husserl, phenomenologists, including Heidegger, have contributed to the development of phenomenological psychology. Brentano had already set aside the British empiricistic theory of mind as consisting of ideas or contents, and wanted to replace it by a theory of mental *acts*. This had shown that the introspectionist, in so far as he wanted to look into his mind in order to determine what was going on (what images one has, for example, when one thinks of something) was misled. The mental consisted rather of ways of intending the world, and describing a mental experience, as Sartre insisted, was describing how the world was presented to the subject. Following upon and extending the Brentano thesis of intentionality, Merleau-Ponty studied 'behaviour' and showed—as against a S–R analysis of behaviour—that behaviour itself was incurably intentional, that in the S–R analysis there was an interesting circularity, and that the Brentano thesis had to be extended to the body as well.[4] What all this amounted to was to appropriate the insights of behaviourism, while rejecting the behaviourists' naturalistic self-understanding. The third psychological theory which phenomenology had to confront was psycho-analysis. Husserl himself had little comment to make on psycho-analysis save making room, in his later works, for 'unconscious intentionalities'; Sartre, as is well known, rejected the Freudian Unconscious as a useless hypothesis, and sought to replace the Freudian by existential psycho-analysis. Binswanger and Boss, drawing upon Husserl and Heidegger respectively, sought to reinterpret and reshape psycho-analysis. Ricoeur, using all the resources of Husserlian phenomenology, attempted a major interpretation of Freud.[5]

Thus phenomenology has confronted, sometimes as critic, but often as interpreter and also as constructive investigator, the three major schools of psychology: introspectionism, behaviourism and psycho-analysis. I will not return to the first two, beyond the brief references here. Today is the era of the so-called 'cognitive psychology'. What can phenomenology tell us about cognition, especially *vis-à-vis* the cognitive psychology? More on this later in this lecture.

This leads me to my third prefatory remark. Within the phenomenological movement, a distinction is made between Husserlian transcendental phenomenology and Heidegger's hermeneutic phenomenology. There are many philosophical issues, answers to which divide the two; some of these are: the question of the priority of consciousness or of existence; the possibility of a transcendental epoché *vis-à-vis* man's incurable being-in-the-world; the viability of a descriptive programme *vis-à-vis* the universality of interpretation. Many of these disputations are ridden with cliches and jargons; some are substantive questions. Psychology has been sometimes influenced by Heideggerean ideas. I propose to return to classical Husserlian phenomenology to bring out its relevance for psychology today.

Many of you must be aware that there is already in existence a whole body of work in phenomenological psychology. For those who want to catch up, I will recommend bibliographical references in Herbert Spiegelberg's *Phenomenology in Psychology and Psychiatry*.[6] The names to be recalled are: from the early Göttingen school, David Katz; from the Wurzburg school, Messer, Bühler, Selz and Michotte; from the Gestalt school which in some form was under Husserl's influence, Koffka, Wertheimer, Gurwitsch, Levin and Metzger; from the Dutch school, Buytenkijk, Van der Berg and Linschoten; in psychopathology, Karl Jaspers, Kurt Schneider, Eugene Minkowski, Ludwig Binswanger and Erwin Strauss. In the USA, William James has been widely regarded as an independent pioneer; other names to be recalled are Donald Snygg, Carl Roger, Eugene Gendlin, Rollo May and Robert MacLeod. A recent anthology of the classical work of the Dutch school *is Phenomenological Psychology: The Dutch School*, edited by Joseph J. Kockelman.[7]

II

In this lecture I will try to lay down what I regard as the fundamental ideas of phenomenology which psychologists either have used or may use profitably.

Methodologically, phenomenology demands—in whatever field it is applied, for our present purpose in psychology—a commitment to descriptive work, and I should add, keeping positing of theoretical entities to the minimum. But description—contrary to the likely initial impression—is not easy to do. As I look out through my window, I see a blooming cherry tree. I may describe my perceptual experience by saying that what is presented to me is a patch of pinks dotted against the background of patches of green—a curious blend of mixed colours floating against the blue of the sky. Or, when perceiving a sequence of changing events, I may describe my experience thus: 'all events seem entirely loose and separate. One event follows another; but we never can observe any tie between them. They seem conjoined, never connected.'[8] This last, I may add, is a quotation from David Hume.

Now, why do I consider these to be bad descriptions? I do so because—as can be easily seen—these descriptions of perception in terms of sensations, patches of colour or discrete bits of events, presuppose a large body of physiological and psycho-physical theory and philosophical theories about the primacy of sensory data. As contrasted with these, consider the following description:

In every external perception, there is reference from the 'genuinely perceived' sides of the object of perception to the sides 'also meant—not yet perceived, but only anticipated and at first, with a non-intentional emptiness: a continuous protention, anticipation of what is yet to come, which with each new phase of the perception, has a new sense.[9]

This is taken from Husserl's *Cartesian Meditations*, and describes how our perception of an object unfolds. First, as I look out and see the building over there, a side of it is presented to me but the other side, the inside, are 'emptily meant', they are not presented but are only intended. As I look at the object from other sides, aspects which were initially only emptily prefigured come to be presented, but with new anticipations.

In describing a mental state, such as anger, fear, anxiety, every attempt should be made to keep out ('bracket') what we may have learnt from other sources (for example, that in such and such experience such and such chemicals are released). What we are to describe is precisely how for the subject, in *that* experience, or in *such* experience, the world is presented.

What I am leading you on to focus upon is the intentional structure of an experience. So let me introduce the concept of intentionality, which is central to phenomenology, and certainly to a phenomenological psychology. Brentano formulated intentionality as the feature of every experience to be *directed towards* some object or other; nothing non-mental has this feature according to him. A fear is fear of something, a hope is hope for something. It is clear that this object of an experience should not be confused with what causes the experience. The object of hope is a future event, yet-to-be, and so cannot cause hope. When one fears ghosts, the ghost—assuming there are no such—could not cause the experience. Two changes need to be made in this simple Brentano thesis. For one thing, since the intentional object may or may not be a real thing out there, what really internally characterizes an experience is its having such and such object. The experience itself has this structure—even if we 'bracket' what things in the world are like. This experience, Husserl pointed out, consists of an *act* and its *noema* (here 'act' is to be understood not in the sense of activity but as a *terminus technicum,* meaning whatever is intentional), it is nothing but a correlation between a *noesis* and a *noema.* In this sense, every experience carries *within it* a meaning, i.e. an interpretation of the object. The object is presented *as* threatening, *as* fearful, or in general, *as* such and such. To describe an experience is unavoidably to describe precisely how, with what significance, its object is presented in that experience. Thus one could, with equal justification, say that the *noesis* interprets or confers a meaning on its object, *and* that in the *noesis* its object is presented with a certain meaning. The two descriptions are equivalent—as much as the wave description and the particle description of a physical phenomenon are, in quantum physics.

Second, as many phenomenologists, such as Merleau-Ponty, pointed out, intentionality does not distinguish mind from body, but defines an area that cuts across that Cartesian distinction. You can overcome the infamous Cartesian dualism either by reducing the putative mind to matter (as does physicalism) or by maintaining that the *bodily* is, in an important sense, a mode of subjectivity. The German language provides two words for 'body,' which come in handy for our purpose: '*Körper*' for body as a physical object (as a proper object for anatomical inquiry) and '*Leib*' for both living body and lived body, i.e. for body as lived from within. In the latter sense, my body is experienced by me not as a thing out in the world, but as (i) a nexus of powers and abilities ('I can raise my arm', etc.) which (ii) confer meaning on the world around, and (iii) as the null-point around which things of the world gather as being 'to the right' or 'to the left', 'in front' or 'behind', 'far' or 'near', 'above' or 'below'. Bodily movement is not intentional in the sense of being purposive or goal directed, but in the more fundamental sense that in being directed towards an object, it confers on that object a meaning or a value. As I start climbing a mountain, my body is so totally absorbed in the task that one could say, as Sartre does, my body is realized in the landscape, bodily fatigue, for example, in the inaccessibility of the top. The body itself is passed over in silence for the task in hand. Illness of the body changes the physiognomy of the world.

If both mental acts such as believing, imagining and desiring and bodily movements are intentional, they both are to be subsumed not under 'consciousness' (recall the objections of existential phenomenologists that body is not consciousness of body), but under a more comprehensive concept, i.e. 'subjectivity'. What intentionality then defines is the realm of subjectivity, which contrasts not with the bodily, but with the *thing-like*. (Whether you would want to regard the bodily subjectivity, if not as consciousness *of* the body, certainly as a pre-reflective consciousness and consequently refuse to identify consciousness with the mental, may be, after all, a matter of deciding upon appropriate designations without being obfuscating or going against ordinary uses of the key terms. Note that Heidegger's use of *'Dasein'* was a radical departure from the ordinary German usage of that term.)

This concept of subjectivity which comprehends our narrowly delimited concepts of the mental and the bodily may then be regarded as determining the field of psychology. The Freudian Unconscious as much as logical operations of thinking and reasoning would belong to its various dimensions. Let me continue further characterizations of intentional subjectivity.

The meaning which intentionality confers on its object (which is the same—as emphasized earlier—as the meanings with which objects are presented to experience) are not creations of an autonomous world-less ego, but are rather taken up from the cultural milieu in which the ego who exercises intentionality finds himself. The *philosophical* issue, much debated within the phenomenological school, whether the meaning-bestowing ego is a worldly entity (the Heideggerean *Dasein*) or a world-less transcendental ego, as so formulated, need not be settled by us, nor does it present a clear picture of the questions at stake, and is therefore more rhetorical than substantive. So for my present purpose I will simply lay it aside. What is important is that the intending ego *both* appropriates meanings constitutive of its culture and, in moments of creativity, interprets, enhances, distorts and reformulates them. Thus subjectivity and intentionality are incurably cultural, as much as a 'culture' is incurably tinged, impregnated and constituted by subjectivity.

This cultural feature of subjectivity leads me to draw attention to two related features, namely to historicity and temporality. If a culture is but sedimented meanings, it is historical; and being historical, intentionality is also temporal. The ideas of historicity and temporality have received a great deal of attention, and also new formulations from the phenomenologists—from Heidegger and Husserl in particular.[10] Temporality as an intrinsic feature of subjectivity is *not*, to be sure, simply being *in* time, as physical processes are, but is that flow of experiencing in which the *now* carries within its structure the past as a retention and the future as a protention, so that around the *now* there is a temporal horizon which, as it recedes into the distant past, intersects with the new and advancing horizons and is retained in memory. This retention leads back eventually to the 'origins' in early infancy and birth; the series of protentions to the ultimate end, as Heidegger first pointed out, to death—both birth and death to be construed not as physical events observed and observable by the third person observer, but as the outermost limits of subjectivity's self-experience, limits without which human subjectivity, raised to the godly, would lose its intrinsic temporality and finiteness.

This last-mentioned finiteness of human subjectivity—as philosophers such as Aristotle and Kant had clearly recognized—is indicated not alone by the natality and mortality which stand as outer and yet internal limits to its self-awareness, but also by a feature that belongs to it at every moment of its life. This is its passivity, or as Kant puts it, *receptivity*. My saying that subjectivity confers meaning on its world should not be construed to mean that subjectivity creates meaningful objects from within. It rather means that there is always a given, passively received, sensory material—which is then 'animated' by a meaning. The life of subjectivity is never free from this material, sensory component, just as it is never merely this: there is no bare sensation that is not interpreted as the presentation of such and such object, no bare impulse that is not interpreted as a desire, love or hope for, no bare feeling pro or con that is not interpreted as an act of valuation. The receptivity of subjectivity is bound to the facticity of the situation as much as to the facticity of the body; the *noema* becomes not an abstract concept but a mode of presentation of a thing over there, the theory of meaning enters into a theory of perception.

I think it is important at this point that we recognize the relation between the meanings subtended by intentionality and by language. This complex relation can be elucidated by the following distinctions, to say the least. First, we shall draw a distinction between a subjective experience as lived, as felt by the subject, and as intentional referring to, directed towards, being of an object. The German language provides us with two words for this—*Erlebnis* and *Erfahrung*. When I perceive an external object, the perceiving is an *Erlebnis* in so far as it is an experience being lived by the subject, it is an *Erfahrung* inasmuch as it is of the tree over there. Thus every intentional experience has a felt, *erlebt* aspect which the scientific theorist may consider superfluous and even recalcitrant for a theory, but which is basic for a subject's mental life as felt by him/her from within. (It is this aspect which Tom Nagel sought to draw attention to by asking 'what is it to be a bat?') Thus, every intentional experience has a non-intentional, reflexive aspect. But, it is only an aspect, not a completed experience for which the other, intentional aspect is needed. Likewise, I would distinguish between pre-conceptual, pre-linguistic meaning and conceptual, linguistic meaning. In drawing this distinction I am indebted to the work of Eugene Gendlin[11] who makes the important point that the same word 'hostility' or 'jitteriness' may stand for an experiential meaning as well as for a 'logical' concept. While admitting that concept and so linguistic expression, does transform the original pre-conceptual, pre-linguistic, experiential meaning, one need not be unnecessarily sceptical about the expressibility of the latter. To mark the transformation, I would distinguish between 'hostility' and 'hostility*'.

What I am driving at is the recognition that we need not be pushed towards an ineffability thesis as also to a privacy thesis. It is a common objection against keeping the ideas of experiencing and experiential meaning at the centre, that it makes psychology as a science, as a theory, impossible. The experiencing is private to the experiencer, so also is the experiential meaning: how then are they available to the scientist? You also tend to be in the grips of the ineffability thesis—thus keeping the door open for a Buddhist-type 'silence'. While agreeing that phenomenology should focus on the experience and its experiential meaning, I want to maintain: (i) that experience is *expressible* and so can be referred to; and (ii) that although the act of experiencing is a private occurrence in the interiority of a subject's mental life, its correlative *Sinn* is, through linguistic expression, or through any symbolic expression, communicable. The *Sinn* always has a generality, a public character. Both the ineffability and the privacy thesis are mistaken.

What I have attempted in the foregoing is to draw a brief sketch of the essential structure of human subjectivity, of that *psyché* which defines the subject matter of psychology as a science. The importance of keeping this structure in mind lies in that it is in the light of this that we can evaluate how good a psychological theory, a given theory, is as a *psychological* theory. In this sense, a phenomenology of subjectivity—not itself a psychological theory—defines the basic framework—or, what Husserl called the 'regional essence'—of psychology.

Now we are in a position to assess the viability of physicalism which claims that the mental is identical with the bodily. Having first determined the intentionality of the mental, its character as a correlation between *noesis* and *noema*, its historicity and temporality, we can then ask if a physicalist theory can have room for these features. Can these features be meaningfully ascribed to brain processes? If the physicalist wants, however, to eliminate them on the ground that a physicalistically describable world has no room for them, he has the right to do so, but we can legitimately ask him why he claims he is giving a theory of the *mind*, a *psychological* theory, and why should a good psychological theory assume, to begin with, that a physicalist world-view provides the ideal framework for psychology to operate. Thus, phenomenology can provide the theorist with a standard, a measure against which to measure its success as a psychological theory—even if phenomenology does not by itself provide a *theory*.

III

In the rest of this lecture, I will reflect on two branches of contemporary psychology and their relation to phenomenology: these are cognitive psychology and psycho-analysis. In general, let us remember, phenomenology will focus on experiencings and their meanings or *noemata*. And above all, it will be a descriptive, and not an explanatory science.

The centrality of the ideas of intentionality and meaning have led many practitioners on both sides to detect a close affinity between phenomenology and cognitive science. In 1982, Hubert Dreyfus spoke of 'Husserl's anticipation of cognitive psychology' by construing the *noema* as a 'rule' 'to synthesize the manifold of experiences into a unified experience of a unified object', and by so broadening the idea of mental activity that it does not require consciousness at all.[12] The cognitive psychologists' affinity to Husserl comes out perhaps best in Jerry Fodor's 'methodological solipsism' as a research strategy in cognitive psychology which proposes a step such as Husserl's phenomenological *epoché*.[13] Both Fodor and Husserl reject 'naturalistic psychology.' Fodor opts for computational psychology and a representational theory of the mind (RTM), in which an internal system of mental representations is posited. The intentionality of a mental state is determined by the *contents* or meanings of the mental representations it involves, precisely in the same way as the intentionality of a sentence or picture depends upon the meanings of the symbols it uses. So, for this theory, there are between mind and world two other entities, a mental symbol and its content. The Husserlian *noema* and the *content* of the RTM are much alike. But Husserl has no mental symbols. Noemata *are* meanings. Now there are two reasons for this difference. The computational theory, despite its rejection of naturalistic psychology, nevertheless wants to conform to an overarching physicalism. The mental symbol or representation permits itself to be given a physicalist interpretation. Phenomenology does not share this anxiety to preserve physicalism. Second, the positing of mental symbols upon which computations are made only by virtue of their formal shapes is an explanatory theory. These symbols are theoretical entities. Phenomenology restricts itself to meanings (which are rather modes of presentation) which are descriptively identifiable. Intentionality need not be accounted for; it is an intrinsic feature of meanings. Phenomenology rejects a causal theory of reference. Cognitive psychology wants to have both a causal theory *and* a methodological solipsism.

A phenomenological psychology would not worry about preserving either physicalism or mentalism. Its chief focus shall be experiencing in all its dimensions and its structures; here again its primary data shall be meanings, both pre-conceptual and conceptual.

Similar brief remarks about psycho-analysis may be in order. Two possible understandings of psycho-analysis need to be avoided from the phenomenological perspective. On the one hand, phenomenology has to be a critique of 'positing' of *theoretical* entities—as much of 'mental symbols' as of the Unconscious. Any entity posited must be accessible to retrieval in consciousness. Phenomenology must also reject any mechanical account of mental life—whether in terms of neurons or in terms of 'repression'. Freud famously used both of the latter languages, and made it appear as if the Unconscious was a theoretical entity posited for *explanatory* purpose. The task, then, of phenomenology *vis-à-vis* psycho-analysis is to open an experiential access into the Unconscious. The early phenomenologists such as Sartre totally rejected Freud, for having posited a thing-like in-itself within the very heart of 'human reality' or being-for-itself, and wanted to replace Freudian psycho-analysis by what came to be known as existential psycho-analysis. There is no doubt also that Husserl, with his emphasis on intentionality as the act of an ego, started with a skepticism about the concept of the unconscious. But in the *Formal and Transcendental Logic*, he writes: 'Far from being a "phenomenological nothing", the "so-called Unconscious," or "universal substratum" where sense is deposited, is limit-mode of consciousness.'[14] In which aspect of consciousness precisely, can phenomenology search for an access to the unconscious? Ricoeur sought for it—not in his Freud' book, but in the earlier *Freedom and Nature*[15]—in the so-called *hyle*. I have referred earlier to the receptive–affective core in consciousness. The *hyle* impinges itself on consciousness, it is not an intentional act. The ego is not a master of its hyletic field. It can be overpowered by it. As Aaron Mishara has pointed out, in Freud's system the sensation and its retention as an unconscious trace are outside of consciousness, consciousness being only *nachträglich;* for Husserl, both sensing and retention occur in consciousness, the retention gradually becomes a *Leervorstellung,* and recedes into the unconscious.[16] What Husserl pursues, in his Freiburg lectures, is a method by which to follow retention into the 'dark sphere' of the 'night of the unconscious'; a new and more radical reduction in which empirical associations—reproductive and anticipatory—are 'bracketed', and a path is opened into the *Urassoziation* in the living present functioning according to passive synthesis of 'similarity, contiguity and contrast' amongst the hyletic data and 'feelings of sensual preference' amongst these data dictated by 'instinctual drives' (but not acts of the ego). The *Urassociation* within the hyletic data falls into two stages: pre-affective and affective, the former being unconscious, the latter on the way to consciousness. The affective syntesis consists in the attractive force or pull that the hyletic field exercises on the ego, thereby 'awakening' the ego and stimulating it into activity. The affective saliences (*Abgehobenheiten*) function against the background of pre-affective background. The threshold between the two fluctuates relative to the greatest affective contrasts within the impressional content. Pre-affective formulation of the hyletic unities occurs prior to the 'awakening of the ego to activity'. The unconscious then, in Mishara's formulation, is 'the furthermost background from which the relief emerges at its lowest point'.[17]

In the hyletic field, Husserl continues, there is conflict amongst affections so that the victorious one suppresses the others, the 'suppression' being also a 'preserving' of the repressed affective force. In the present field, there is something which comes to the advantage of the repressed and awakens it. We have here the rudiments of a phenomenological theory of the unconscious.

CONCLUSION

In this lecture I have attempted to present the relevance of Husserlian phenomenology for psychology. In so doing, I have consciously departed from the tradition of using Heideggerean *Dasein-analytic* for that purpose. I hope to have been able to show that Husserlian phenomenology *directly attacks* the problems of psychology, suggests research strategies which can be fruitfully pursued, and I hope, to the benefit of working psychologists.

The greatest contribution of phenomenology for psychology is to pre-determine the field of psychology as *the field of* subjectivity in terms of (a) the pre-intentional hyletic experiences and (b) intentionality which confers meaning on the *hyle* and constitutes the meaningful objects of experience. I have given a somewhat detailed account of the structure of intentionality, and have suggested that a psychological theory be evaluated in the light of these structures.

If we take the phenomeonological method seriously, we have to describe the *noemata*, or meanings, from the perspective of their producer, namely the subject. The serious methodological problem, of course, lies as to how the investigator can have access to the subject's experiential meanings. Get rid of the privacy-assumption, and keep in mind the expressibility thesis—we would find a way out of the sceptical challenge. One of the pervasive prejudices of the Anglo-American analytic philosophies is that the mental is private, that the bodily is public. Phenomenology fundamentally challenges this.

As a phenomenologist, I will tell the psychologists: do not regard physics as your model. Do not aim at squeezing your theory of the *psyché* into the physicist's world. The physicist is no closer to reality than you are. Don't worry about ontology—much less about a physicalist ontology. Let the philosopher worry about that, about the possibility of a unified view of things. The mysteries of the mental processes are enough to keep you challenged and engaged.

NOTES

1. E. Husserl, *Logische Untersuchangen*, 2 vol. (Halle-Max Niemeyer, 1900–1901).

2. E. Husserl, *Phänomenologische Psychologie* (Husserliana IX) (The Hague: M. Nijhoff, 1962).

3. E. Husserl, *Die Krisis der europäischen Wissenschaften und die transzendentale Phänomenologie* (Husserliana VI) (The Hague: M. Nijhoff, 1954).

4. M. Merlean-Ponty, The *Structure of Behaviour* (Boston: Beacon Press, 1963).

5. P. Ricoeur, *Freud and Philosophy: An Interpretation* (New Haven: Yale University Press, 1970).

6. Evanston: Northwestern University Press, 1972.

7. Evanston: Northwestern University Press, 1987.

8. David Hume, *An Enquiry Concerning Human Understanding*.

9. E. Husserl, *Cartesian Meditations* (The Hague: M. Nijhoff, 1960), p. 44.

10. E. Husserl, Zur Phánomenologie des inneren Zeitbewusstseins (1893–1917). (Husserliana X), (The Hague: M. Nijhoff 1969) and *Die Krisis*. Also M. Heidegger, *Sein und Zeit* (Tübingen: Niemeyer, 1927).

11. E. Gendlin, *Experiencing and the Creation of Meaning* (New York: Free Press, 1962). Also J.N. Mohanty 'Experience and Meaning', in: David M. Levin (ed.), *Language beyond Post-Modernism*. (Evanston: Northwestern University Press, 1997), pp. 17.

12. H. Dreyfus (ed.), *Husserl, Intentionality and Cognitive Science* (Cambridge, Mass: The M.I.T. Press, 1982), esp. The editor's Introduction, p. 11.

13. Jerry Fodor, 'Methodological Solipsism Considered as a Research Strategy in Cognitive Psychology', in *Husserl, Intentionality and Cognitive Science*.

14. E. Husserl, *Formal and transcendental Logic*, Eng. tr. D. Cairns (The Hague: M. Nijhoff, 1969), p. 18.

15. P. Ricoeur, *Freedom and Nature: The Voluntary and the Involuntary*, Eng. tr. Evazim V. Kohak (Evanston: Northwestern University Press, 1966).

16. A. Mishara, 'Husserl, Freud: Time, Memory and the Unconscious' *Husserl Studies*, vol. 7, no. 1, 1990, pp. 29–58.

17. Ibid., pp. 31ff.

chapter

eighteen

Remarks on Wilfrid Sellars' Paper
on Perceptual Consciousness*

When called upon to comment upon Professor Wilfrid Sellars' contribution to the symposium on 'Consciousness', I could not but accept the invitation, for I knew that a paper by Wilfrid Sellars must offer what any commentator would want—substantial and provocative philosophical thought; the temptation to respond to that sort of challenge was too strong to resist. On reading his paper, I was comforted that like me he did not see an unbridgeable gulf between phenomenological analysis and conceptual analysis; amazed by the skill with which he has practised phenomenological reduction by gradually 'thinning out perceptual commitments', and intrigued by some of the theses that he seems to me to be defending. In these remarks, I will first turn to three such theses. With two of them, I find myself in substantial agreement, so I will spend some time in elaborating them in the way I would like them to be understood. With the third I disagree. That I concentrate on these alone is not in any way to be construed to suggest that I do not think many of the other things he says in this essay are important; in fact, they are all so unique that they deserve the minutest scrutiny. The three theses on which I will concentrate are as follows:

1. In paragraph 12, Sellars writes that although acts of believing are not linguistic, 'they are sufficiently analogous in essential structure

---

*Cross currents in Phenomenology, (eds) Bruzina and Wilshire, The Hague: Nijhoff, 1979.

and function to the sentence tokens which express them in candid speech, for it to be appropriate to make an analogical use of semantical terminology in describing them'. This strikes me as a most intriguing and yet essentially true thesis. It is also basic to the essay, for the account of perceptual consciousness follows rather closely the guideline of the sentences that would most appropriately express such consciousness.

2. In section IV of his essay, Sellars tells us something about how far sheer phenomenology or conceptual analysis can take us; it can take us only to the recognition of 'the somehow, other than believed in, presence' of such-and-such object and not beyond it. I agree with this, but only in part.

3. Feeling the need for going beyond phenomenology and conceptual analysis, Sellars introduces 'visual sensations' as theoretical postulates, formulates again an 'analogy between manners of sensing and perceptual attributes of physical objects' (compare the analogy in thesis I) and after undertaking a 'thinning out of perceptual commitments' proceeds to advance the thesis—for me, the most intriguing of all—that the referent of 'this' in the demonstrative subject term of the sentence expressing the 'reduced' perceptual consciousness is nothing other than a sensation. At this stage of my thinking on this essay, and to the extent I have been able to understand what he is doing, I am convinced that in this he must be wrong.

II

An occurrent act of believing is a mental act. This act is expressed in a sentence such as 'This paper is white'. There is a clear sense in which the act of believing is totally unlike a linguistic event (unless one wants to construe it as sub-vocal speech). An utterance of the sentence, however, is a linguistic event. Further, the act of believing that is appropriately expressed in the sentence 'This paper is white' should be, not numerically but structurally, the same act as is expressed in the sentence 'Dieses Papier ist weiss'. And yet these two are different linguistic entities, their utterances are different linguistic events in a sense in which two utterances of the sentence type 'This paper is white' are not. In an important sense, the concept of 'linguisticality' is relative to some language or other. The structural identity of the two acts must then be independent of the differences of languages in which they are expressed, and must be grounded in what is invariant in the midst of those differences. According to a dominant philosophical tradition, what is invariant is the *proposition* or the thought expressed in the two sentences. A proposition is linguistic in the sense that, by definition, it is the *sense* of a declarative *sentence*, although it is non-linguistic in the sense that it is an abstract entity, a *sense*, and is invariant, for example, between what is expressed in 'This paper is white' and 'Dieses Papier ist weiss'. One way of making sense of the claim that acts of believing, though not themselves linguistic, are 'sufficiently analogous in essential structure and function to the sentence tokens which express them' is to distinguish between an occurrent act and its *content* as two inseparable aspects of a believing and then to say that the content is *propositional* (and so is analogous to the sentence). It should be noted that in this context 'content' does not mean a real phase or component of the act, but what is believed in precisely as it is being believed in, something which Husserl sought to capture by the word 'noematic sense'. Such a distinction can be made also with respect to acts other than believing: in each case, we would then have two act-moments. Two occurrent acts are by definition numerically different acts; the same act cannot recur. However, of two acts we can say that they are both acts of believing; and of two acts of believing, we can say that they have the same content. Thus, that an act is an act of believing and not, let us say, an act of doubting, expresses its 'quality'; and that it is *of* a content *p* expresses its act-matter. Two acts of believing which have the same content agree both in their quality and matter; in Husserl's language, they have the same intentional essence. Here we have a criterion of identity of acts for purposes of conceptual analysis or eidetic phenomenological description: acts having the same quality and the same matter, i.e. having the same intentional essence, may as well be regarded as the same.

Now we appear to have a clear sense in which to speak of the structure of a belief as being analogous to the structure of a sentence. The content of a belief, the *what* one believes in, is a proposition which is the sense of a sentence. That sentence not only expresses the sense, the act's matter, but also (in a slightly different sense of 'expressing') the quality of the act. The act of believing finds expression in a declarative sentence, an act of doubting in a problematic one. If not the isolated sentence by itself, then certainly the context of discourse, and such features as intonation, spacing and gesture, bring the quality of the act into expression.

It may be argued that although the proposition believed in has a structure analogous to the structure of the sentence expressing the act

of believing, to say that the act itself has that or an analogous structure is highly misleading, if not false. To be able to appreciate the
extent to which it is not misleading, it is necessary to emphasize that
mental life is not a uni-dimensional succession of acts and states,
but to borrow Aron Gurwitsch's suggestive phrase 'a correlation or
parallelism between the plane of acts, psychical events, noeses, and a
second plane which is that of sense (*noemata*).'[1] For such a conception of consciousness, to every act there belongs a sense which is not
a real component or phase of that act but its intentional correlate.
This view is different from another which is very much like it and
was widely held at one time: the view that an act of consciousness is
of an object (which may be a physical object or an abstract entity),
but the object even when it is an abstract entity is as much independent of the act as a perceptual object is independent of the act of
perceiving it. It is in this latter view that one could say that the act is
not propositional, though its object may be. But in theory of consciousness for which an act and its sense are inseparable, the
propositional character would directly belong to the sense and indirectly to the act whose sense it is. It is owing to such considerations
that Husserl held that 'linguisticality' *(Sprachlichkeit)* is a most universal feature of consciousness, that every noematic sense is 'expressible',
that the logical meaning in fact is the expression. I would go even
further and assert that since the linguistic act itself is an intentional
act and so a modality of consciousness, and since every act is essentially 'expressible', the linguistic act (of speaking) is that subset of the
total domain of acts into which the entire domain can be 'mapped'.

While this is the way I would like Professor Sellars' thesis to be
understood, I would however insist that there is a 'surplus' in
consciousness over its most candid linguistic expression, and there
is a serious risk if the 'analogical' nature of the relation is forgotten
and replaced by identity or even strict isomorphism. The 'surplus'
may be indicated, in the first place, by saying that although every
perceptual consciousness—with which we are here specifically
concerned—is in an important sense aware of itself, this aspect of
its being, its translucency, is not 'reflected' in the sentence expressing
the perceptual consciousness by any 'analogous' structure. There is
also another aspect of the situation, more tangible than the first
one. The same perceptual statement, 'This paper is white' may express
a perceptual consciousness which is a seeing that this paper is white
or also a perceptual consciousness which is a seeing that the white is

the colour of this paper. Linguistically, the statement may be construed as answering the question, 'What is the colour of this paper?' or as answering the question, 'Of what is this white the colour?' What this shows is that perceptual consciousness is underdetermined by its object and is not fully reflected in the sentence expressing it. In fact, for a proper analysis of the sentence we need to consider the context with a view to determining the perceptual consciousness itself—for, as Cook Wilson had long since pointed out, in one case the subject term would be 'This paper', in the other case 'White'. Finally—and this is the last of the points I want to make in connection with the relation between an act and the sentence expressing it—although one may speak of the 'subject' and 'predicate' of the belief itself, it is necessary not to forget that there is a difference between the pre-predicative, perceptual 'as' and the predicative 'is'. A thing's *looking* as something is not the perceiver's *judging that* it is such and such.

These remarks are not intended to be construed as if Sellars errs on these scores. Far from it: what he has said is consistent with these and I have tried to make explicit what I thought to be implicit in the total significance of his remarks.

III

This brings me to the second thesis of Sellars, which is that sheer phenomenology or conceptual analysis can take us only up to a recognition of 'the *somehow*, other than as believed in presence' of such and such object and not beyond it. I have said that I agree with it but only as subject to qualifications.

Let us recall that 'the somehow other than believed in presence of a cube of pink in physical space facing me edgewise' is, according to Sellars, common to veridical as well as non-veridical perception. In veridical perception, there is something real out there: a cube of pink ice in physical space facing me edgewise. But if my perception was in fact a hallucination, the perceived cube of pink ice did not exist out there and yet there was something standing before me, something that was being perceived as a cube of pink ice. Back again to veridical perception: let us apply phenomenological reduction, and set out of action belief in the real existence of the object. What is still left over is a relation between perceptual consciousness and its object. In the reduced perception we still find the perceived as such to be a cube of pink facing me edgewise in physical space; but—as Husserl writes—'all these descriptive statements, though very similar in sound to statements concerning reality, have undergone a radical modification of meaning . . . in virtue, so to speak, of an inverting change of signature'. This 'cube of pink facing me edge-wise in physical space' is the intentional correlate of the reduced perceptual consciousness, it is not a real component of that con-sciousness, it is neither in the mind nor out there, though 'being out there' is a component of its *sense*. Hence its *somehow* character. It is the Husserlian noema. The cube of pink has not, because of the reduction, forfeited the least shade of content from all the phases, qualities, characters with which it appeared. Only everything has been changed from an ontological predicate to a 'meaning'. There has been, if I may use Quine's well known metaphor, a 'phenomenological ascent' from the talk about things and their qualities to the talk of a complex structure of meanings and its components.

Now why does Sellars think that there is here a philosophical task beyond phenomenology, that the mere isolation of the noema leaves unexplained something, to explain which he takes recourse to the theoretical concept of 'sensation?' Since the '*somehow*, other than as believed in, presence of a cube of pink ice facing one edgewise' is common to veridical and non-veridical perceptions of a cube of pink ice facing one edgewise, there is still the philosophical task of accounting for that distinction, and it is for this purpose that the concept of sensation and the appeal to causal processes appears relevant. Sellars is perfectly right, in my view, when he says that the visual sensations are not yielded by phenomenological reduction, but postulated by a proto-scientific theory. But if the task of phenomenology is to 'explicate' the distinction between veridical and non veridical perception in the sense of finding the 'equivalent' of that distinction within the reduced consciousness, then this can be done and has been done—roughly as follows. First, within the structure of the *noema* one has to locate such properties as 'real', or 'being out there'. Hence, although the noema itself has a *somehow* nature—we do not know where to locate it—it contains, in the case of perceptual consciousness, the predicate 'really out there', for this, property belongs to the very *sense* of the physical object *qua* perceived. The full implications when made explicit of the noematic predicate would include the presumption of a certain coherence with the *noemata* of other perceptual acts having 'the same' object. The *sense* of this sameness again, on its part, needs a similar explication. The claim of a perceptual consciousness to be veridical is the claim of a *noema* to being harmonious or congruent with an infinite number of such noemata. Similar explication is needed for the appraisal that a perceptual consciousness is non-veridical.

IV

The thesis of Sellars which for me is most difficult to understand as well as to accept is, that the ultimate referent of 'This' in 'This cube of pink over there . . .', particularly after what he calls the thinning out its perceptual commitments, is nothing other than a sensation.

As far as I can see, Sellars' crucial move is:—Begin with a statement about:

This cube of pink over there facing me edgewise.

Phenomenological reduction leaves us with a statement about:

This *somehow* (cube of pink over there facing me edgewise).

In this reduced statement 'This' refers, not to the cube of pink ice over there, for *ex hypothesi* there is none. It therefore refers to what is *somehow* a cube of pink ice over there facing me edgewise. And the sensation is indeed that.

I find the following problems in this move:

1. When Sellars writes, 'the sensation is indeed that in the experience which is *somehow* a cube of pink over there facing me edgewise', note that he has removed the brackets that had enclosed the expression 'a cube of pink . . .'. This is significant, for with the opening of the brackets what the expression refers to is a thing—not a *noema*—and if it is not the thing out there it may conceivably be the sensation.

2. He says the sensation *is* that in the experience which is indeed somehow a cube of pink . . . Now, I fail to see how sensation which is a theoretical entity can be *in the experience*. Yet if it were not in some sense in the experience, it could not serve as the referent of a perceptual statement which has been stripped of its ontological commitments.

3. Though in accordance with his principle of analogy laid down in paragraph 44 the sensation may *somehow* be a cube of pink, yet a sensation does not possess the *somehow* presence with which phenomenology had to stop. Is it possible that he is using 'somehow' in the two cases differently? If sensation is indeed that whose recognition earlier provided the point of terminus for phenomenology, it would not also be the theoretical entity that it is intended to be. If it is a theoretical entity, it has a very precisely definable mode of be-

ing; it is far from being the somehow presence that I encountered in non-veridical seeing.

4. Even if according to Sellars the perceiver does not conceptualize his sensation as a sensation, it should be in principle permissible—if his theory of ultimate reference is to be accepted—to replace the demonstrative phrase in some way by a name or description of the sensation *qua* sensation without engendering absurdity.

5. As far as I can see, if the sensation indeed is that which is *somehow* a cube of pink over there facing me edgewise, my interpretation of Sellars' second thesis as amounting to a recognition of the perceptual noema must be wrong, for a sensation is not a *noema* and a *noema* is not a theoretical entity.

While thus I find it difficult to accept his account of the ultimate referent of 'this' in the reduced perceptual statement, I nevertheless agree with his distinction, in the case of a statement of the form 'This S is p', between the complex demonstrative constituent ('This S') and the predicate 'is p'—the former being a pre-supposition that is *taken* and the latter being what is believed about what is so taken. This is a valuable distinction, which to my mind is consistent with the following analysis of the constitution of the perceptual judgement of the form 'This S is p':

'This S' designates what is the object of a simple apprehension. This object is held in grasp, while an act of explication analyses it and fixes upon p as a determination of what is so held in grasp by an act of synthesis (which is originally perceptual, not judgemental or predicative—as a result of which a judgement of the form 'This S is p' is made possible. But this new objectivety or state of affairs may itself be objectified in an act of simple apprehension and an act of explication and a similar synthesis (at first perceptual, not predicative) may generate a judgement of the form 'This S (p) is q', That there is always a taking, a presupposition prior to believing *that*, corroborates the phenomenological thesis that all perception takes place within the horizon of typicality and pre-acquaintanceship.

V

I propose to end this commentary, so long restricted to Sellars' stimulating thoughts, by making a few observations, not quite unrelated to his essay, but having a more general relevance to the theme of 'consciousness'. It is only in the fitness of things that his essay is devoted to perceptual consciousness, for in an important sense, and according to a long metaphysical tradition, all consciousness is basically perceptual. Readers of Husserl's writings are impressed by the fact that the perceptual model, more specifically, the model of visual perception, weighs so heavily on his thinking. In fact, this has been a familiar criticism against him. On the other hand, we also know how in his *Logical Investigations* linguistic acts are taken up first, and how the central theses that are established with regard to these acts—namely that every such act has a *sense* as distinguished from reference, and further that in understanding an expression, or meaningfully using one, there is a meaning-intending act that supervenes as its were upon a sensuous act of (visual or auditory) presentation, interprets it and forms an indissoluble unity with it—are then extended to all acts of consciousness, so that every act is said to have its noematic correlate whose central nucleus is its *sense* and in every act there is found to be a meaning-giving or interpreting function that 'animates' the so-called hyletic component. Now, what we find here is that the linguistic model is made to apply to the paradigmatic intuitive act, i.e. the perceptual act. The problem, for Husserl interpretation, is: which model was primary for him? Did he interpret the linguistic act as if it involved an inspection, a mental seeing as it were, of meanings and categorial objectivities? Or, did he rather interpret perceptual acts as if they involved the sort of interpretation of data and the sort of sense-reference distinction which we find in the case of linguistic acts? It has been the contention of hermeneutic phenomenology that all human experience is interpretative (of itself and of its world), which is set in opposition to the allegedly Husserlian emphasis on the givenness of objectivities. On the one side, there is the model of the text, on the other, the model of perception of the pre-given natural world. My submission is that, not only for a true and deeper understanding of Husserlian thought, but also for an adequate philosophy of consciousness, it is necessary to see that both these models need to supplement each other—not as though there are two different types of consciousness, one of which fits the one model and the other fits the other one, but as though every act of consciousness is both intuitive and interpretative. What at one level is an interpretation, is at another level an intuited datum. Just as the fact that the meaning-intending act is an interpretation is not inconsistent with the claim that there is, in an important sense, a grasping of meaning, so the fact that in perceptual consciousness there is an interpretation of what is given is not inconsistent with the claim that the object is bodily given in perception. Consciousness is both intuitive and interpretative in one.

NOTE

1. A. Gurwitsch, *Studies in Phenomenology and Psychology* (Evanston: Northwestern University Press, 1966), p. 138.

chapter

nineteen

Thoughts on the Concept of 'World'*

Trying to think about the *world*, I cannot but begin with the sharp and precise formulations Kant gave to this concept. The Kantian thesis may be briefly stated thus: if by 'world' we mean nature, which is the proper subject matter of investigation by mathematical physics, the system of sensible things and events ordered in space and time and connected by principles such as causality, then the world is indeed constituted by the human mind with its a *priori* forms of intuition, space and time, and its *a priori* forms of understanding, i.e. categories such as substance and causality. The mind, however, *receives* the basic data, i.e. the sense-impressions upon which its *a priori* forms work, which they order and synthesize, thereby constituting an order of phenomena which, precisely because it has constituted it and to the extent that it has done so, the mind can, as is evidenced by mathematical physics, know *a priori*. As far as Nature is concerned, Kant conceded that mathematical physics can deliver to us its true nature. In the third critique, *Critique of Judgment*, however, Kant asked: how can this nature, mathematical in structure, be also purposive and beautiful.

Pursuing the Kantian theme further, we need to distinguish between the world as nature and world as an infinite totality. If physics is the science of the former and is justified in its claim to

The Visva Bharati Quarterly, Vol. 43, 1977–8.

give us knowledge about it, metaphysic's claim to deliver to us knowledge about the latter is spurious. To know an infinite totality is to posit an infinite series as completed. Kant showed, in various ways, that such a positing involves hopeless contradictions. The 'world as a whole' or 'totality of all things' is an inconsistent concept. In this essay I do not propose to elaborate on this Kantian dialectic, but rather depart from the problem-situation which we inherit from Kant. The leading question for me is: 'How shall we think the concept of world such that we can avoid the Kantian antinomies, and yet appropriate the Kantian insights?'

In answering the question, I shall suggest two propositions, the first of which is closer to Kant's first thesis but involves a radical reformulation of it, and the second, following the lead of contemporary phenomenology, resolves the problem of totality in a manner more satisfactory than Kant's. The first proposition is: the world of physics is indeed a construction, not out of atomic sense-impressions but out of pre-scientific worlds. The second proposition is: what is given is not—and here Kant is undoubetedly right—the totality of all things, but the world as the all-comprehensive *horizon* within which everything whatsoever is given and thought of. After I have elaborated these two propositions, I shall return at the end to the theme of 'totality'.

II

It has, rightly I think, been pointed out that Kant did not overcome the Humean atomistic psychology according to which our experience is built out of simple, atomic and discrete impressions. Such simple impressions or sensations, far from being the given par excellence, are rather constructs, *theoretiaal* entities, presupposing an entire nexus of theories, especially physics and physiological psychology. The physical sciences could not then be regarded as constructions out of them as building blocks. Taking into account, then, the insights of contemporary phenomenology, we can say that all experience, even the simplest and the most 'primitive', is intentional and meaningful and locates its objects within a world. But, not for all experience, this correlative world is the world of physics. The expression 'world of physics' is ambiguous. For one thing, it means the world of 'scientific entities' (elementary particles, energy quanta, waves, etc.); in another sense, it means the world of experienceable things and events determined and governed by laws of physics and for whose explanation the scientific entities are posited as theoretical constructs.

Nature, as Kant understood it, is the world of physics in the latter sense. It is important, for my present purpose, to emphasize that this is not the world as we live in it, as we perceive in pre-scientific experience, and as we relate to in everyday life. Husserl sought to capture this pre-scientific world precisely as it is experienced in everday life by the historically decisive expression 'life-world'.

In this essay I shall refer to only some important aspects of life-world. First, the space and time of the pre-scientific world, or as they are experienced prior to scientific determination, are not the Euclidean space and the one-dimensional, irreversible and uniformly flowing time which Kant held to be the forms of intuition and in which, in his view, sense-impressions are ordered. In fact, lived space and lived time are qualitatively diversified and are not yet merely quantitative dimensions of ordering. Let me recall such distinctions as profane space and sacred space, space that is threatening (as in a strange place) and space that is reassuring (as in home), far and near (one who is near in the physical space may indeed be far away in the space of communication), musical space and the space of paintings, the space as experienced in walking and the space as experienced in dancing. We find similar phenomena in connection with time. The time of religious experience is not one-dimensional and irreversible. Celebration of religious events is a reliving of those events, of the return of the cycle. Even day to day secular experience of time is marked by qualitative distinctions which are expressed by such locutions as 'a moment seemed to be an age'. Lived time does not flow at a uniform speed. To *explain* such distinctions as being due to subjective interpretations or colourings is to make use of a Cartesian dualism between the subjective and the objective, which is an intellectual achievement, historically accomplished and consolidated, and to which life-world is prior and anterior.

It is also not true that the life-world is not characterized by causality. But the causality of life-world is not yet the strictly physical causality of natural science. Causality is rather undistinguished from interest and motivation. Since the subjective and the objective are not yet separated, the concept of purely physical event causing another purely physical event is lacking in the life-world. In fine, life-world is the field for inexact, vague concepts rather than the exact concepts of geometry, physics and eidetic thinking. Shapes are more or less circular, rather than perfect circles. It required a great deal of intellectual achievement to be able to idealize the life-worldly forms, shapes and modes of connection so as to arrive at the geometricization and mathematicization of space, time and causality, and thereby at the idea of the world of physics. I distinguished earlier between two senses of the world of physics. In one sense, it is the *explanandum*, the world of 'purely' physical things, events, connections and processes; in the other sense, it is the *explanans*, the world of 'minute' entities, particles and waves, and mathematical laws. It is important to recognize that the *explanandum* and *explanans* need each other and presuppose each other. The idealization that makes possible the world of 'purely' physical things, events, connections and processes, also makes possible the positing of theoretical entities as explanatory constructs, and what are at first idealized constructs also determine the way we perceive the world and therefore also the world we perceive.

At the source of the constitution of the *one* objective world, Nature, there lies the role of our body. Piaget has shown that for children, at a certain stage in their learning process, their own bodies are not objectified as items in the phenomenal space in which they perceive sensory data. In Piaget's theory constitution of an objective world in objective space requires objectification of one's own body. Phenomenologists such as Scheler and Merleau-Ponty have distinguished between lived body and objective body. Lived body is body as felt from within. It is not one thing amongst others, but rather that unobjective 'zero-point' around which all other objects centre and from which they derive their significance. It is not so much a totality of parts (i.e. hands, feet, etc.) as a nexus of powers and abilities through which the world around becomes 'practically' meaningful. A 'horizon' of practical possibilities surrounds the lived body, which contains not so much objects of cognition as fields for 'I can'. However, the body is *also* an object, even if it is never fully objectified. Or, rather any objectification of my body leaves an unobjective background of felt body. I will not go into the steps in the process of this objectification. What I want to point out is that in the constitution of one objective world, eventually the world of physics, objectification of *my* body (in so far as I, and so also you, belong to that world) plays a decisive role.

Amongst the other factors that determine the constitution of the one objective world, we should mention language. The world-making role of language was never so much in the forefront of human consciousness as in our times. I will recall only two aspects of the situation. For one thing, from the contentual point of view, a language determines, as Sapir and Whorf have demonstrated, how the world is cut out into different entities, what sorts of distinctions can or cannot be made in one's world, and what ontological categories ('substance-quality' or 'event-occurrence') are basic to it. Out of these incommensurate languages and their associated worlds, the language of science—truth-functional and extensional—stands out as the correlate of the one objective world of physics. The transformation, through idealization, of many languages into the one extensional language of logic (and mathematics), goes hand in hand with the construction of that one world. With this intellectual achievement, both 'language' and 'world' lose a major component of their original senses. The formal language is not any longer *spoken* by any one, it is no one's own language, it does not embody any community's intentions, just as the world of physics is no one's, no community's own world. It is the world as it is when all human subjectivity is 'removed' from the scene. A new tradition, paradoxically, emerges: the tradition of science. Space and time 'become' geometrical and physical, body 'becomes' a thing, languages 'become' logic, history and tradition 'become' archaeology.

What I am contending is that Nature in the Kantian sense is *constructed* out of the many pre-scientific worlds and not out of atomic sense-impressions. These pre-scientific worlds are not constructed in the sense of spontaneous, historical achievements, but are passively *pre-constituted* in the appropriate modes of experience: aesthetic, religious and everyday life of interest. In each of these, it is not an individual who makes his world. The individual *finds* himself in a world, the world handed down by a tradition which is but a sedimented structure of meanings inherited from the past. The scientific world has become such a tradition, inherited but also in the process of being restructured and reshaped. These many worlds however, are not eliminated in favour of the scientific, they coexist with it—which is the same as saying that we, the modern men, live in many different worlds, at many different levels, though men differ as to which one of these worlds functions, for him, as the dominant organizing principle.

III

We have been concerned uptil now with *one* concept of world, namely the concept of the world of physics, understood either as the *explanandum* or as the *explanans* of physics. Although, in either sense, the scientific world is a construction, an accomplishment made possible by several moves, yet it also determines, influences and markedly changes the way we pre-scientifically perceive and live in the (pre-scientific) world. The scientific tradition, as a tradition, impinges back on the life-world; in fact it is a major component of the modern man's life-world, progressively encompassing and transforming the way we relate to nature around us and our fellow human beings. I am referring to phenomena of technology, of growing objectification, of treating persons as though they were numbers in computerized data banks, of the ecological problems arising out of *using* nature, of the gradual loss of the feelings of respect and reverence for the world around. A new naivete is replacing the old, pre-scientific naivete—a naivete that, unaware of its origins, looks upon what is indeed *a* historical accomplishment of *a* tradition as though it were *the* reality, and which consequently mistakes a *methodology* for an *ontology*.

At the same time, there is *another* concept of world which has come into prominence in phenomenological literature. This is the concept of the world as *horizon*. Let me introduce it with the help of the familiar *gestalt*-theoretic concepts of figure and background. If all perception, and indeed all experience, has the figure-background structure, and if what is at first a background can be thematized and so transformed into a figure, which would be a figure only against some other background—it seems reasonable to speak of a background which can never be thematized, which can never be a figure, just because all figure-background structuring and re-structuring take place against it. Such a background would be none other than the world understood as the ultimate horizon within which both science and common sense have their moving space. In this sense, then, the world is not a theoretical construction, not the correlate of a specific attitude (religious or aesthetic, for example), not the totality of all things (which Kant condemned as a dialectical concept). It is important to appreciate the last point. The world as horizon is not the world conceived as a totality. The totality is never given, but ever recedes as a task. The idea of the totality of all things is a regulative, but not a constitutive idea. It is not given. The world as horizon is not an ideal for thought. It is rather given, not as a theme or figure to be sure, but as the ever present context for anything else to be given. Husserl used the expression 'pre-givenness' to convey this sense. The

242 • EXPLORATIONS IN PHILOSOPHY

Kantian problem is given a new twist and brought to an insightful solution.

What, then, of that totality which, Kant said, can never be an object of knowledge? There is no doubt that even if scientific thinking constructs its own world and phenomenology is satisfied with the discovery of a universal, unthematic, world-horizon, metaphysics in the traditional sense and religion need the concept of totality. With regard to this concept, I will make only a few very tentative remarks.

There is a strange anomaly in Kant's handling of this concept. While on the one hand he denies its cognitive *validity*, at the same time he seeks to give a *genesis* of the concept in cognitive terms, i.e. as a regulative ideal arising out of the speculative reason's search for the unconditioned and connected with the forms of *inference* exactly as the categories of understanding are related to the forms of *judgment*. It seems to me that Kant was right in his critique of the concept of totality, but wrong in his account of its genesis. If the concept has no cognitive validity, its origin has to be sought elsewhere than man's cognitive faculty. In this regard, I find certain ideas of Heidegger more promising. Reflecting on the possibility of asking the paradigmatic metaphysical question about *all* things, Heidegger finds the origin of totalization in non-cognitive experiences such as encounter with death or groundless anxiety, experiences which lead one to say, 'Nothing matters any more, nothing makes sense'. As nothing makes sense, this nothingness contrasts with the world as a whole. There has taken place, even if momentarily, a totalization such that all things, taken together, have lost their significance for one who is living through the appropriate experience. Now, there is no doubt that such a totalization does not deliver a permanently conceptualized world as a whole. But the important point is that only a being who has the possibility of experiencing such deep existential anguish could think *meta*-physically about world as a whole—even if he can never *know* it.

If this is *an* individual's awareness of a sudden and evanescent totalizing experience, great art, especially epic poems, have constituted for tradition the framework within which the world has to be contained. This happens by speaking of heaven and hell, the gods and Destiny. It is no wonder that the Kantian critique and the consequent *disruption* of the solidarity of the world could only have been possible in an age in which that grand genre of epic art was not, and is no longer, possible. Today, we live in the unstable equilibrium between worlds and the unitary world of science. Our only hope for stability lies in recovering the world as horizon. We can have glimpses into a totalization that is offered by experiences intrinsic to human existence. But the solidarity of the totality of the world, so magnificently present in the consciousness of antiquity, has been disrupted and lost for us.

chapter

twenty

*On Philosophical Description**

T hat one of the tasks of philosophy is to describe is fast becoming one of those points where extremes tend to meet in philosophy. The historical influences which have led to this have, no doubt, been chiefly: phenomenology with its insistence on the descriptive method in philosophy and the recent anti-metaphysical schools with their shattering attacks on the speculative method. However, the appreciation of the role of description in philosophical activity is to be found in very different quarters. Leaving aside the phenomenologists with their more well-known adherence to the descriptive method, we may quote here two philosophers of very different persuasions. Thus writes Whitehead: The primary method of mathematics is deduction; the primary method of philosophy is descriptive generalisation.[1] 'Metaphysics is nothing but the description of the generalities which apply to all the details of practice'.[2]

Wittgenstein writes: 'We must do away with all *explanation*, and description alone must take its place'.[3] 'Philosophy may in no way interfere with the actual use of language; it can in the end only describe it'.[4]

A more recent author, P.F. Strawson, calls his major work *An Essay in Descriptive Metaphysics*, and assigns to it the task of describing the actual structure of our thought about the world.[5]

**Philosophical Essays: First Series*, Kalidas Bhattacharya (ed.), Santiniketan, 1969.

In this essay, I propose to deal with certain questions of vital importance to any conception of descriptive philosophy, no matter whether such a philosophy remains a mere phenomenology or claims to be a metaphysics. The questions with which I propose to occupy myself all concern the idea of philosophical description, and they may broadly be formulated as follows:

1. How is a philosophical description different from a description that is not philosophical?

2. How is a true philosophical description different from a philosophical statement which only purports to be descriptive but is not really so?

3. How are the descriptive and the speculative components of a philosophical doctrine, or of a system, related to each other?

It should be obvious that these questions are intended to clarify the meaning and the nature of description as a philosophical activity, and to relate it to that speculative endeavour which has traditionally been regarded as the very core of philosophizing.

II

Some preliminary observations about the concept of description in general may be in order. First, the idea of description necessarily relates to the idea of intuition: one describes what one intuits. If a statement p be a descriptive statement, then there must be an intuition i whose datum p purports to describe. By 'intuition' is here meant a mode of awareness such that if a subject s intuits an object o, then one can also say that o is given to s. One may very well describe theoretical constructs or acts of constructing such entities only in so far as the construct or the acts concerned are given to the person describing them. But the construct itself is not a description of anything else, it does more than merely reporting some data of some intuition. Second, what is described or sought to be described need not be obvious. One who is out to describe need not just open his eyes and see. The subject matter of a possible description may in fact be hidden. It may lie below the surface and it may be necessary to go beyond the obvious to uncover it. It may be implicit and require to be made explicit for the purpose of description. Similarly, what is to be described need not be fully determinate, simple, atomic etc.; the indeterminate, the complex and the structured may equally well be described.[6] It follows that the task of describing does not necessarily exclude the exercise of thought, the practice of analysis, the activity of reflection. One may indeed think, analyse and reflect, not in order to construct an intellectual system but to render explicit what is implicit or to make obvious what was hidden. The satisfactoriness of a description depends, objectively, on its faithfulness to what is sought to be described; and it is to be tested in the long run by its ability to make the others see for themselves the phenomena concerned.

Description is to be contrasted with (i) inference, (ii) framing of explanatory hypothesis, (iii) constructing interpretative frameworks and theoretical models.

III

We may now ask: how is a descriptive philosophical statement to be distinguished from a non-philosophical, ordinary descriptive statement? 'This wall here before me is white, smooth and hard' is a non-philosophical descriptive statement. It purports to describe the object of my present perceptual experience. Or, 'I have a pain' is a non-philosophical description of my present experience. As contrasted with these, consider the following statements which are both descriptive and philosophical:

(i) 'All that is coloured is extended;'
(ii) 'All conscious states are *of* something.'

Seeking to distinguish between these two groups of statements, we are at once struck by the fact that the non-philosophical statements purport to describe concrete particular events, things, places, situations or experiences, whereas the philosophical statements purport to describe what, for lack of a better expression, we may call *essential* relations or structures. After saying this, however, it is necessary to warn against certain very likely misgivings. First, no commitment is thereby made with regard to the ontological status of the so-called essences. The characterization is entirely phenomenological and not ontological. What the statements (i) and (ii) purport to describe are facts which hold good of all of a specific of cases, and are very different from facts about singular events, things, places or situations. It may be pointed out that scientific law statements also purport to hold good of a specific type of cases and yet they are neither philosophical nor descriptive. This, however, is no point against the contention that philosophical statements which are descriptive are distinguished from ordinary, i.e., non-philosophical statements by virtue of being descriptions of essential relations and structures. The scientific law statements are not descriptive; their functions are different. Further, they are not essential either: they do not state necessary truths. If they are empirical generalisations they are probable truths, and if deductive formulations they are constructed models in accordance with which empirical phenomena are to be interpreted, explained or predicted. In any case, they are neither descriptive nor essential.

It should generally be admitted that there cannot be a philosophical statement which claims to have only a degree of probability. The necessity of a philosophical statement may be either analytic if it follows from the established proposed meanings of the terms used, or synthetic if it claims to describe a non-linguistic fact which itself holds good for all of a type of cases.

In the ontologically neutral sense in which philosophically descriptive statements have been characterised as essential, the statements of logic and mathematics may also be claimed to be so: they hold good of their respective domains universally and necessarily. But are they descriptive? There may be, we do not deny, non-descriptive statements which are universally and necessarily valid of their domains, but are we not seeking to distinguish between the various type of descriptive statements?

It has already been pointed out that the essential character of philosophical descriptions does not commit us to any particular ontological theory of essence, but it does rule out nominalism, indeed it rules out any ontological theory for which only particulars exist. Likewise, to say that these essential statements are descriptions does not entail that there is an essential insight into, an intellectual or eidetic intuition of the facts concerned. The idea of philosophical description stands or falls with the idea of intuition.

IV

To the distinction proposed in the preceding section between philosophical descriptions and non-philosophical descriptions it becomes necessary to add another.

The descriptive statements of philosophy permit, I should think even demand by their very nature, a three-fold interpretation. I should rather say they describe facts—let us call these 'philosophical facts'— which permit, by their very nature, to be looked at from three different points of view. They may be looked upon as linguistics or meaning-structures; or, they may be regarded as ontological structures; or again they may be regarded as structures of subjectivity or consciousness. Let me elucidate with the help of an example. Consider the philosophically descriptive statement. 'There are universals as well as particulars', or the statement. 'All conscious states are *of* something'. The first of the two may mean either that any language, to be a language, must contain both singular and general words, that, in other words, a particular-free and a nominalistic language both are impossible; or, that the world consists of the two radically different sorts of entities; or, that there are two radically different modes of consciousness, perception and thought. Similarly, the second statement may either be about a feature of mental words, or about the mental states or processes themselves (in the present case, the second and the third aspects would seem to fall together). The events, entities, states and processes which non-philosophical descriptive statements purport to describe are, of course, both designata of linguistic expressions and also objects of consciousness, but they have also, *qua* such entities, states and processes, i.e. *qua* objects of such description, a being independent of being designated by an expression and being objectified to consciousness. Not so in the case of the philosophical facts which are such they they not only admit of such alternative formulations but even demand it in the sense that for a complete, adequate and integral understanding of their nature it is necessary to keep this three-fold possibility in mind. Linguistic philosophers who hold that philosophical statements are concerned with linguistic meanings, and transcendental phenomenology which reduces such facts to noetic functions or their intentional correlates are both guilty not of error but of inadequacy. They do not perceive—largely under the influence of their ontological prejudices—the whole truth about philosophical facts. Each of these alternatives supplements the others and makes up for their inadequacies: together they constitute the total nature of philosophical facts.

V

After having tried to distinguish, in the preceding two sections, between ordinary, i.e. non-philosophical, descriptions and philosophical descriptions, we may now turn to the second question on our list, the question, namely: How is a true description in philosophy different from a philosophical statement which only purports to be descriptive but is not really so? Here again it would be helpful to proceed with examples.

Let us consider the following example of a philosophical statement which only pretends to be descriptive but is not really so. Hume writes: 'All events seem entirely loose and separate. One event follows another;

but we never can observe any tie between them. They seem *conjoined,* but never *connected*.[8] As contrasted with this, the following appears to be a genuinely descriptive philosophical statement:

There belongs to every external perception its reference from the 'genuinely perceived' sides of the object of perception to the sides 'also meant'—not yet perceived, but only anticipated and, at first, with a non-intuitional emptiness (as the sides that are 'coming' now perceptually): a continuous *protention,* which, with each phase of the perception, has a new sense.[9]

Why do I consider the first as a pseudo-description but the second as approximating towards a genuine description? It seems to me that there is one and only one way of exposing the pretensions of a statement to be descriptive or of confirming the genuineness of its claim, and this consists in asking, Does the alleged description conceal any ontological or epistemological presupposition or not? A genuinely philosophical description should not be based on any such presupposition; it should not be founded on any ontology or epistemology just because it alone is able to found one.

Thus the Humean statement owes its seeming obviousness to the fact that its presuppositions have an air of deceptiveness about them. The statement quoted above, for example, presupposes amongst other things, atomistic psychology and Hume's own theory of meaning as formulated in Section II of his *Enquiry* (a theory which pretends to be descriptive but is in reality a recommendation).

As contrasted with this, the statement of Husserl exhibits a sustained effort to delineate the actual process of external perception as given to consciousness, without letting scientific or any other ontological preconceptions interfere. It may be worthwhile to contrast with it the sense-datum theory of perception which no doubt purports to be faithful to the given but whose conception of the given is vitiated by scientific, psychological and epistemological preconceptions. It presupposes, for example, the reality of sensations, which on its part is based on a psychological atomism, a notion of psycho-physical causality and the constancy hypothesis, but is not warranted by the evidence of consciousness.

A genuine philosophical description then must not make use of what it knows of in other ways, through commonsense or from the sciences (which is not to say that it should reject them or should doubt their validity). It should try to get hold of the primitive phenomena exactly as they exhibit themselves in consciousness. This is not, in the first place, to say that descriptive philosophy should remain at the level of phenomenology and cannot aim at metaphysics. All that is being said is that description in philosophy should not presuppose metaphysics or an ontology. Only then can it provide the foundation for a metaphysics or ontology. In the second place, we seem to be back with the problem of unreflective immediacy *versus* reflection. There are in fact two kinds of reflection. One kind of reflection, the more familiar sort, questions, analyses, interprets explains, enquires into the conditions of the possibility of the given, and led by any one or more of these tasks, constructs theoretical models (as in the sciences) or speculative systems. Let us call it reflection$_1$. There is, however, another sort of reflection (which again is not quite the same as introspection or *anuvyavasāya*) which aims at catching hold of the unreflective experience prior to its distortion by preconceptions. This is not, as may be supposed, an instantaneous 'directing one's glance towards' but involves a strenuous effort at recognizing preconceptions as preconceptions, at unravelling sedimented interpretations, at getting at presuppositions which may pretend to be self-evident truths, and through this process aim asymptotically at the pre-reflective experience as such. Let us call it reflection$_2$. A genuine philosophical description has to make use of reflection$_2$, which has to cultivate— by the very nature of its business—the skill of looking at, or rather getting at, pre-reflective experience without disturbing it. It is no valid objection to say that this ideal can never be reached, and so no description in this sense can ever be possible. For, we can only lay down the task to be achieved, the goal to be pursued. But to guarantee that any particular philosopher or any particular statement achieves this task, or reaches the goal is beyond our present task. One may at best distinguish between good and bad descriptions, between more or less adequate ones. The situation is not unlike that in the sciences or in speculative metaphysics.

Reflection$_1$ is not denied. It has an important function, whether as scientific or as speculative thinking. But it can build only on pre-reflective experience. The precise significance, however, of descriptions based on reflection$_2$ for the sciences and for speculative thinking are different. In the next section we shall be concerned with the latter half of this problem.

VI

We may now take up the question, How are the descriptive and the speculative elements of a philosophical system related to each other?

It is possible to find in every metaphysical system some descriptive core (and the descriptive core is not only made the spring-board for speculative flights but itself gets transformed beyond recognition in course of such a flight). Thus, for example, the Platonic two-world theory is surely based on the descriptive core of the mutual irreducibility of sense-perception and thought (of which another transformation is the Kantian two-faculty theory). That Kant's transcendental idealism contains a large descriptive core has been recently shown by Strawson,[10] but had been emphasized much earlier by Nicolai Hartmann. One may try to do the same with regard to Whitehead's grand system of metaphysics.

What interests us here is to detect the various ways in which the descriptive finding is used for speculative purposes. We want to find out the various modes of speculative flight from the descriptive spring-board. If we could find all the various ways in which this is done, we would have a complete list of the modes of speculative thinking. But in the absence of an *a priori* clue one can be sure neither of exhaustiveness nor of the systematic character of such a list. Kant reduced all the various modes of speculative moves first, into one: the move from the conditioned to unconditioned; but then under the influence of his general architectonic, especially of the threefold classification of inference, subdivided it into three. We cannot here undertake such an *a priori* classification, but would satisfy ourselves with the humbler task of isolating by empirical survey a few striking speculative moves. Some of these moves are:

(i) *Generalization*: Every descriptive finding pertains to a certain region of phenomena. Speculative philosophers sometimes generalize it over some other regions of phenomena, far beyond the limits within which it could have intuitive support. I will give here two examples of how this is, or could be, done.

Samuel Alexander held the view—as is well known—that mind enjoys itself and contemplates its object, meaning there-by that every conscious state is of something and at the same time immediately aware of itself. Now this undoubtedly is a sound philosophical description, leaving aside the question of an adequate linguistic formulation. However, Alexander does not rest satisfied with this, but in the true spirit of a speculative metaphysician proceeds to generalize this over all regions of being. For, this is what he writes: ' . . . we may say that any finite "enjoys" itself and "contemplates" lower finites'. Thus each level has its specific "enjoyment" and what it "contemplates" is what from the nature of the case can be revealed to it, and so far forth as it can be revealed.'[11]

A similar extension may possibly be given to Brentano's thesis about intentionality.[12] It may be held that in so far as anything—not excluding material bodies and living organisms—refers beyond itself, it also possesses mind; in other words, that that element of self-transcendence is precisely its mind. Only a short step takes you to pan-psychism.

(ii) *Filling in gaps*: The speculative metaphysician does not tolerate the existence of gaps amongst phenomena, and therefore, in the interests of *system*, proceeds to fill in such gaps. Thus, consider the phenomenological-descriptive thesis regarding the radical distinction between sense-perception and thought, between the acts as well as the objects given in them, the sensible particulars and the ideal essences. Not satisfied with this provisional dualism speculative philosophers try to reduce the one to the other by showing its 'origin'—which involves the filling in of gaps, of reducing the heterogeneity of phenomena to a homogeneity. This also involves denial of discontinuity amongst phenomena.[13] A satisfactory descriptive philosophy should admit and respect discontinuity where the same is intuitively given. Most varieties of monism, ontological as well as epistemological, exhibit this sort of move.

(iii) *Search for generic concept*: The speculative metaphysician collects descriptive cases, but is too eager to bring them under a generic concept. Thus, starting with the descriptive thesis that there are material bodies, living organisms, minds (all constituting the real world) and ideal entities, like the mathematical ones, he seeks for a generic concept of Being, common to all these, whereas a descriptive metaphysician would remain satisfied with the concept of Being as an analogical concept. To make this point clearer, it may be necessary to explain briefly the distinction between generic concept and analogical concepts. If G is a generic concept with a, b, c, and d, as its instances then of course a, b, c, and d are different Gs, as, for examples, Plato, Socrates, Aristotle and Kant are different philosophers, but they are so in so far as each of them contains the properties which go to define G. But supposing N to be an analogical concept of which u, v, w and x are instances, then it is not only the case that u, v, w and x are different N, but they are, as N, different: in other words, they are radically different. (Material bodies and minds, are not only different real entities, but are radically different entities, that is as real entities they are different.) In such case, the search for a generic character is futile and the imposition of one leads to a speculative construction.

Let us take another example of this move. We find different types of intentional directedness: the intentionality of mental states, and the intentionality of bodily behaviour. Now, the speculative philosophy would like to find out a common source for both, or would regard the one kind of directedness as a reflection or epiphenomenon of the other (which is move *iii*); in effect, the concept of intentionality would be for him a generic concept. The descriptive philosopher, satisfied with the radical difference evidenced by phenomena would prefer to regard the concept as an analogical one. It hardly needs to be mentioned that the moves *(ii)* and *(iii)* are closely related.

(iv) *Exclusive recognition of one favoured mode of description*: It has already been emphasized that philosophical facts are such that they demand three alternate and yet mutually supplementary modes of description, the linguistic, the ontological and the subjective. Now, the speculative philosophers, largely under the influence of their ontological pre-conceptions, are prone to accord recognition only to one of them and to deny the other modes of description. Examples of these are: (1) the Platonic hypostatization of abstract entities; (2) the linguistic thesis that philosophy is concerned only with linguistic analysis; and (3) the idealistic thesis that philosophy is concerned with consciousness alone with its functions.

(v) *Enquiry into the conditions of the possibility of a descriptive finding*: Speculative philosophers seek explanations: Why should a fact be what it is? What are the conditions of its possibility? Thus, accepting the thesis of intentionality, they may go on to ask 'What makes this self-transcending reference possible? They may ask, in other words, How is it possible that consciousness should be able to refer to what is yet beyond itself? This kind of question usually leads to a monistic answer. It would seem that consciousness can refer to what is yet beyond only if consciousness and its object were not as different or as independent of each other as they appear to be, i.e. if there were some sort of unity underlying their apparent difference. There are various forms of such monistic solutions: objective monism (in the manner of behaviourism or neo-realism of Holt's variety), subjective monism, Absolute monism and neutral monism; or, it may be a transcendental idealism of the type of Kant.

All the above make the descriptive philosopher a tragic philosopher, and the speculative metaphysician a happy one. A genuinely descriptive philosophy is bound to be characterized by a tragic sense not merely because everywhere phenomena exhibit discontinuity and gaps which he would not fill in, but also because he is haunted by the gap which continues to persist and which he only tries to make up asymptotically, between philosophic reflection and unreflective experience. His is thus a never-ending endeavour, his is an open system. The speculative metaphysician, on the other hand, closes the system; by means of reflection₁, he constructs a system in which every item of experience finds a place, a role or a reconstruction: nothing is left out. All conflicts are solved to satisfaction, the tragedy of reflection is once and for all eliminated.

This list of four different kinds of speculative moves does not claim exhaustiveness, but it may serve as a beginning for further enquiry.

VII

Brief remarks may now be in order on two different questions concerning philosophical description. First, it may be useful to enquire how many different kinds of description there could be in philosophy. It may appear as if to be a description is, for a statement, to represent the fact described as a photograph represents the original, or even as Wittgenstein used to take a sentence as 'picturing' a fact. However, to describe is not to picture. Here again Wittgenstein himself cautions us against the danger.[14] Husserl who laid so much emphasis on the descriptive method in philosophy did not quite see the problem of the logical relation in which a descriptive sentence would stand to the fact described. However, he did explicitly reject the picture theory of meaning. For him, I should think, a sentence is descriptive if the meaning–intention expressed in it is fulfilled in corresponding intuition, where the intention and fulfilment coincide. The emphasis is on the meaning-intention, and not on the sentence considered as a physical entity with its constituent parts, i.e. words. However, be that as it may, we may distinguish between the following types of description in philosophy:

(1) *Pure, direct description:* Where the description directly pertains to the essence of the phenomenon concerned. Such an example is Brentano's thesis of intentionality and the Mīmāṃsā thesis of the *svayaṁprakāśatva* of consciousness.

(2) *Description by negation:* A description may seek to focus on the distinctive peculiarity of a region of phenomenon through a series of negations rather than through some positive characterization. In other words, one may seek to describe an X by saying that X is not p,

X is not q, etc. Such descriptions, though useful, must take the help of some premise, in order to serve their purpose, for in order that the series of negations may bring out the distinctive peculiarity of X and serve to demarcate from it everything else, it is necessary to add the premise that p, q, r, . . . exhaust all characters save one within the universe of discourse.

(3) *Description by series or approximation*: One may describe an X by arranging phenomena, with which one is relatively better acquainted or whose descriptions are already at hand, in such a manner that they all form a series which points towards X as its limit. Whitehead's method of extensive abstraction may in this sense be regarded as a method of description. Thus, it may be said that when he is defining a point in terms of 'abstractions' extensive he is giving a description.

(4) *Classificatory description:* One may also describe a region of phenomena by classifying it into its sub-regions. Thus a descriptive ontology may begin with a classification of the principal regions of being, for example in Hartmann's case: the real, the ideal and the hybrid regions. But it is important to be aware that such classificatory schemes may well hide unrecognized preconceptions. In fact it is in this kind of description that it is most difficult to achieve the ideal of presuppositionlessness.

(5) *Hermeneutic description*: This is the kind of description practised by Heidegger in his *Sein und Zeit*. Briefly speaking, there are two distinguishing marks of this method. First, this kind of description is not confined to what is immediately given, to what is obvious, but tries to uncover what is hidden and implicit. In the second place, what it is after are the hidden *meanings*. Heidegger of course calls them 'interpretations', but they should be clearly distinguished from the interpretations of scientific or speculative thinking as also from the preconceptions or presuppositions which all sound philosophical description, as we saw, has to avoid. The interpretations (*Auslegungen*) or meanings which Heidegger seeks to uncover are those which constitute the very essence of a certain region of being, namely *Dasein*. It is important to bear in mind that this method of hermeneutics applies only to human existence or *Dasein* for it belongs to the very essence of this kind of being to have meaning and significance. However, even here it requires the utmost circumspection to remain on the purely descriptive level and not to indulge in speculative flights. In this respect, it is instructive to compare the hermeneutic description of human existence such as we find in *Sein und Zeit* and the rather esoteric significance claimed to have been

uncovered in Heidegger's later works. In this connection, Spiegelberg's warning is worth bearing in mind:

In any case, not until the anticipations of hermeneutics can be followed up by an elucidation which will turn the full light of intuitive clarity upon them is there much hope for a genuine expansion of the scope of 'descriptive' phenomenology.[15]

(6) *Description of phenomena in the making*: One may distrust all objectification as being a distortion of phenomena and try to catch hold of the very process by which phenomena arise (which are not quite the same as physiological or physical or psychological process of perception), the 'origin', as some phenomenologists would say, of the world. In fact this is what Merleau-Ponty does in his *Phenomenology of Perception*. He is interested neither in the fully determinate world posited by the sciences or by commonsense nor in the fully indeterminate mass of experience (the sort of sentient experience, for example, of which Bradley speaks), but in the phase of transition from indeterminacy to determinateness. It is this mid-region in which he is interested just because it is this which for him represents the true and original phenomena, the two extremes being products of construction. Thus what interests him is not how we perceive a determinate physical object with its determinate qualities, but how the determinate object comes to take shape through phenomena which themselves are not determinate.

(7) *Linguistic Description*: Needless to add, today the most profitable kind of description in philosophy is the linguistic description of meanings. But this heading by itself leaves room for a large variety of things to be done, ranging from the Austinian variety of linguistic phenomenology to Heidegger's variety of hermeneutics. In these cases also we have to ask, which linguistic description approximates more towards the ideal of presuppositionlessness and looks at the linguistic phenomena as they give themselves without imposing upon them one's favoured logical, epistemological or ontological preconceptions.

VIII

From the above account of philosophical description, it should have been clear that there are various themes to which a descriptively-oriented philosopher may apply himself. He may apply himself to definite regions of being, he may apply himself to human existence in particular; he may seek to describe the structure of consciousness, or of the world; he may even be interested in describing the correlation which obtains between the structures of consciousness and the world or what Husserl calls the noematic–noetic correlation. The type of description he would need or would find most convenient to offer would partly depend upon the theme he chooses to apply himself to.

It is worthwhile, in the light of these remarks, to make a critical examination of the descriptive elements in some of those modern philosophers whom we quoted at the beginning of this essay. However, this essay has been meant to prepare the ground and to make a beginning of a study of descriptive method in philosophy. If it has been successful in doing that my purpose for the present will be deemed to have been fulfilled in spite of the fact that I am fully aware of the rather sketchy nature of my doing the job.

NOTES

1. A.N. Whitehead, *Process and Reality* (New York: Hamper Torch Books, 1941), pp. 15–16.
2. Ibid., p. 19.
3. L. Wittgenstein, *Philosophical Investigations* (Oxford: Basil Blackwell, 1953), p. 47.
4. Ibid., p. 49.
5. P.F. Strawson, *Individuals* (Anchor Book, 1963), p. xiii.
6. For this, see J.N. Mohanty, 'The Given', in *Proceedings of the Delhi Philosophical Colloquium* (India International Centre, New Delhi, 1963).
7. The above remarks may be regarded as a partial explication of K.C. Bhattacharya's statement: 'Speakability is a contingent character of the content of empirical thought, it is a necessary character of the content of pure philosophic thought.'
8. D. Hume, *An Enquiry Concerning Human Understanding* (Progressive Publishers, Calcutta, 1967), pp. 61–2.
9. E. Husserl, *Cartesian Meditations*, Eng. Tr. by Dorion Cairns (The Hague: Martinus Nijhoff, 1960), p. 44.
10. Strawson, *The Bounds of Sense. An Essay on Kant's Critique of Pure Reason* (London: Methuen, 1966).
11. S. Alexander, *Space, Time and Deity* (New York: Dover Publications, 1966), vol. II, p. 104.
12. Professor J.N. Chubb tells me that this in fact was upheld by one of his Bombay teachers.

13. For this, see J.N. Mohanty, *Edmund Husserl's Theory of Meaning* (The Hague: Martinus Nijhoff, 1964).

14. Wittgenstein, *Philosophical Investigations*, p. 99, articles 290, 291.

15. H. Spiegelberg, *The Phenomenological Movement*, vol. II (The Hague: Martinus Nijhoff, 1960), p. 697.

chapter

twenty one

A Case for Idealism*

In order to make out a case for idealism, I will, in this essay, first present two forms of idealism in their bare outlines (these two being, in my view, the most interesting and defensible forms) and then a set of premises for an *argument* for idealism. I will then respond to what are the more pertinent difficulties with these, and finally, make some general remarks regarding idealism as a theory.

I. VERSION 1

The colossal joke is that things are as they are . . . we need only take them in their phenomenality . . . the essence of the essence is to manifest itself. (Hegel)

The idea of the first form of Idealism I owe to Hegel's *Phenomenology of the Mind*. My account of it reflects what I understand his central project in that book to be, but not the details of his scheme. Let me begin by assuming that there are many different forms of consciousness, such as sensation, the perceptual, scientific, ethical, moral, aesthetic and religious. Each such form of consciousness is *internally* characterized by—let me further assume—(a) its own conception of what is *real* (to which its objects conform), (b) its own criterion of *truth* and (c) its own naivety which consists in regarding its objects as

*A lecture delivered at All Souls College, Oxford, on 11 October 1989.

an absolute other, as being-in-itself. Thus, for example, for sensation, the world consists of bare particulars, the 'this' -es, and truth consists in certainty. For perceptual consciousness, the world consists in things such as sticks and stones, substances with qualities, truth consists in adequacy or correspondence of cognition to its object. Scientific consciousness replaces perceptual things by such objects as atoms, molecules, or, as one wants to say today, quanta, charms and quarks, or also abstract objects such as laws of increasing orders of generality; truth consists in explanatory power and predictive value. The details of this account can be improved upon, and my own formulations on this occasion can be, without doubt, considerably improved upon. What is important for my present purpose is the idea that a domain of objects of a certain kind is the *correlate* of a certain form of consciousness. In accordance with (c), *within* each such form of consciousness, one is a realist. As long as I confine myself to the naive perceptual consciousness, the objects of such consciousness will be taken to be independent of that mode of consciousness. As long as I am a practising scientist, I will be—by virtue of the built-in naivety of scientific thinking—a scientific realist. Likewise, within the naive religious consciousness, the believer is a realist. Thus, the intuition of realism with regard to any domain of objects, is rooted in the built-in naivety of the corresponding form of consciousness. Philosophical reflection, for the first time, exhibits this naivety *as a naivety*. If only we could arrange these forms of consciousness in a hierarchical order, and lay down a path of reflection which would lead from the lower to the higher—in which case, the naivety of one form of consciousness will be expressed and overcome in the other, then it could be demonstrated—as Hegel claims to have done—that every ontology is the *correlate* of a phenomenology and cannot be sundered from it. To be able to show this, one needs to launch a critique of a form of consciousness. It would not do, however, to show that perceptual consciousness, for example, falls short of the demands of scientific theory or of the grand demands of Hegelian metaphysics (enshrined in the dictum 'The Truth is the whole'). What is needed is to be able to show that as a form of consciousness is made (pardon this figurative mode of locution) to tell its own story, i.e. state its own ontology and its own conception of truth, it falls into incoherence—an incoherence that demands that we move on to a 'higher' form of consciousness for which a new domain of objects 'comes into being'. The central point of this narrative is that any ontology consisting in positing a domain of objects has a necessary correlate: a form of consciousness. To restate a point made earlier: realism captures a primitive feature of every form of consciousness, i.e. its built-in naivety, the inveterate tendency to reify the object domain by severing it from the domain of consciousness. Idealism captures the reflective 'discovery' of this 'forgotten' process. Reflection succeeds in 're-enacting' the process of constitution of the object domain—forgotten and reduced to 'anonymity'. If only this process had a closure, then we would have a form of consciousness which is not itself characterized by a naivety, but which, fully reflective and transparent, sees all reified objectivities as but its own posits, but also retains its grip on the earlier phases gone through—such is what Hegel calls absolute knowledge for which all reality is spirit.

II. VERSION 2

From this grand Hegelian vision, let me take you to what, by comparison, would be a *micro*-theory about individual intentional acts and their objects. This theory is *not* however quite unlike that grand macro-theory, for it too operates with the idea of *correlation* between consciousness and objects in the world. For an object of a certain type, say O, we have—in this theory—intentional acts of a certain type, say A, such that a O is 'originally' presentable as an O only through an act of that type. Thus material objects *qua* material objects are originally presented only through sensuous perception (derivatively in memory, imagination or thought). One then would say that O-objects *as such* are constituted in A-acts. Another way of putting the same thing is: The *sense 'O' is constituted* in A-acts. Consider, now, an arbitrarily chosen object: the coffee cup I have on my desk. It can be regarded as a material object, or as an artifact, or as a cup, or as an art-object—to name a few. Each of these may be regarded as a *sense* attaching to it. There are also such broad categorial predicates as 'an existent' or 'a thing' or 'an object'. It is possible to correlate to each of these *senses* a nexus of intentional experiences of a certain sort, such that when something is the object of experiences of a certain sort it is regarded as bearing that sense. Thus: to 'being a material object' correspond actual and possible perceptual experiences (by more than one subject) concatenated in appropriate manners; to 'being a cup' correspond perceptual, kinaesthetic ('I can take it up in a certain manner') and practical ('I can use it in a certain manner') experiences of specifiable kinds; to 'being an art object' correspond aesthetic experiences directed towards it; to 'being existent' correspond acts of belief; to 'being an object' correspond any intentional experience of which it is the intentional object.

As is rather well-known, Husserl put existence under brackets, and 'reduced' the real thing to an intentional object. Thus, the initial step was to show that the intentional object *qua* intended, i.e. precisely as it is intended, is the correlate of intentional experiences ordered in certain specifiable manners. This thesis, however, leaves realism in tact, for it has already left the real existence of things out of its thematic focus. But that can only be a provisional device. If my above chain of thinking makes anything clear, it is that the distinction between the real thing and the intentional object is not only provisional, but also a *vanishing* distinction. For whatever descriptions one gives of the real thing (its reality, existence, thing-hood, or anything else) surfaces within the intentional content as a constitutive *sense*, and so points, conceptually, to intentional experiences of some sort or other.

It is in this sense, then, that the world is the correlate of consciousness. Consciousness both belongs to the world and *presents* the world. As belonging to the world, it is mundane; as *presenting* the world, it is transcendental.

The *reality* of the world is not denied; it is originally 'bracketed' in order to be reduced to a *sense*, a *categorial predicate* and then exhibited in its constitutive source. For this idealism the world is out there, not *within* consciousness, for consciousness, construed as intentional, has no 'within' where the world could possibly find a habitat or from which it could be expelled to save realism. It is, however, still idealism in the sense that the *sense* of the world *qua* world—of things in the world *qua* the things they are taken to be—is made possible by structures of *our* intersubjective and historically developing intentional experience.

III AN ARGUMENT

In addition to the two forms of idealism that I have outlined, I promised at the beginning to formulate an argument for idealism, that has dominated thinking on these matters—this time, in the Indian tradition. The argument has the following premises:

P1. Every consciousness, besides being of whatever happens to be its object, is *eo ipso* consciousness of itself. (The principle of transparence—*Svaprakāśavāda*.)

P2. Every state of consciousness has an intentional content internal to it—a content (*ākāra*) which represents to it the object of that act. (Principle of content—*jñāna sākāra-vāda*.)

P3. The *truth* of a cognitive state is apprehended along with that cognitive state itself (Principle of intrinsic truth—*svataḥprāmāṇyavāda*.)

A conjunction of these three premises yields a strong idealism. How this idealistic thesis is to be understood, depends upon how one construes the concept of 'content' in P2.

Consider P1 and P2 together. In accordance with P1, when I am perceiving this coffee cup before me, I am also aware of my perceiving, my perceptual consciousness itself. According to P2, the consciousness has a content, and since the consciousness shows itself (according to P1), its content is also 'revealed'. If the content were different from the object (as realism would have it), then I would have, in my awareness, three distinct things: the perceptual consciousness, the content 'this coffee cup' and the object, i.e. the thing coffee cup. But I do not notice, when I am seeing the cup, three such things. What I do notice are only two things: my consciousness and the cup over there. In accordance with P2, my consciousness has a content, which as a consequence of P1, is 'manifested'. It follows, then, that the putative object, 'this coffee cup' is but a content of my consciousness.

It may be suspected that so far the argument has focused upon a contrast which is indifferent to truth and falsity—a contrast that belongs to the perceptual consciousness, no matter whether my perception is veridical, or not. If this is so, then one may argue that when my perception is veridical, there must be something other than that contrast, something serving as the extramental measure of truth—a real coffee cup out there. At this point, P3 comes in handy.

P3 has two components: first, the thesis that truth is an epistemic concept—not a merely ontological or a merely semantic concept. In other words, truth concerns a cognitive claim, not a relation between two non-cognitive terms nor the referent of a sentence. The second component of P3 is the thesis that a cognitive state occurs *eo ipso* with a claim to truth, so that as we are conscious of it (P1), we are also conscious of its truth-claim. When I perceive this coffee cup, I am conscious of so perceiving, and also I am conscious of the intrinsic truth-claim of my perception—ie. to say, I make that claim *ab initio*. A cognition consists in making such a claim. Claim to truth initially characterizes a cognitive occurrence.

Our realistic intuition persists. Is there not a distinction between truth-claim and *actual* truth? Let the former be an epistemic notion, the latter is not. The first component of P3 precisely amounts to saying that 'actual truth' over and above 'truth-claim' is a spurious concept. For one thing, 'truth' (*prāmāṇya*) is a property of a cognitive state, not of a sentence or of a proposition. In the second place—and this is more pertinent to the argument—to know is *eo ipso* to make a truth-claim, and as, in accordance with the principle of transparence, the cognition itself is apprehended so is its truth-claim (in accordance with P3). Since to know, to be *prama* and to be known as *pramā* all collapse (extensionally) in one single instance, there is no unknown *pramātva*, what then do progress of knowledge, more evidence, better reasoning, establish over and above the initial truth-claim? The point of P3 may be restated thus: Knowledge is never known as (for it never is) indifferent to truth or falsity. It is taken as true, not proved to be true. And it is taken as true *as long as it is not proved to be false*. It is proved to be false if the truth-claim is defeated by subsequent experience, or if the cognition under consideration leads to pragmatic frustration.

IV. SOME EXPLANATORY REMARKS

As promised, I have presented two *versions* of idealism which seem to me to be promising, and an *argument* for idealism that seems strong enough to deserve serious consideration. Within the scope of this essay, I do not hope to be able to defend those versions or this argument. To defend the argument, one must defend the premises P1–P3. Suffice it to say that they are at least reasonable enough. In lieu of the sort of thoroughgoing defense that an idealist needs to mount, I have set for myself a more modest task: to make a reasonable case and to see what prospects show-up for an idealist position.

First, some explanatory remarks regarding the two versions. It is most important to note that both the versions use 'consciousness' both in a deep and a wide sense. The *deep* sense departs from the superficial understanding of mind or consciousness as a container *containing* ideas or mental contents, and understands it as fundamentally *intentional*, as intending an object, a situation, the world, in some manner or another. A certain familiar form of idealism, which construes things to be *ideas* in the mind of some one or other, is then incompatible with both versions. Things are rather understood as intentional objects. P2 or the Principle of Content needs to be suitably construed. The content is not a *real* part of one's mental life—not the 'idea' of the empiricists. It is rather akin to the Fregean *Sinn* and the Husserlian *noema*—with certain necessary modifications in the case of perception.

The *wide* sense goes beyond the usual restriction of 'consciousness' to the theoretical cognitive states, and extends 'intentionality' to the *practical* and *actional* states as well. The senses that things have derive as much from the theoretical–cognitive intentional acts as from the practical and actional intentionalities.

Furthermore, it is worth bearing in mind that the mental is being construed as transcendental. This is not simply a rhetorical device. It is not as though a Kant or a Husserl simply duplicated the mental world by positing for every type of familiar mental function, an unfamiliar transcendental one: for empirical imagination, transcendental imagination, to recall but one well-known Kantian thesis. What may seem to some a redundant trick, is, in truth, necessitated by the realization that what is called the 'mental' permits, by its very nature, of this two-fold interpretation. Let me leave aside for the present the curious fact that what is often regarded by some as the paradigm case of the mental—a pain, a twitch or any such 'nomological' dangler—is, for others, merely bodily states, and that these latter philosophers regard such things as thoughts and theories, social practices and political institutions as truly 'mental', *geistig*, intentional. Such things as beliefs and thoughts, hopes and desires, actions and practices may be regarded either as occurrences within the real world order to which they belong or as conferring sense on that world: in the former case, they are empirical, in the latter case, transcendental.

The last of the 'explanatory' remarks is this: when in version 1, to each form of consciousness, there is a correlative domain of objects, a world, so to say, or in version 2, consciousness constitutes a world or rather the meaning-structure that a world is, in no case the world is itself 'mental' in the sense of being a real part of a mental life, in both cases it is a *correlate*. No 'world' without a form of consciousness, no sense without a sense-giving consciousness; likewise—one should add—no consciousness without a world that it is of. Transcendental idealism since Kant, through Hegel and Husserl, recognizes this. Consciousness and world form a unity, such that they are both abstractions from the ongoing and developing experiencing-of-the-world. To detach the world from the concrete whole is as much an abstraction, as is to detach consciousness from what it is of. The history of consciousness is the history of constitution and re-constitution of worlds, of emergence of new worlds, and dissolution of the old.

V. REVISION OF P1–P3

Now, whereas the two versions of idealism are mutually compatible—the one a macro-theory, the other a micro-theory, the one a historicist and diachronic, the other a static and synchronic theory, some of their common theses do not mesh with some of the premises of the argument presented in III. Let me, in particular, draw your attention to P1, ie. the Principle of Transparence, according to which every consciousness, besides being of whatever happens to be its object, is *eo ipso* conscious of itself. Now both the versions of idealism I have laid out require that consciousness not be aware of some of its accomplishments. In version 1, I introduced an idea of 'naivety' which characterizes every form of consciousness—the naivety which requires that every form of consciousness be *realistic*. This naivety is nothing other than an unawareness on the part of consciousness of its own constitutive function. The Principle of Transparence would not allow it. Nor would the principle allow that forgetfulness of its constitutive function which the other version also requires. In fact, any theory of constituting requires some opacity, so that what is constituted is *presented* as being given. However, we need not outright reject the Principle, what we need is to weaken it and replace P1 by P1*, which I would call the Principle of Phenomenological Accessibility according to which reflection can *uncover* the workings of consciousness, that consciousness can be made transparent, if not at the moment of its functioning, certainly to subsequent reflection. I believe, in this modified form, the principle can still function in the structure of the argument for idealism formulated in Section III. But the new principle would certainly introduce a tension which the argument as previously stated had no inkling of.

For, now that we have introduced the idea of *deep* structure (and function) of consciousness, we have to make room for a similar fissure in the conception of the 'content' of consciousness—requiring a suitable emendation of P2 of the Principle of Content. The realists' *object* (the coffee cup over there) is the surface-level *content* of perceptual consciousness. Reflection reveals that consciousness *was* at work constituting this content, the nexus of senses that it is. This is the *reduced* content of the consciousness caught by reflection in the act of constituting. A quasi-realistic distinction between content and object is then recognized, of which one is assigned to the pre-reflective and the other to the reflective experience of what is *the same*. The principle of content needs then to be modified to:

P2*: Every consciousness has a *surface* and a *deep* content.

With this, a certain measure of consistency has been retrieved between those versions of idealism and that argument for idealism.

VI. SOME PROBLEMS

Several problems remain—more than I can handle in this essay, or even later on. But some deserve immediate attention. There are three objections traditionally pressed against idealism. Let us see what happens to them. First, how does one account for the receptivity of sensations? (This was called, within German idealism, the question of 'deduction' of sensation?) Second, there is the notorious question about the scheme-content distinction which underlines much of transcendental thinking since Kant and which has been the target of much recent criticism. Third, where does causality fit in in all this? (This question was discussed by Fichte, Schopenhauer and the Buddhists, among others.) Let me make brief remarks on each of these, when considered in the context of the idealist position expounded here.

As for the first: if we were examining an idealism, such as Fichte's which *deduces* all the epistemic apparatus from one single principle (in Fichte's case, the principle of the ego or self-consciousness), the problem of sensation (with its receptivity) become insuperable. For us now, the concept of 'sensation' represents a form of consciousness which has its correlative domain of objects (the world of bare 'this'-es), so *that* problem (which Kant also had to face) does not arise. What does arise, however, is the question, whether sensory experience does not need a causal explanation in terms of some available scientific theory; with *this* question we have moved to the third of the three problems listed above, namely the question of causality. For version I, the Hegelian, the scientific–causal explanations in terms of minute bodies and laws characterizes scientific *Verstand*, a form of spirit whose correlative object domain is the world of such bodies and/or forces organized by laws of increasing order of generality. Thus, the scheme has a place for causality—not as an overarching metaphysical category, but as characterizing the object domain of scientific consciousness. For Version II, 'causality' characterises material objects nothing is a material object if it does not causally impinge on other such, so any account of the *sense* 'material object' must take into account this feature of them, and must answer the question, how such 'sense' is constituted—in what experiential structures. As regards the scheme-content distinction the following remarks should suffice: unlike the Kantian version of transcendental idealism, neither of the two versions I have expounded requires a scheme-content distinction. Instead of an absolute content, the bare given, what we need at most is a *relative* content—so that what is interpreted, is always a given *world*, which is itself a meaningful structure, not a bundle of uninterpreted data. Thus, there are worlds behind worlds—never any rock-bottom content or uninterpreted given.

VII. 'ABSOLUTE KNOWLEDGE'

I have expounded two versions of idealism—drawing upon ideas of two of the very best: Hegel and Husserl. These two philosophers had not only given a *general* account of what idealism is, they carried out the general project into some specific details. These details were largely determined—apart from the general nature of the project— by some other preconceptions they had. Hegel, for example, was guided by some idea about where the spirit *was* moving, and through what crucial stages. This accounts for the specific ordering, in his work, of the various forms of consciousness. Husserl was guided by what he took to be the structure of *the* world: a hierarchical structure, matter at the base, the organic life, animal mentality, human mind, social ordering and spiritual acts—arranged in the order. This accounts for the way the general project of analysis of the constitution of 'sense' is carried out in the second volume of the *Ideas*. I am not here concerned with a specific project. I prefer to follow the following principle. There is, in my view, no unique way of structuring the world or history. But whichever account we *choose*, we still would have the general project to be carried out in accord with that choice. In other words, the idealist project does not commit us to any particular picture of the world or of history. It is neutral as against competing versions.

There is, however, one aspect of Hegel's project that I wish to briefly reflect upon. The series of forms of consciousness, in Hegel's *Phenomenology*, culminates in what he calls *Absolute Knowledge*. In course of a conversation with Hilary Putnam, I suggested to him that my preference was for an open-ended picture—one which retained a series of forms of consciousness but did away with a final closure. Putnam surprised me by saying that he preferred to have

'*Absolute Knowledge*', for such a conception helped to preserve the intuition that there was a way things really were in the long run, and so to preserve his realistic intuition. But one may construe *Absolute Knowledge* not as putative knowledge of the supposed real nature of things (as contrasted with the preceding forms of consciousness where we had only appearing worlds which is what could preserve our realistic intuition) but as knowledge of the way human spirit, growing through history, has posited, shattered and reconstructed and restructured worlds as well as, *pari pasu*, understood/interpreted itself.

This world-constituting function is assigned in today's locution, to discourses and/or conceptual frameworks. Between such conceptual frameworks and discourses are interposed 'ruptures' and 'breaks' across which our ability to provide intelligible accounts of origin or transition is said to be fundamentally faulted. I do not wish to take that route leading to relativism. The 'worlds' I have talked about are not those of the relativist. We understand how one arises out of the other. Philosophical reflection enables us to grasp them in their origins. This is why, I prefer the language of 'consciousness', which comprehends the other locutions, and frees us from the grips of their alleged relativistic implications.

VIII. REMARKS ON 'IDEALISM'

Have we, in the end, *understood* idealism to an extent that could enable us to possibly say, we know it is the truth about things? Here is what Hegel, supposedly the idealist *par excellence*, says of idealism. After saying that idealism, as a theory, is 'the conscious certainty [on the part of reason] of being all reality', Hegel adds: 'It merely gives the assurance of being all reality, it does not, however, itself *comprehend* this fact.' (*Phenomenology of Mind*, Bailey tr., p. 274–5)

It is a bare assertion, a mere assurance, to which there are counterimposed other equally intuitive certainties (realism, for example).

Such is idealism as a *theory*, which historically appeared as one system amongst others. This empty and formal certainty is given filling when we trace the history of the spirit (which is the mind-world correlation in its various forms), 'the forgotten pathway' as Hegel calls it. Idealism, in this sense, is a path, whose *sense* we acquire by reflecting upon the history of mind. Husserl gave an account of the same mind–world structure a-historically—excepting in the *Crisis* where he claims to show how the world of modern physics *arises* out of the pre-scientific life-world.

There is a widely held view according to which realism is not a theory but a pre-theoretical, possibly instinctive, view of things—while idealism is a theory, a speculative theory at that. I wish to maintain that this is wrong. The everyday view of things, the view of commonsense is as little realism as idealism; it does contain, though, features which serve as spring boards for both.

Index